Edwin Abbott Abbott

Through nature to Christ

The ascent of worship through illusion to the Truth

Edwin Abbott Abbott

Through nature to Christ

The ascent of worship through illusion to the Truth

ISBN/EAN: 9783744745529

Printed in Europe, USA, Canada, Australia, Japan

Cover: Foto ©Lupo / pixelio.de

More available books at **www.hansebooks.com**

THROUGH NATURE TO CHRIST:

OR,

THE ASCENT OF WORSHIP
THROUGH ILLUSION TO THE TRUTH.

BY

EDWIN A. ABBOTT, D.D.,

Formerly Fellow of St. John's College, Cambridge.

London:
MACMILLAN AND CO.
1877.

[*The Right of Translation and Reproduction is Reserved.*]

TO

The Memory of the Blessed Dead

WHO NEXT TO CHRIST

HAVE HAD MOST POWER TO HELP THE LIVING

BY DESTROYING DEATH

AND BY MAKING THINGS INVISIBLE REAL.

PREFACE.

Two classes of people deceive themselves with respect to the worship of Christ, some supposing that it is unnatural but demonstrably right, others that it is unnatural, and therefore confessedly wrong. The object of this book is to undeceive both classes, by inducing both to ask themselves what Worship is and what Christ was, and by proving to the former class that Worship implies much that is beyond the province of logical demonstration, and to the latter class that there is a natural Worship of Christ, based upon recognized truths of humanity, and including Art and Science, as well as Morality, within the scope of its life-giving influence.

CONTENTS

	PAGE
INTRODUCTION	3

PART I.—WORSHIP.

CHAP.
I.—What is Worship	31
II.—The Danger of Anthropomorphism .	39
III.—The Religion of Humanity	53
IV.—The Symmetry of Worship	65
V.—Illusions .	72

PART II.—THE WORSHIP OF NATURE.

VI.—The Illusions of Non-Human Nature	93
VII.—The Illusions of Sacrifice	115
VIII.—The Illusions of Seers	129
IX.—The Illusions of Death	141

CONTENTS.

CHAP.	PAGE
X.—The Illusions of the Family	158
XI.—The Illusions of Society	173
XII.—The Gains of the Worship of Nature	197
XIII.—The Deficiency in the Worship of Nature	204

PART III.—THE WORSHIP OF CHRIST.

1. CHRIST PURIFYING THE REVELATION OF THE FAMILY.

XIV.—The True Method of Creating Worship	221
XV.—The True Worship	232
XVI.—The True Forgiveness and the True Sacrifice	249

2. CHRIST PURIFYING THE REVELATION OF SOCIETY.

XVII.—The True Society	269

3. CHRIST PURIFYING THE REVELATION OF NON-HUMAN NATURE.

XVIII.—The True Attitude to Non-Human Nature	281
XIX.—The True Spirit of Science	299
XX.—The True Spirit of Art	328
XXI.—The True Revelation of Death (the First Part)	345

CONTENTS.

CHAP.	PAGE
XXII.—The True Revelation of Death (the Second Part)	367
XXIII.—The Past Worship of Christ	391
XXIV.—The Present Worship of Christ	400
XXV.—The Future Worship of Christ	413
APPENDIX.—On a Possible Origin of the Miraculous Element in the New Testament	435

INTRODUCTION.

THROUGH NATURE TO CHRIST.

INTRODUCTION.

To the very large number of the young who, year by year, are rejecting Christianity because they say they find themselves unable to believe in it, I wish to suggest the natural worship of Christ. The word natural is often ambiguous, and Christ is so far above us that He must always be called, in a certain sense, supernatural: but it is a worship which, at all events, shall not call upon them to believe anything that is unnatural or incredible. I shall begin by assuming that righteous Worship means love, trust, and awe carried to their highest limits. I shall then ask my readers to review with me the gradual growth of worship, together with the gradual progress or redemption of mankind before the coming of Christ. Next, I will ask them to consider a small part of such records of the life of Jesus of Nazareth as are perfectly natural and readily credible. Then, after a review of His influence, both upon His immediate disciples and also upon the world during the last eighteen centuries, I shall ask them to reflect upon the part thus played by Jesus in accelerating that progress or redemption. It will naturally occur to us then to consider whether there is not a certain consistency in the work of redemption as it was wrought before Christ, and in the work of redemption as it was wrought in Christ, so that the progress or redemption of mankind, taken as a whole, would appear to have been, as it were, the work of one and the same Spirit. I shall then appeal to them whether the fact that they may feel obliged to set aside the whole of the miraculous element in the Bible as essentially non-historic, should reasonably prevent them from recognising in Christ the supreme expression of this Spirit of progress or redemption, and whether they do not naturally feel themselves drawn to love, trust, and reverence Him. The last question that I shall put to them will be whether there is any other being or collection of beings to whom or to which they are prepared to accord more of love, trust, and awe, than they are prepared to accord to Jesus of Nazareth. If they can honestly answer that there is no other, then I would beg them to bear in mind that they are Christ's true worshippers, and would earnestly ask them not lightly to separate themselves from Christ's Church.

The great cause of present disbelief seems to me to be this, that Christ is commonly so presented to the world that men do not love Him, do not even care about Him so much as about a brother or an intimate friend. It is not historical faith that is just now most needed to make men Christians; it is love and trust— that sort of affection which we call *personal*. Now one great reason why people do not love Christ is that they do not believe that He was Man. What

INTRODUCTION.

I desire to do then is, to inspire the belief that He was human, by showing that He worked upon the laws that govern humanity—spiritual laws, of course, but still the same spiritual laws that govern men. In other words, Christ wrought signs, forgave, converted, manifested Himself to His disciples after death, and bequeathed His Spirit to us in accordance with the same laws by which common men perform corresponding acts. Approaching Jesus of Nazareth in this way from the side of His humanity, we should, as it seems to me, be more likely to believe *in* Him, instead of believing facts about Him; and this kind of belief seems just now most needed and most rare.

I know that one obstacle to the worship of Christ is the supposition that His influence does not cover all the departments of human life. It is fancied—how idly I shall try to shew hereafter[1]—that Christ only teaches us morality, and that He has no attitude at all toward science, while He absolutely discourages art, and is hostile to the pleasures and graces of life. Fully to expose the absurdity of such an assertion would be a task requiring more space than I can devote in a work not specially devoted to the Life of Christ; but I hope to show at least that it is baseless, and to prove that if a man desires to obey the precept of Goethe and "to live resolutely in the Whole, the Beautiful, and the Good," or, in other words, to give due homage to science, to art, and to morality, he cannot do this better than by striving to live in conformity with the spirit of Jesus of Nazareth.

The life and work of Christ seem to have experienced,

[1] See Chapters XIX and XX.

of late, very unscientific treatment at the hands of those who profess to be most devoted to science. Those who look on His work as natural, and on Christ Himself as merely human, would seem to be bound to explain on what natural law He worked, and what must have been the nature of the Man who could produce such results. But they have in general either evaded the problem, or offered none but most unsatisfactory solutions of it. Reading M. Comte's interesting and suggestive review of history in the fifth volume of his *Philosophie Positive*, while the following pages were passing through the press, I was struck with the apparent incapacity of the writer to recognize the life of Jesus as a fact. For the death of Julius Cæsar that eminent philosopher has more space to spare than for the death of Christ. He attributes the enthronement of morality above all human existence—which he justly calls "the most fundamental principle of social life"—not to Christ, but to "the profound wisdom of Catholicism:" and the character of Jesus Himself appears to him to be the fabrication of the "social genius" of "les premiers philosophes qui ont ébauché le Catholicisme," which "social genius" succeeded in erecting Him into a type "universel et actif, alors admirablement adapté à la direction morale de l'humanité ; et dans lequel, en cas quelconque, les plus chétifs et les plus éminents pouvaient également trouver des modèles généraux de conduite réelle." To my mind there is no miracle in the records of the miraculous that would be so incredible as such an "application of social genius" on the part of the "first philosophers of Catholicism." Many scholars have felt a difficulty in believing that the *Iliad* sprang from the brains of more than one poet: but what is all the supposed genius of the Homerids as compared with the collaborative art which enabled the Christian philosophers to fabricate the character of Christ?[1]

Yet M. Comte's inadequate appreciation of Christ as a Person influencing mankind, and of Christianity as a simple allegiance to that Person, is probably shared by a large number of writers in the present day. Many, besides Comte, find it too difficult—partly, I suppose, because it is too inconveniently destructive of cherished hypotheses—to attempt to apprehend Christ as a human Being, to be approached in the same spirit in which we approach the greatest and noblest of human beings.

To me Christ's work becomes none the less admirable, and He Himself none the less worthy of worship, for being regarded as natural, and as a pre-ordained part of the development of mankind. Of M. Comte's *Review of History* it may be said, as I believe Mr. Darwin has said of his own theory of evolution, that it adapts itself admirably to Christian teleology. Throughout the pages of the fifth volume of the *Positive Philosophy* history is described as one continuous redemption of the human race; no retrogression, nothing abortive, nothing wasted; whatever is, is right; something or other, whether one

[1] Vol. v. p. 306.—" L'instinct philosophique du Catholicisme lui a fait remplir spontanément, de la manière la plus heureuse, cette condition indispensable, en la conduisant à faire passer, pour plus d'efficacité pratique, ses types moraux de l'état abstrait à l'état concret, épreuve vraiment décisive, qui, en un sujet quelconque, manifesterait aussitôt l'exagération effective des conceptions initiales : c'est ainsi que les premiers philosophes qui ont ébauché le Catholicisme, se sont complu naturellement, dans l'application de leur génie social, à concentrer graduellement, sur celui auquel ils rapportaient la fondation primordiale du système, toute la perfection qu'ils pouvaient concevoir dans la nature humaine ; de manière à l'ériger ensuite en type universel et actif," &c.

calls it Providence, or the Word of God, or Destiny, or Humanity, or Nothing, is continuously guiding mankind toward the truth. Subject to a few deductions, where M. Comte's prejudices may have slightly warped his judgment, the greater part of his historical review would commend itself to me as eminently Christian. Putting the Word of God where Comte puts Nothing, I find myself in almost complete accord with him, and my only quarrel with that suggestive treatise would be perhaps that, while professing to prepare the way for the destruction of the spirit of theology, it is itself almost too obtrusively theological. For, admitting that a great deal of the work of Jesus which was once supposed to violate the laws of Nature, is, on the contrary, in accordance with Nature, I am driven to a conclusion quite different from that of the sceptics. If all that Jesus has done has been nothing but the natural influence of mind upon mind, than I am driven to exclaim, How powerful must have been the mind of Him who has been thus naturally able to influence mankind for eighteen centuries! Is it possible, I am forced to ask myself, that the graceful hero of a Galilean idyl, so exquisitely sketched by M. Rénan, can have had in him the stuff to make a Shepherd of the spiritual Israel and the Founder of the New Jerusalem? And then, glancing at other solutions of the perplexing problem, I say to myself once more, "If, in spite of Catholicism, and in spite of Protestantism, and, in a word, in spite of Christianity, the spirit of Christ, by its mere natural influence, has yet succeeded in permeating and imbuing the world so that even now, at this distance of time, we are preparing for some new manifestation of

His presence, some new revelation of His truth, then can we possibly hope ever to understand Him, or ever in the faintest way to apprehend His marvellous nature, unless we approach Him with the recognition that He was a Healer of Souls, a Seer of things Invisible, a Spirit in communion with the Realities of the Universe, a living man endowed with stores of vital force sufficient to revivify a decrepit world?"

But there is a very serious obstacle, hitherto unmentioned, in the way of the acceptance of a natural or positive Christianity by the English people: I mean the general ignorance of history, and of that "teaching by illusion" which has always formed a part of Nature's training of every individual and of every nation in the world. The New Testament, if it proceeds from God, may not improbably be presumed to contain this same all-pervading element of illusion by which God has taught us in the world. But the English mind rebels obstinately against the notion that it can be a man's duty to disentangle illusion from truth: Englishmen feel themselves at once absolved from search (at least in spiritual matters) as soon as they are told that the heap of truth contains some falsehood in it. "I never will believe in lies," was the answer once made to me by an able mathematician, one of the most honest and straightforward of men, when I ventured to suggest that the New Testament contained some things that were not literally true. The retort has a good moral ring about it: but when analysed, it is not much more sensible than the utterance of that firm believer in the literal inspiration of the Bible who is recorded to have said: "Touch the headings of the chapters of the Bible! Touch a syllable in the Bible, and I would not pick it out of the gutter."

Time and illusion seem to be as natural elements in God's spiritual training of mankind as they are in Nature's training of the senses. Those at least who accept the Scriptures must accept this truth. From the time when the Father of the Faithful is said to have left house and home for the sake of the Faith of God, nearly two thousand years are recorded to have elapsed before the Chosen People of God could be prepared to receive the Revelation of the Promise. What wonder then if, after the coming of the Promised Word, another two thousand years should be required to enable mankind to rise to the full meaning of that divine and astounding utterance? Again, a thousand years before the coming of the Word, God in His wisdom permitted the Religion of the chosen people to attain compactness and definiteness at the cost of spiritual purity; and the first Temple defined and sensualised the worship of Jehovah. In the same way, a thousand years after the coming of the Word, God united and hardened Christendom into that great Church of the days of Hildebrand, which, as we Protestants think, at once preserved and contaminated truth. But, as the Prophets prophesied against the sensuous superstitions of Israel, so our German and English prophets have prophesied against the superstitions of Rome; and, thanks to them, we are now partly free. Partly, but not wholly. Still lurks among us the leaven of materialism. Still Christ is not trusted, because not understood. Christ, living and moving among thoughts or realities, and speaking of them as real, was even during His life often misunderstood by His disciples, who, when He spoke of realities or thoughts, misinterpreted Him, as though He meant unrealities, that is to say, things. Christendom followed in the same path of misunderstanding, and to this day we are still in danger of burying His language of reality under our gross and unreal explanations. The world is the metaphor, Christ the reality. But we cannot expand our metaphor into its simile until we have overcome the delusions of the world through faith. At present the world is too strong for us, and we babble as though the world were real and Christ's words unreal.

It may indeed be urged that the faith of the early Church depended upon those very details which I would now allow Christians to put aside or to suspend their judgment about, as being comparatively unimportant. But to this I should reply that, although the early Christians may have *thought* that they believed in Christ because of these details, and may have based their polemical treatises upon these details, as being most definite and best adapted for argumentative purposes, yet in reality the true disciples of Christ have always believed in Him on spiritual and not on material grounds. They have believed in Him, not because He occupies a visible seat on this side or on that side of God, but because He is felt to be exalted in spiritual power, sitting enthroned in the human heart, inseparable from the conception of the King of kings; not because His tangible flesh rose from the grave, but because *He* rose from the grave triumphing over death; not because His body, but because His Spirit and His nature were the direct offspring of the Eternal Father. The confession of St.

Peter was, as I have attempted to show hereafter,[1] the birth of Christian Faith : and the faith of St. Peter which called down the blessing of Christ, was faith, not in the Incarnation, nor in the Atonement, nor in the Resurrection, nor in the Sacraments, nor in the Church, but simply faith in Jesus Himself.

I have said above that I address myself principally to the young. I do so, not because I would not gladly address myself to the old as well, but because I could not hope to persuade those who have grown old in scepticism; and in the attempt to succeed, I should probably fall into a kind of argument and language which would not be equally adapted for those to whom I specially appeal. I say it with profound sorrow that, when the heart has been contentedly familiarised for many years with a spurious Christ, mentionable in the same breath with Mohammed, there is not much chance that, during this present existence at all events, a man will ever return to the true conception of Christ. Faith in Christ appears to me to be not a demonstrable matter, like the Pons Asinorum, but the product of a life of effort, and the result of many influences, the influence of parental and school training, the influence of society and of the Church, the influence of the memory of the dead, of public and private prayer, of the hope of immortality, of the continual reading of the Scriptures, and above all of self-denying and philanthropic labour. The resultant of all these potent influences cannot be conjured up by any magical charm for one who during the years of mature manhood has learned comfortably to dispense with these, or many of

[1] See Chapter XV.

these influences, and to do well enough without Christ. Yet, convinced as I am that if not in this, then in some future existence, every human being will be conformed to the image of the Son of God, I would ask even older sceptics to consider whether a purely natural consideration of the life and work of Christ might not lead some of them to feel not entirely satisfied with those negative solutions of the phenomena of Christianity in which they are at present acquiescing.

Again, in the beginning of this Introduction it was stated that the reader should be called on to believe nothing that was unnatural or incredible : now it may be urged that I am inconsistent in laying stress, as I undoubtedly do, upon the faith in the immortality of the soul. But I never said, nor intended to say, that nothing is credible except what is proved by the direct evidence of the senses or by logic. However, since some good men of the present day disbelieve in immortality and yet retain a belief in God, it is worth while justifying the stress we lay upon the faith in immortality, especially because the disbelief in it often proceeds from a stern resolute love of truth, even when painful, and from a hatred of pleasant self-deceptions. "We should like to believe it," they say, "but that is no reason why we should believe it; rather it is a reason why we should be on our guard against believing it." I do not admit the force of this argument thus broadly stated. No doubt we ought to be on our guard against believing anything simply because it is *pleasant;* but the reason why we believe in immortality is, not because it is pleasant, but because it is *right*. We who believe in a righteous God, feel that He can never have implanted in the hearts of men (not to speak of Jesus) the feeling of sonship and the hope of eternal communion with Him, without intending *in some way* to satisfy this aspiration. If God could have thus cheated us (not to speak of Jesus), by forcing the noblest and purest of men to long for gifts which He did not intend to give them in any shape whatever, then we feel that He would be a bad god, a god not to be worshipped. I grant that if this hope of immortality had produced more mischief than good, then it might be plausibly argud that God is not responsible for it—

"Sua cuique Deus fit dira cupido,"

—but this cannot seriously be maintained. The evil qualities of human nature have no doubt in some cases perverted the belief in immortality, as they have perverted the belief in Christ; but, on the whole, whether art or science or morality be considered, it will not be gainsaid that (in times past at all events) the progress or redemption of mankind has been accelerated and not retarded by the faith in a life beyond the grave. This faith was the source of the strength of all the saints and martyrs of the Church; it breathes through the life of Christ, and through Him it has enthroned morality in the hearts of mankind. Now we are asked by those who disbelieve in immortality, to assume that this absolute trust of Christ, which has been the uplifting of mankind, has been absolute hallucination. We reply, we cannot assume this: it is not merely unpleasant, it is *wrong*.

It is urged that there is no evidence for the belief in immortality. There is certainly none for those who do not believe in a God, nor for those who do not believe in a good God. But for those who believe in a Father in heaven the evidence of the heart will seem not untrustworthy. *If* God is a Father, is it not reasonable to suppose that He is leading us to know Him and to believe in Him in somewhat the same way in which the best of earthly parents lead their children to believe in them? The logic of the family is not the logic of the laboratory or the dissecting-room; and if the universe is not a laboratory nor a dissecting-room, but a family, may it not well be that, whenever we attempt to approach Him, the Heavenly Father requires us to study a different grammar of assent from that which serves to master the secrets of science. A child does not, or should not, say, "I should like to believe in my father's honesty or my mother's purity; but that is no reason why I should believe it; rather it is a reason why I should be on my guard against believing it." Love and trust go for something in the family. In the same way we ought to feel towards the Parent of all. We ought—if we believe in a God—to have something of the same passionate affection and trust for Him that we have for our human parents and dearest friends. "Shall not the Judge of all the earth do right?" seems to me a perfectly reasonable argument. In a word, sanguineness and hopefulness, duly controlled, appear to me moral virtues, ultimately leading (even though it be through illusion) to true intellectual conclusions. The universe speaks to us through parents, wife, and children, and says, "Do not merely reason about me, but trust me," and the universe ought to be trusted. But many people, nowadays, when they speak of the voice of Nature, mean, not the voice of the universe, but the voice of the universe *minus* humanity—a very different and a very one-sided thing.

But it may be urged that "our visions of immortality, though eminently useful in past times in promoting the moral progress of mankind, may be, after all, mere illusions which, having once served their purpose, may now be discarded: God teaches men by illusion; why may not immortality be one of these illusions?" Now I am ready to admit that when we talk of immortality we are talking in the dark of what we can barely, even in the faintest manner, apprehend. Imagine a number of seeds underground conversing together about their future existence, and agreeing that their size and weight will probably be greatly increased, and that their existing faculties of imbibing moisture, of swelling and rotting, will probably be indefinitely magnified—and we may form some faint, some very faint, notion of the darkness and earthiness amid which we throw out words at that leaf and bloom of developed humanity, which we ought perhaps to regard (if we could) as independent of space and time. It is possible, no doubt, that the hope of immortality may be in some respects an illusion; but it will be shown hereafter that it is *characteristic of illusions to contain a satisfying truth*.[1] No believer in a good God ought to deem it possible that the noblest aspirations of humanity and of Christ, the type of humanity, are baseless lies. All that I contend for is that there is some truth and reality in store for us

---

[1] The word "illusion" is, throughout this treatise, used to denote the errors of healthy nature, as distinct from "delusions," the errors of morbid nature. See Chapter V.

corresponding to our conception of the immortality of the soul, and that the reality will be infinitely superior to our present impotent apprehension of it. In all this there is nothing incredible or unnatural : and to believe otherwise is not only an error, it partakes of the nature of a sin.

The apparent ignoring of immortality by Israel may no doubt be used with some force, to show that a great nation may with impunity dispense with this faith. But it is one thing for a Church in its infancy to dispense with an advanced conception, and quite another thing for the same Church in its maturity to retrograde from that conception, when it has been attested by the blood and agonies of martyrs, and by the life and death of such a spiritual authority as Jesus of Nazareth, and has been made the basis, through centuries, of a superstructure of hope and morality for mankind, all of which is liable to, and would be in danger of, collapsing should the foundation be removed. Our objectors may retort, " The hypothesis is not *pleasant*, but it must be faced ;" but we reply, "The hypothesis is *wrong*, and therefore cannot be true." Immortality is essential to faith in the Eternal Father, therefore immortality, in some shape or other, is a certainty. It was not essential to Israel, but it is essential to Christendom. A child of seven years old—what need has he of a faith in immortality, he who in the natural hopefulness of childhood looks on nothing as mortal, and is resentfully surprised at death when it invades what he loves ? But the father of that same child, standing by the death-bed of his only one, and looking forward to a life void of the old familiar joys, has he no need of it ?

Now this is just the difference between the old Israel and the new. Israel in old times looked forward to an eternity of natural existence upon earth; we in modern times can have no such prospect. Science warns us that within a certain time—say ten thousand or ten millions of years, it matters not which, for our argument—this habitable globe will become uninhabitable, dragging down to destruction the human race. Placing ourselves then in imagination upon the decaying earth, the day before the final dissolution of mankind, we ask what room is there for trust, or even for awe, which are constituent elements of Worship? To know that when this ball of clay shall have made but one more revolution, then Homer and Dante and Shakespeare, yes, and Christ Himself, will have vanished into space, and be as though they had never been, is that a thought provocative of trust? Rage, indignation, revolt against the accursed Fate that brought us into being, these feelings on this hypothesis are all conceivable; but from what point of view can the Positivist feel trust or awe, contemplating this *finale* of the pageant of humanity? Surely, if the human drama is to end thus, and is not rather to prove but the first play in a trilogy or in many trilogies, then, after all, both Christians and Positivists too must alike confess themselves mistaken, then verily there *is* a God that destroyeth the earth, and as the curtain falls upon the stage of despairing Humanity, we shall cry *Plaudite* to Satan.

It will be seen, therefore, that no dogmatic preconception, but rather the simple definition of Worship, forces me to lay stress upon the hope of immortality. For if worship is nothing but a combination of love, trust, and awe, then it would seem to me that those who are—not suspending their judgment about, or entertaining hopes of, immortality, for that is a different matter—but living without any kind of hope of immortality—must find it very difficult indeed to feel for anything or any person that combination of feeling to which we have given the name of Worship. God forbid that, while I assert the difficulty, I should deny the possibility. No doubt many now disbelieving in immortality will hereafter stand nearer to the throne of God than many now believing in it. Love (as well as trust and awe) is an element in worship; and who can limit the potency of love in compensating for lack of hope and trust, and even of reverence? Possible it is, no doubt, that some pure unselfish natures may feel a perfect willingness to be absorbed into the unconscious world, their work being done. But even to these I would say, though you may be ready to give up immortality for yourself, can you so readily give it up for the great heroes of humanity? Can you bear to think that Christ is mortal and that a time will come when even His influence will be extinct?

But the class to which I desire more especially to address myself consists of those who have not given up the faith in immortality, I mean the young, and more especially those who, after having been educated at our public schools, are entering, or have just entered, the universities, and are just experiencing the transition into the atmosphere of sceptical thought. The danger of young men at this stage consists, sometimes, not in believing too little, but in believing too much. Many of them are, perhaps, in the habit of basing their faith in Christ upon a great mass of propositions to which they have hitherto given unhesitating assent. Hearing some of these propositions denied, and the denial taken for granted in large circles of educated society, and being forced to confess that some parts at least of the old basis of their belief are unsound, they suddenly find the whole structure of their faith shaken with the shaking of the foundation. The want of knowledge, and the rashness, and the truthfulness of youth, result too often in a premature conclusion. From the most foolish superstition there is often a rapid passage to the most foolish unbelief. Not knowing enough of history to recognize how often illusion contains truth, not knowing enough of human nature to recognize the subtle and powerful influence of mind upon mind in the spiritual processes[1]

[1] Compare the well-known words of George Eliot, which have always seemed to me to form one of the best commentaries upon the Incarnation, and one of the best introductions to the Epistles of St. Paul : " Blessed influence of one true loving human soul on another. Not calculable by algebra, not deducible by logic, but mysterious, effectual, mighty as the hidden process by which the tiny seed is quickened and bursts forth into tall stem, and broad leaf, and glowing tasseled flower. Ideas are often poor ghosts, our sun-filled eyes cannot discern them, they pass athwart us in thin vapour, and cannot make themselves felt. But sometimes they are made flesh, they breathe upon us with warm breath, they touch us with soft responsive hands, they look at us with sad sincere eyes, and speak to us in appealing tones ; they are clothed in a living soul with all its conflicts, its faith, and its love. Then their presence is a power." If it were necessary to point out any one work in which the spiritual laws described by St. Paul are best illustrated, I mean the animalism of the " life according to the flesh," the purifying pangs of the awakening to a consciousness of sin, the divine but painful power given to human beings of bearing one another's burdens, of imputing righteousness, and of remitting sins, and in a word, the whole process of the Atonement, then I should say that in no work of modern days are the invisible processes by which Christ has conquered, is conquering, and is destined to conquer the world, so clearly exhibited as in *Daniel Deronda*. It is true that no mention of the name of Christ lies within the possibilities of the book, and the blank suggests an artistic as well as a spiritual deficiency. None the less, the blank in *Daniel Deronda* seems to me to bear a plainer testimony to Christ than is borne by the attempts of many other authors to fill the blank.

described in the New Testament, and not knowing enough of science to recognize how many things called supernatural and rejected as incredible are really both natural and credible—they fly at once to the conclusion that Christianity is exploded. It is to this class that I appeal, having myself found by experience that it is quite possible to suspend my judgment about almost all those details of the record of the Gospels which would cause any difficulty to any educated sceptic, and yet to feel a faith in Christ confirmed by each passing year, and especially by the hopeful and fascinating suggestions of recent scientific discoveries.

Remembering my own difficulties and struggles, let me most earnestly beg the undergraduates of both universities to learn to practise more resolutely and more patiently than at present the art of "suspending the judgment." If I had read Strauss' *Life of Jesus* three years before, instead of three years after, taking my degree, I should have, in all probability, at once cast off faith in Christ. But years of subsequent study have led me to a point where I can recognize considerable force in many of the arguments of Strauss, and yet remain a Christian. I venture to think that many other undergraduates of the present day, working hard for their degrees, are, no less than I was, deficient in the leisure and perhaps also in the knowledge of human nature, necessary to read Strauss with advantage. At such a time the right course is to follow Bacon's advice: "Antiquity deserveth that reverence that men should *make a stand thereupon*, and discover what is the best way;" and by "antiquity" I mean not merely antique dogmas, but habits, public and private prayer, thoughts of the dead, purity of word and deed, conscientious diligence and self-denying action.

Are we not too apt to shut our eyes to one of the best proofs of Christ's presence, I mean His handiwork in our hearts and in the hearts of those around us? The New Testament will always remain one of Christ's most conspicuous signs, but it is not the only, nor the most important sign. I claim for the great work of the redemption of mankind, and for the traces of Christ's influence on men, the same respect and attention that is so eloquently claimed by Mr. Frederic Harrison for the progress of humanity: "We see," he says, "in this provision, all the signs of concert and connection, as if it came from love and mind . . . We know that the humblest rag and coarsest basket in which the beggar-child is laid were all produced by human hands, working with fruitful activity under some intelligent aim, and with some honest feeling at the bottom of it." Precisely similar phenomena do I see when I look around me even in our present imperfect human society. In churches, hospitals, schools, and prisons, in shops, and offices, and courts of law, in works of art and of fiction, and in the columns of newspapers, which represent our every-day life, I recognize, amid heaps of grossness and vulgarity, a certain "honest feeling" which I trace back to Christ. Things are bad as they are; but they would have been infinitely worse but for Him. When I turn, not from Aristophanes or Martial, but from Thucydides or Horace to modern life, I am at once struck with the presence of a different moral atmosphere; when I look into my own heart, and try to penetrate the minds of those who are nearest to me, everywhere I discern that the texture of our humblest thoughts of goodness, and of our coarsest feelings of righteousness, show traces of the kindly handiwork of Christ, and the words of the psalmist naturally rise to my mind, "O Lord God of hosts, who is like unto Thee ? Thy truth, most mighty Lord, is on every side." Again, when I turn from modern life to the pictures of the earliest ages, sketched or suggested in the works of Sir John Lubbock and Mr. Darwin, I cannot fail to recognize that the redemption worked by our incarnate Lord is but a harmonious part of the great redemption of humanity which has been in progress since the creation of mankind, and that the same Word of God in Jesus, and out of Jesus—if I may so speak without offence—has been redeeming mankind by the same influences, and in accordance with the same laws. Looking forward to the future, I seem to recognize with even greater clearness, that if mankind is not to fall back into anarchy and barbarism, if civilisation in its true sense—I mean the power that makes men citizens—is ultimately to prevail and to bind the world together, the victory will be owing, not to the mechanical arts or sciences, nor to the unaided might of reason helping men to discern what is expedient, but primarily to that same power of love, and self-sacrifice, and faith in a divine Fatherhood, which has proved so strong in Jesus of Nazareth. Wherever Jesus of Nazareth is worshipped, there I see, at all events, comparative progress and morality; wherever He is not worshipped—in China, in India, in Asia, and in the savage tribes scattered through America and Africa—there I find stagnation or decay.

Mohammedanism, which threatened to supplant the worship of Christ, is now, after many centuries of trial, found to be destitute of the regenerative principle, and potent only for destruction ; Buddhism has long been lifeless ; it may be said without exaggeration that at this moment the ruin of Christendom would mean the ruin of the world. The conclusion is forced upon me, that if ever mankind is to attain that full development to which we give the name of Salvation, Jesus of Nazareth and no other must be the Leader of our advancing hosts, and in His name, and in no other name under heaven, will society eventually triumph over the disorganizing principle of selfishness, and be built up into a Temple of God. History, ancient and modern, conscience and common sense, and the common facts of daily life, all point to Christ as the source of the spiritual life of Christendom, and the type of the spiritual life of the whole of mankind since the creation, so that unintentionally and unconsciously I find myself falling into the language of the Fourth Gospel, and naturally confessing that the Spirit of Jesus of Nazareth is the Life of the World. Feeling, therefore, with Mr. Harrison the absolute need of some "real power to revere, some ever-present goodness to love, some faith which can explain and guide my life," I am naturally drawn to worship this Life of humanity, this ever-present Power of progress, this Spirit of self-helpful love, this Word of God, which to me is represented by the Spirit of Christ. I appeal, then, in like manner to those who may feel that they cannot accept in their entirety the tenets of the Church of England, to pause at least before they reject the clear and unmistakable evidence which points out Christ as "a real power to revere, and an ever-present goodness to love." Let them not shrink from the charge of adopting a Christian Positivism, if it is to be so called: provided that it is a real, uncontroversial, unwavering, satisfying heart-shaping worship, loyalty to Christ will be far better—called by whatever name—than many current forms of mere dogmatic Christianity.

One last word as to my own religious position. "Before serious men will listen," says Mr. Harrison to a man who wishes to persuade others in matters of religion, "he must tell them what he believes himself." I believe, then, in the spiritual reality of every article of the Creeds. The Incarnation, the Resurrection, the Atonement, the Ascension are to me not mere historical facts, nor theological dogmas requiring mere otiose assent, but profound spiritual realities. Believing that God did not begin to be Love some eighteen hundred years ago, but that He was Love from all eternity, I find myself under the necessity of conceiving Him as being from all eternity, not a solitary Being, but—how inadequately soever words may express the thought— one with some other Being, whether called a Word, or a Son, or by whatever name. When I try to conceive of the Creation, and of God (so to speak), in action upon the world and upon mankind, it seems natural to conceive of Him as working through this manifestation of Himself and to use the language of the Psalmist who tells us that, "By the Word of God were the heavens made." But if this be true of inanimate Nature, in a far higher sense does it seem to be true of man. I am therefore not using Biblical language because it is Biblical, but the language that expresses my inmost convictions when I say that the Word of God is present at the birth of every human being, and is the source of all goodness in every human heart. But if this be true of all men, even of the worst, then, when I come to throw out words at the supposed origin of the personality of Jesus of Nazareth, I feel that to declare that He was merely "inspired by the Word of God" by no means expresses the reality even up to the mark of possible adequacy; nor do I find any other words that express my heart's conviction so well as those which declare that "In the beginning was the Word, and the Word was with God, and the Word was God. . . . And the *Word was made flesh* and dwelt among us."

But while I have no doubt or misgiving at all as to the divine nature of Christ, I have grave doubts as to the historical accuracy, or as to the correctness of the literal interpretation of the miraculous element in the narrative of the New Testament. Not that I deny the possibility of a miracle, or that I should decline to believe in a miracle upon sufficient evidence: but the evidence usually accepted as sufficient appears to me quite insufficient (especially in the face of another probable explanation of the origin of the miraculous element in the New Testament), nor do I see any present probability of supplementing it by fresh evidence. On the other hand I recognise the clear distinction between the miracles of the New Testament and the lies of the Apocryphal Gospels,[1] and I at once admit that, without a belief in the literal accuracy of these miraculous narratives, the faith in Christ might never have been preserved for us through the fall of the Empire and

[1] See Appendix.

the Middle Ages. Some of the miracles, therefore, I should recognize as being historically accurate, but supernatural only in degree, and not in kind; the rest I should consider as subsequent accretions round the historical narrative, often containing some spiritual truth, and not implying in the narrators any intention to deceive, but not historically accurate. About some details of the Incarnation and the Resurrection I suspend my judgment, not knowing whether they are literally as well as spiritually true, and inclining to the belief that they are not literally, but only spiritually true. My readiness to suspend my judgment on these points is the greater because my faith in Christ as the Word of God is quite independent of them. If it should be demonstrated to-morrow by irrefutable evidence that the first chapter of St. Matthew's Gospel and the first chapter of St. Luke's Gospel are not historically accurate, I should none the less continue to believe that Jesus is our Incarnate Lord and one with God. On the other hand, if it should be demonstrated to-morrow that those chapters are historically accurate in every detail, then I should welcome the demonstration as containing comfort for many Christians, and also as suggesting new and hitherto undreamed-of laws of nature; but (unless I much deceive myself) I should not change a prayer, a hope, a thought about Christ, I could not trust in Him more fervently for such historical demonstrations, or worship Him more devoutly as the divine Saviour of mankind. I wish to show to others who may go somewhat beyond my position that it is quite possible to reject the miraculous as essentially non-historic, and yet to retain the worship of Christ.

And oh! the indescribable peace in having attained some fixed platform of faith, whence one can look down undismayed at all that criticism and all that science may discover, and feel able to say, "My faith can be shaken by none of these things; a Christian I am, and a Christian I shall remain to my life's end. Nothing can alienate me from Christ except a paralysis of the faculties of loving, trusting, and reverencing. While God spares these to me I can as soon avoid seeing with my eyes open, or hearing with the ears unclosed, as I can cease to worship Jesus of Nazareth, the Son of Man, and Son of God."

PART I.
WORSHIP.

CHAPTER I.

WHAT IS WORSHIP?

WHAT is meant by worship? That men have in them the faculty of worshipping, and a craving for some object to worship, is as patent a fact as that they have the faculty of loving and a craving for some object to love. If there are exceptions to this rule, they are but exceptions. As there may be, here and there, individuals who are so immersed in self that they neither love nor care to love anyone, and seem altogether destitute of the power of loving—I say seem, for I do not believe in the existence of such a person—so there may be among nations, here and there, a savage tribe so undeveloped or degraded that it may seem, if we may trust report, to have lost, or never to have possessed, the faculty of worshipping. But whether in the individual or in the nation, such a state of things is recognized by all students of human nature as anomalous and monstrous. Great philosophers in old times may have doubted, and some philosophers in modern times may have repeated the doubt, whether the craving for an object of worship is healthy, and whether the faculty of worship ought not to be repressed. But no one, so far as I know, that is to say, no one whose *dictum* would deserve consideration, has so completely closed his eyes to the facts of human nature as to deny the assertion that we have a faculty of worshipping and a natural desire to exercise it.

But worship is of very different kinds. As the faculty of faith is neutral and colourless, and assumes the hue of its object, so it is with worship. We do not need the testimony of Lucretius to tell us that religion—which is another name for systematized worship—has often done men more harm than good, engendering or fostering baseness, cruelty, and superstition: the accounts of modern missionaries and travellers tell the same story, and accumulate against worship a heavy list of charges. This is, of course, no reason in itself for endeavouring to eradicate the tendency of worship from human nature. The faculties of eating and drinking, perverted to gluttony and intemperance, have wrought great harm to mankind; the affections of compassion and of resentment, ordinarily called virtues, have produced the effects of vices when carried to harmful excess; yet no one desires to suppress these natural faculties and affections; everyone feels that the object should be, not to suppress them, but to direct them rightly. So it is with worship. It has done great harm, but it has, in the judgment of most of mankind, done greater good. In any case it is inherent in all but anomalous and diseased natures, and, therefore, the question should be, not "How can we suppress worship?" but "What is the best kind of worship, and how can we encourage and develop it?"

Our question, therefore, resolves itself into this: "What is the best kind of worship?" This may seem a question almost as difficult to answer as the question, "What is the best kind of food?" which must necessarily be complicated by many considerations of climate, race, habits, and the like. Nevertheless, as physiologists would be able, penetrating beneath individual peculiarities of this nature, to reach the laws by which food acts upon the human body, and to assert that in every case that kind of food is the best which tends best to supply the waste in the different elements of the bodily frame, so theologians would, I think, be justified in saying, without respect to the characteristics of oriental or western nations, Latin or Teutonic, that in every case the best worship is that which best develops in us love, trust, and awe.

Worship, in itself, means, of course, etymologically, no more than "attaching worth to anything," it may be to wealth, health, fame, art, or God. Accordingly some writers have urged the necessity of recognizing all kinds of worship, and have endeavoured to widen the meaning of the word to the very utmost. It has been recently maintained with singular ability that the name worship may be extended so as to include admiration.[1] The power of admiring, it has been urged, is that which keeps the life of men fresh, sweet, and pure, and makes the essential difference between the religious and the irreligious mind. Now it is quite true that a certain kind of admiration, drawing a man out of himself and making him look up, has something in common with worship. The admiration of a child for the bubble at its brightest, the admiration which made Wordsworth's heart leap up in childhood when he beheld a rainbow in

---

[1] See a series of papers in *Macmillan's Magazine*, 1875, 1876, 1877, entitled "Natural Religion."

the sky, undoubtedly contains elements of worship : and this kind of admiring tendency, as compared with the purely animal self-absorbed condition which knows what it is to lust, but not to admire, may fairly be called religious, while the latter condition is purely irreligious. But, although this distinction is important, I should fear that to lay undue stress upon it would be ambiguous and misleading. The common use of the word scarcely admits of the tension proposed to be given to it. I scarcely know whether the able author would, or would not, claim as favourable to his use of the word the well-known line,

"For fools admire, but men of sense approve."

But in any case the word admire is so often used, without any of that elevation mentioned above, to describe the feelings with which one regards mere ornaments and articles of luxury, that I doubt the expediency of substituting it for the more familiar term worship. After all, our business is mainly not with the different kinds, but with the best practicable kind, of worship, just as the physician's business is, not to consider how many kinds of new food there may be in the world, but only what is the best food for his patients. We will assume, then, at all events as a working hypothetical definition, that righteous worship is simply a combination of love, trust, and awe. It will follow that whatever it may be for which a man feels his combination of love, trust, and awe, carried to the highest limits of which his nature is capable, this, and nothing else, is the object of his highest worship. He may be quite unconscious that he is worshipping this object, and may even assert that he is worshipping some other object. Such unconsciousness is by no means uncommon; but none the less, a man actually worships (in the best sense of the word worship) nothing but what calls out in him the highest love, trust, and awe.

Applying this test to ourselves, we shall at once recognize how much of our so-called worship is unsound and unreal. Indeed most people have very little active faculty of real worship. All have the faculty, but it is either dormant or undeveloped; dwarfed by our grossness and servile fears. With most of even the higher kind of worshippers, worship means little more than awe, with perhaps a tinge of trust, and hardly any love. With the lower sort, worship means awe untinged by either love or trust: and unmixed awe of this kind is nothing better than cringing terror. But with the highest, on the other hand, awe is almost supplanted by the fervour and passionate devotion of love and trust. Abraham in ancient times has been handed down to us as a pattern of this highest type of worshipper; and in modern times St. Francis also was a veritable "friend of God," one to whom the awful rigidness of nature suggested no fears, who hailed the air and water and fire as brothers and sisters kindly though firmly helpful, so that law was swallowed up in will, and awe in love. It is well that we should be reminded by the lives of Abraham and St. Francis and by the life of the Highest of all, that this and none other, pure and unmixed love, is our ideal of worship: yonder, high up, attainable in the end by all of us, is the high pinnacle of superhuman worship. if we had but the wings of faith to waft us to it. But, for the present, such worship is too wonderful for us, we cannot attain to it: we commonplace people are in danger of despising or distrusting whatever we do not revere with a reverence approaching to fear; and therefore for the present we cannot entirely exclude awe from our definition of the best worship.

This leads us to our next question, What are the legitimate objects of worship? It might be thought at first that some human being would best satisfy our requirements: for what can we love and trust so well as a wife or child, a father or mother, or a dear friend? But the element of awe is wanting, or not sufficiently developed, at least except from quite young children towards their parents: and though we may trust the will, we cannot trust the power and wisdom, of human beings. Nevertheless when any human being, in greatness and goodness far above our level, calls out in us affections of love, trust, and awe in a very high degree, our feelings for that human being approximate to worship. Indeed if such a human being—say Socrates or St. Francis —makes us feel more love, trust, and awe than we feel for our conception of the Supreme Being Himself, then, talk as we may about worshipping Him, we are not really worshipping Him, but St. Francis or Socrates. Little children are habitually in this state. They pray each night and morning to the Father in heaven, but their hearts are fixed on the father or mother on earth. They love and trust and reverence their parents more than anyone or anything else; consequently they must be said, in accordance with our definition, to worship their parents. In such worship there is nothing to be ashamed of, it is natural and healthful for the souls of children. But food that may suit children may not be best for men. The mischief is, that hundreds of thousands of men are in a condition infinitely worse, to all appearance, than that of little children, worshipping God with their lips, but in their hearts having a conception of Him far inferior to that which a good man would form of Socrates or St. Francis.

For such people it would clearly be a positive gain that they should be elevated from their gross and perverse conception of a God to some decently pure conception of a reasonably good Man. But further, even for the purest and highest it would appear that, in some sort, humanity must form the object of worship. If we desire to find objects of love and trust, and to keep these faculties of love and trust in constant exercise, it is to human beings that we must look. We cannot love or trust anything that is not in some sense human. If therefore by a "person" is meant a being capable of loving and being loved by mankind, then it may be said with perfect truth and reasonableness that, by the very nature of worship, men are unable to worship any but a Person.

But in the worship of a mere human being, a certain element is wanting. There is a feeling, higher than fear, with which we contemplate a stormy sea, or hear the crash of the thunder-clap, or gaze upward toward the infinitely distant stars and faintly try to realise the immensity and wonderfulness of the material world. This feeling, which we call awe, we do not feel for the best of living men, nor for the heroes of the past, but solely for the vaster phenomena of non-human Nature. Rightly controlled and balanced, this feeling is recognized by us as purifying and sobering our hearts, suppressing in us the tendency to insolence and self-conceit, and yet not quenching nobler aspirations. When our hearts ascend in worship, this feeling of awe chastens without degrading the feelings of trust and affection. It is not terror, it is not servile dread such as a jungle-dwelling Indian may feel for a cobra or a tiger, or a European may feel for cholera or diphtheria. Terror can never raise anyone : but true awe casts out terror, and always has a tinge of reverence and trust. But if awe is to be an element in worship, then it would seem that the object of worship must be, in some sense, "not ourselves."

What then is our conclusion? The object of our worship must be human and liable to human affections and sufferings; or else we cannot love Him. He must be elevated above human sins and failings; or else we cannot trust in Him. He must be superhuman and in some way one with non-human Nature; or else we cannot feel awe for Him. If therefore anything or any person can satisfy these different, and seemingly incompatible, requirements; if any one can call forth in us to their highest extent our faculties of love and trust, and at the same time that awe which we seem to be capable of feeling for non-human Nature, but incapable of feeling for any ordinary man—such a being concentrating and reconciling in himself the diverse revelations of Humanity and Nature, will be the one true legitimate object of human worship.

CHAPTER II.

THE DANGER OF ANTHROPOMORPHISM.

WE have shewn that the legitimate object of worship for human beings must be, in some sense, human. But it may be urged, " in making this assertion, are you not guilty of anthropomorphism? Instead of speaking about a Person, still more about a Father, had we not better adopt as the name for the object of our worship some circumlocution that shall either avoid or conceal the danger? We never know how anthropomorphic we are, and can never be too cautious against the anthropomorphic temptation." Such a warning has a curiously deterrent effect for many, even educated persons. Many are as much afraid and as ashamed of subjecting themselves to the charge of anthropomorphism as though they thought it next door to idolatry. But a little consideration will shew that anthropomorphism is not a danger, but a necessity imposed upon us by the very conditions of our nature, and that those very philosophers who most bitterly decry it must either practise it unconsciously, or in the successful attempt to avoid it, must fall into a greater danger. To avoid anthropomorphism in religion is like avoiding the act of breathing in life. The anthropomorphic atmosphere encompasses the soul as the air surrounds the body, and as we cannot avoid breathing except by dying, so we cannot avoid anthropomorphism except by spiritual death.

As usual, the difficulty has arisen from not defining terms. Anthropomorphism—in the sense in which it is often condemned by modern theologians—simply means forming a conception of God derived from the conceptions of men; and this is in no sense a thing to be ashamed of. Anthropomorphism is not idolatry, but something very different. Idolatry means the worshipping an image. Now a graven image or picture is incapable of growth, and cannot expand with the growing conceptions and emotions of the worshipper. Consequently idolatry stiffens and hardens our conceptions of God, and is to be avoided as a sin. There would have been no sin in idolatry if statues of Apollo or Athene could have adequately represented the best and noblest attributes of man. The sin of idolatry was that it passed over the highest attributes of humanity, such as truthfulness, goodness, justice, compassion, and the like, partly because they were in the idolatrous times of old unduly neglected, but partly also because the sculptor's marble could not so easily represent them as it could represent the more superficial and attractive attributes of strength, speed, and beauty. Anthropomorphism is a mental act, not liable to the same dangers, and therefore not liable to the same prohibition. What is forbidden is, not anthropomorphism, but bad anthropomorphism. In other words—to tear away the imposture of fine-sounding terms which are so often used to conceal thought—we are forbidden to derive our conceptions of God from what is lowest, but not from what is highest, in the nature of man.

I do not see how any difficulty should arise here for those who have ever fully considered that all thought can only be expressed (for ordinary purposes) by language, and that all language is based upon our sensations of material objects. There is not a virtue, nor a vice, nor a quality in anything whatsoever, however immaterial in nature or subtle in distinction, that is not described by some name, which (either as a whole or in its parts) was originally applied to material, and thence transferred to immaterial, objects. In some words the transference can be traced at once, as in the words "spirit," "excellence," "virtue:" in others the connection is less distinct, but obviously the rule is without exception. So far, therefore, as the nature of God is to be conceived in thoughts expressible by words, so far we must be indebted for our conception of Him to the conceptions derived from what we see, hear, touch around us, from our sensations of things in heaven and things on earth and things in the water under the earth. No law of God or man prohibits so necessary an idolatry as this. Only, as the ancients selected their best Parian, or ivory, or gold, and jewels for their material idols, so must we give good heed that for the stuff of our invisible anthropomorphism we select not the coarse grit of earthly power and majesty, but the ethereal substances of justice and love. To erect such a statue of the Supreme in the temple of his heart is the duty of every human being. At hand, thickly strewed at our feet, near the threshold of our homes, yes, in our homes themselves, lie the materials for our sculpture, the deeds of the heroes of Israel and of the great men of our own nation and of our own days, the love of parents and of children, the patience and self-denial which we admire in others and strive to practise in ourselves, all these are so many fragments, great or small, precious or common, that help us to accomplish that great theomorphic and anthropomorphic task which is the be-all and end-all of our existence.

Can then man make God in his own image? No, he is himself made in God's image (so we Christians at least and Jews believe), and while appearing to form God after his own likeness, man is in reality accepting that revelation of God which is conveyed by man's own nature and by the nature of the men around him. Even those who may be disposed to reject the teaching of Moses, that man is made in the image of God, must be prepared to admit that there is nothing unreasonable in it. If there be indeed a divine Creator of the world, then, of all His works, none is so likely to reveal His nature as that "piece of work" called man. God reveals Himself not only through the Bible, but also through the revelation of humanity, through history, through biography, through the daily intercourse between man and man. He is the Supreme Light that lighteth every man that cometh into the world: by studying the broken reflections of the divine splendour in human nature we can approximate to the divine reality itself. Greece and Israel are at one in asserting this possibility; for if Moses tells us of man made in God's image, Plato adds that "there is nothing more like God than the man who is as just as man may be."

This human creature, at its lowest bordering on the apes, at its highest touches a superhuman sphere which we call divine. Moreover, it is not only variable and versatile, but progressive. As in beasts and birds and fishes, and even in the vegetable creation, diversities of individual characteristics suiting environment are developed and propagated till the old and lower forms are superseded by the newer, so it is with men. Brute force and cunning and mere intellect, each developed in turn to the utmost, are intended to prepare the way for something higher, for some closer approximation to Him who has been revealed to us by the name of Love. What the body is to the mind, that the mind is to the soul, the faculty of worship ; so Pascal tells us, and our consciences assent to it. But if this be so, and if all the triumphs of art and intellect of which Greece and Rome can boast, are not to be weighed for a moment in the balance with a single act of genuine self-sacrifice, then it may well be that the present general diffusion of humanity, compassion, and goodness (side by side with the development of justice) may place this age far above the glorious times of Greece and Rome, in spite of our artistic deficiencies.

Nor is it only in the race that progress may be traced. Each individual contributes to the general progress of morality more than might be expected of him. Some men, of course, contribute more harm than good, and all contribute some harm as well as good. But mankind has a natural and beneficent tendency to ignore the evil and to store up the good works of the dead. What Antony said is a rhetorical falsehood : it is not true that " the evil that men do lives after them." On the contrary, the evil is often buried with them, while the good is treasured up unto a life beyond their life.

Few write the biographies of bad men, scarcely any one writes the biographies of petty men: they are left to oblivion, while the examples of the great and good are handed down as guides for posterity. Even of the few bad great men the lives are not written because they are bad, but because they are great; and the badness is held up to the reproach of posterity. Thus history serves as a kind of filter for each generation, removing the impurities of the traditions of the generation before. As it is with the conspicuous heroes of nations so it is with the most commonplace of us. We pass away, but our work remains. The evil of it is forgotten or forgiven, but the good is gratefully remembered and idealised by our children; and our imperfect lives, exalted by their gratitude, remain to make a generation, perhaps better and nobler than our own, regret their degeneracy from their ancestors. This is God's law, not ours—the law of human progress. We can and do sometimes break it, as we break His other laws; but it stands none the less as His law, that each generation shall rise nearer to Himself through the mediation of the generation before.

Consciously or unconsciously, some worship we must adopt, for worship, like breathing, is a necessity; and were anthropomorphism ever so dangerous, it would seem to be the least dangerous of the courses open to us. For by the necessity of language it would seem that any definition of the conception of God must, so far as it is not pure negation, suggest either a being human in respect of the highest attributes of humanity, or else some being inferior to humanity. Take, for example, the well-known definition (how skilfully and gracefully advocated every one knows) that God is "the Eternal not ourselves, that makes for righteousness." Now, what is meant here by the word *makes*? For the word necessarily calls up three, and only three, kinds of " making;" either " making " voluntarily, as a man makes; or "making" instinctively, as a beast makes; or " making " neither voluntarily nor instinctively, but unconsciously, just as an eddy or current may be said to " make." [1] Of these three kinds of " making," which is meant? If the first, you are anthropomorphic; if the second, you are zoomorphic; if the third, you are azoomorphic. Supposing each of these three hypotheses to be dangerous, I should prefer the first as the least dangerous. But if you say that you prefer not to define what sort of " making " you mean, and that you will leave this an open question, then I should reply that such a use of words rather conceals than reveals thought, and conveys (as perhaps indeed it is intended to convey) no revelation whatever of the nature of God. Moreover, in practice, it appears to me that any one endeavouring to apply this definition of the nature of God would be unable impartially to suspend his judgment between the three conflicting images suggested by it, the human, the animal, and the inanimate. Unless he combines them all three together, or two together, into some portentous mind-idol, he will practically accept one of these images to the exclusion of the other two. Either, therefore, God will be conceived as in some sense human, or else you will be driven—for the alternative of animalism is in these days

[1] I understand the word " make " to be used in the sense which it has in the phrase, " to *make* for a goal : " but the argument is independent of the sense of " make," and simply insists that the " making " can only be conceived as voluntary, or instinctive, or unconscious.

impossible—to conceive of Him as a gigantic growth, a huge machine with certain powers of self-motion and self-change, but still, disguise it as you may, a machine.

It may be replied that the "Eternal not ourselves," representing as it does the tendency of the Universe, includes human as well as non-human nature, and therefore cannot be called a machine. But the object of worship will in that case consist of two parts, humanity, and an environment of machinery disposing humanity to righteousness; and we must either worship one of these two parts separately or the two conjointly. Now if we worship humanity by itself, we are worshipping "ourselves." But if it be said that each individual worshipper may worship Humanity *minus* himself, and that this is the meaning of worshipping "an Eternal not ourselves," then, in the first place, I do not see how the epithet Eternal can justly be applied to "Humanity *minus* oneself;" and in the second place, the worship is reduced to the well-known Religion of Humanity, about which we shall have something to say in the next chapter. But as to worshipping the other part of the Eternal separately, I mean the environment of humanity, how can we worship it, that is, how can it inspire us with love, trust, and awe, if we know nothing about the source or author of it, so that, for all we know, it may have come into existence by chance, or to serve as the amusement of some "careless gods," after the type of the deities of Epicurus? And lastly, if we feel unable to worship either of the two parts of the Universe separately, why should we feel moved to worship the two parts conjointly, since we may be worshipping nothing but "ourselves," placed by chance in circumstances favourable to righteousness ?

Let it be once admitted that genuine worship must imply love and trust, and the spurious nature of this machine-worship will be at once detected. One cannot love and trust a machine. It may be urged that for a machine unerring in the accuracy of its operations one does feel a certain kind of trust, as in the case of the calculating-machine; and this kind of trust may appear to be called out by the unvarying operation of the laws of nature. But it is not so. So far as one may be said to have trust or faith at all in a machine, it is trust in the conscientious labour or the skill or the wisdom of the machine-maker: about a machine in itself one may have knowledge or conjectures, but no trust.[1]

[1] It has been suggested that this statement is controverted by the well-known love and trust which the sailor feels for his ship, feelings which, in him, are quite independent of any thought of the maker of the ship. This is true: but though, when he thinks of his ship, the sailor does not think of the maker, he does think (perhaps unconsciously) of himself and the crew. The ship, under *his* guidance, and care, and skill, has battled successfully against storms and foes, and (partly through ignorance of the fixed laws of Nature obeyed by the vessel in its every movement) he imputes to the wood and canvas something of his own merit and volition. In fact, his love for the vessel is love, not for it as a machine, but for it as something higher than a machine. The ship is *she*, not *it*, to the sailor. As soon as steam takes away her eccentricities and caprices the sailor begins to love her less, *because she is becoming a machine to him*. Go a step further, and take away another element of uncertainty by substituting iron rails for the sea, and you still further diminish the possibility of love or trust, by increasing the absurdity of imputing personality. Go one step further still, and take away the steam which gives the appearance of voluntary motion, and the impossibility of love and trust becomes patent. Who can love and trust a system of pulleys, or a pump ? Take Turner's great picture as an illustration. When we look regretfully at the fighting *Téméraire*, tugged to its last berth by the fussy little steam-tug, we see in the great ghost-like vessel in the back-ground, no mere collection of spars and planks, but a noble phantom of English Victory, protesting against the desecration of being treated *like a machine*, and broken up into so much firewood.

But it may be suggested that we have not done justice to the definition of God above-mentioned, in taking no notice of the word "eternal." The use of the word is artistic, as suggesting the most sacred and awful of associations, calling up a great deal that is not strictly implied in the epithet. But if the word is to be applied to a machine or a tendency, surely there is nothing so very grand or worshipful implied by it. To say that anything lasts for an infinitely long time is, after all, not much more—weighed as a claim to worship—than to say that it fills an infinitely large space : and if we all agree that there is something poor and vulgar in admiring anything merely because it is infinitely big, why should we esteem it as in itself a god-like attribute that anything should last for a time infinitely long ? To worship an "eternal," simply as eternal, is not worship, but only a kind of awe, and not a very noble kind of awe either. The question rises at once, "An eternal *what?*" The answer is given, "An eternal that makes for righteousness." But still the question must be repeated, "an eternal *what?*" For as the calculating-machine, though it makes for arithmetical accuracy, is not in itself reasonable or wise, so the righteous-tending machine, if it be nothing but a machine or a tendency, cannot be in itself righteous. Neither the calculating-machine, nor the world, nor any other conceivable thing or system of things, however wonderful and complicated and beneficent, can possibly inspire trust, except so far as it points back to a righteous Will. Assume for a moment, with the Persian poet, that the Eternal looks on the drama of the Universe as a chess-player on a game at chess, and that, just as a chess-player may habitually make white win, so the Eternal makes righteousness win :

> "We are no other than a moving row
> Of tragic shadow-shapes that come and go
> Round with the sun-illumin'd lantern held
> At midnight by the master of the show :
> Impotent pieces of the game he plays
> Upon this chequer-board of nights and days,
> Hither and thither moves, and checks, and slays,
> And, one by one, back in the closet lays."

Now in all this assumption there is nothing inconsistent with the conception of God implied in "the Eternal not ourselves that makes for righteousness;" yet who would worship an eternal chess-player because he makes white win? And why worship an Eternal for making righteousness win, any more than for making white win, if we do not know that He makes righteousness win because He *loves* righteousness?

Why should we be so ashamed of anthropomorphism? Who would not twenty times sooner worship a man than worship a tendency? Supposing that it were certain that there is no God, what would be the being or collection of beings that would most call out our love, trust, and awe? Surely the human race; or, if it must needs be one being, then some one man, living or dead. If, for example, we had to choose between worshipping any of the dead phenomena of a godless Nature, the sun because of its brightness, or the sky because of its suggestions of infinite space, or night because of its peace, or time because of its infinite duration, or the law of attraction because it keeps the world together, or Socrates because of his lofty and discursive intellect, his love of truth and contempt of death—who but an untutored savage, or one of Nature's civilised valets would hesitate a moment? The dread of anthropomorphism seems to me to be sometimes encouraged by vulgar admiration for what is ostentatious, and by a vulgar contempt for those quiet and domestic processes of human nature, in virtue of which we approximate to God. Familiarity with human greatness has bred contempt in petty minds, and to the valet no master is a hero. But if we had Christ's insight to discern the sacred image in the heart of the most commonplace and sinful of human beings, then almost every man would be to us, in some sort, a mediator by whom we might draw nearer to God. On the other hand, if, in forming our conception of God, we put away the human side of revelation, and if, instead of this, we substitute a "tendency" or "an eternal, not ourselves, that makes for righteousness," what is this but practically to ignore the highest teaching of Nature, and to introduce in its place a strange doctrine of a new God who is indeed little better than a refurbished representation of the Vortex or Whirlpool recommended for worship by the young Athenian in Aristophanes—

"Δῖνος βασιλεύει τὸν Δί' ἐξεληλακώς."

"So, because you cannot express the attributes of God except in human words, therefore you regard a human being as God! A strange consequence!" The objection is neatly put, but it does not quite accurately exhibit our present position. Hitherto we have only reached thus far: we find that mankind has, and always has had within the memory of man, a faculty called "worshipping." It is of course open to assert that this is a bad faculty, like the faculty of envying, or that it was a good faculty once, but is now obsolete; with those who would assert this we are not now dealing, but only with those who recognise the necessity of some kind of worship. We say that worship has been, and is, at its best, when it combines love, trust, and awe for the object worshipped. But the objects of worship are called gods or a god. It follows that the best kind of worship will recognize no god or gods but those who are capable of being loved, trusted, and reverenced. But a being capable of being loved, trusted, and reverenced is by us called a "person." Hence we say that the best kind of worship will recognize no god or gods, but a person or persons; and, therefore, if our worship speaks of God as a Person, we have no reason to be ashamed of it.

Beyond this point we have not yet passed, except so far as to hint that, *if* there is a good God, and if anthropomorphism is a necessity to human nature, then so far from there being anything absurd in His leading us to Himself through anthropomorphism, there is something monstrous and almost blasphemous in the supposition that He should have made anthropomorphism a necessity to us, and yet a lie. We shall try to show hereafter that the whole of the training of Nature would lead us to believe that anthropomorphic worship is not a lie. Call it an illusion, if you please; but if so, it is an illusion containing truth. By raising men from brute force to cunning, and from cunning to reason, by raising them from attention to memory, and from memory to comparison, and from memory and comparison to love, and from love to all morality, Nature has been teaching even sceptics and atheists that, *if* Nature is to be approached by men in our highest and purest spirit, then we are to approach Nature in the spirit of love, trust, and awe, that is, with the feelings with which we approach a Person.

CHAPTER III.

THE RELIGION OF HUMANITY.

ALTHOUGH no single human being may seem to be a fit object of worship, humanity, as a whole, may seem to have higher claims. Nature herself may seem to dictate a worship of this sort. To the little child the parents stand in the relation of gods. As the child grows older, the circle of those to whom he looks up enlarges. The great men of his own nation working in the present, the great national heroes of the past, the heroes of all nations and of all times, step in, each in turn, to be the objects and supports of a growing faith. As our standard of morality rises, and history makes noble deeds more and more familiar to us, it becomes less and less possible to fasten upon this or that individual as the one ideal to whom we can attach our faith. The heroes of the present seem dwarfs in comparison with the heroes of the past; and these, in turn, when compared with one another, are seen to have had their weaknesses and imperfections. Of all the heroes of the world it is true that they generally know but one or two deep spiritual truths; "they have earned faith and strength so far as they have done genuine work, but the rest is dry, barren theory, blank prejudice, vague hearsay; their insight is blended with mere opinion."

As soon as this is felt, it is perceived that the virtues of individuals are but reflections of one greater light, to the knowledge of which we must approximate by combining all that is best in each individual. In some periods of the world's history the State has represented this combination.[1] Men have loved their country with something of the passionate affection that we feel for wife or children, and have laid down their lives for Israel, Athens, Sparta, Rome. Englishmen know that this feeling is not yet extinct: and if love can be tested by self-devotion, then the word "love" is not abused when we say that the Greeks and Romans "loved" their country. Yet the State cannot satisfy the aspirations of the faculties of trust and awe. A State can be compared with States as a man can be compared with men, and can be found wanting: a state, as well as a man, can lie, cringe, oppress, decay, perish. How can one stand in awe of a thing so imperfect?

For this reason some men of wide studies and deep sympathies in modern times have felt that no State could ever suffice as the object of worship, and that our aspirations can only be satisfied when they include, in the scope of adoration, the whole of mankind, past, present, and future. Here, it might be thought, we have reached at last the outermost circle which has been widening for us since our childhood from the centre of the family. A man may discern faults in his own

[1] I am aware of the distinction drawn by Fichte between the State and the Nation. But the word Nation does not apply to Athens, or Sparta, or the Greek cities generally; and I desire to use the word State to imply all that is conveyed by the Greek word πόλις.

ancestors, may even refuse to sympathize with the policy of his own country, but what human being will dare to deny to the collective human race the tribute of trust and awe as well as affection? Individuals may perish, nations decay, but humanity abides for ever to be worshipped—or at least as long as human beings remain endowed with the faculty of worshipping. If men could live and die in old times for Rome or Athens, why should not men in modern times live and die for mankind? What element of worship need be wanting in our feelings towards universal humanity?

There is something very beautiful and attractive in this religion, but it seems to me to require definition. In the first place, where shall we find, summed up in a worshippable form, the worshippable attributes of humanity? We spoke just now of the possibility of worshipping England; but clearly it is not possible to worship England protecting her interests in the East by conniving at Turkish misgovernment, or England protecting her interests in Ireland by oppression and cruelty. If we are to worship England we must worship her in the act of emancipating the slaves, or in the act of combating the ambition of Napoleon, or in the act of gradually working out the problems of constitutional government and religious tolerance. In the same way, if we are to worship humanity, we are not to be expected to worship humanity cannibalizing, or oppressing, or retrograding, or stagnating; the object of our worship is clearly to be humanity progressing. Where, then, are we to find humanity in the act of progressing, that we may go to the very fountain-head of the worshippable essence and adore the Spirit of Progress? If we are to be true Positivists and take things as they are, putting aside metaphysical speculations and vague theories, where is progress at this moment to be found? The answer must be, in Christendom and in Christendom alone. Wherever Christ is not worshipped, there humanity is not progressing. Clearly, then, if we are to be true Positivists, humanity is to be worshipped through Christendom. But again, how, and in what aspect are we to worship Christendom? For when we look to the present and past of Christendom we find that, around an undying seed of progress, there has always been a mass of retarding corruption. Shall we, then, worship Christendom striving to resist her own pure principles, or striving to conform herself to them? Clearly the latter. We must, therefore, worship Christendom in the act of striving to enthrone morality as the ruler of human life. But if we ask, what nation, or collection of nations, or what man, or collection of men, most contributed to this enthronement, then, if we will act like true Positivists and not shut our eyes to facts, we must confess that the supreme author of this divine enthronement was a man called Jesus of Nazareth, who, however much he may have been misunderstood and however much his life may have been distorted by legendary accretions, did undoubtedly enthrone morality in his own heart, and transmitted to generation after generation of his disciples an influence which has enabled them to imitate him, and which is even now the source of life and spiritual strength to the whole of the progressive part of mankind. If, then, we desire to worship Christendom, we find ourselves inevitably driven to Christ as the summary of Christendom. Thus, therefore, step by step we seem naturally led on from the worship of humanity to the worship of progressing humanity, and from the worship of progressing humanity to the worship of Christendom, and from the worship of Christendom to the worship of the Spirit of Progress in Christendom : and this Spirit of Progress we find incarnate in Christ.

Worship of humanity in this sense, so as to include Christ, or rather so as to include humanity in Christ, would seem to me both reasonably and spiritually satisfying. For it presents humanity to us in the dependent attitude of a Son growing in grace and knowledge, through trust in an eternal Father. If in this spirit we worship humanity, then by implication we worship the Father also : for the one thought is inseparable from the other. Such worshippers of humanity I therefore claim as Christians. But the worship of humanity against which I protest is that which professes to regard Christ as a human being, and yet, whenever it speaks of humanity, means humanity *minus* Christ. This is not true Positivism, for it ignores facts. It ignores the undeniable influence exerted by Jesus of Nazareth upon mankind, and gets rid of Him as an inconvenience, despatching Him, in a phrase, as " the real or ideal founder of Christianity," and proceeding to show how Christianity was elaborated afterwards by " the first philosophers who sketched out Catholicism." How can we be fairly asked to give the name of the Religion of Humanity to a religion that thus ignores the greatest human being that ever lived, and the very source from which the Religion of Humanity sprang ?

Humanity, unless it points to some divine fulfilment of the ideal which it suggests, so far from inspiring me with trust and awe, fills me with distrust, shame, and indignant perplexity. If there is no Supreme Goodness and Wisdom to whom we can entrust the burden of miseries and wretchednesses of this existence, the care of developing and perfecting all that is here imperfect and undeveloped, and of ultimately destroying sin, then I confess I am utterly unable to feel anything but scorn, hatred, and contempt for myself and my fellow creatures. Like Swift or Pliny, one would in that case turn with relief from men to horses and pigs, those higher classes of animated beings who have not been mysteriously tormented with insatiable and ridiculous aspirations. Without some kind of Will directing the struggle, the mere spectacle of struggling humanity—though it has happened hitherto to struggle upwards and not downwards—would either strike me like the spectacle of a chaos, or of a machine. The progress would appear a mere fortuity or an automatic necessity; in neither case causing either trust or awe.

Again, the ordinary religion of humanity, rejecting or ignoring a life beyond the grave, appears to be bound up with a belief in the everlasting progress of mankind upon earth. Now, if there were really a certainty that we might live for evermore upon this earth, not indeed preserving our individuality, nor even remembered by name, but made perceptible to the hearts of others by our influence for good, however slight and petty, treasured up to all eternity; if we knew that each good deed of ours wrought in this passing instant would produce its harvest and seed-time of good deeds multiplied infinitely for infinite ages of posterity, then perhaps the hope of such an eternity of diffused existence—if it may be called existence, as perhaps it may—might supply sufficient motive for action even though we had laid aside the hope that we should ever meet again those for whom we are working in this world, and that we should ever know that Being, the knowledge of whom seems to us to be eternal life. But science will not suffer us to cherish this hope of an eternity of influence on earth. Science expressly warns us that a time will come when this habitable globe, losing its vital warmth, will become an extinct creature like the moon, dragging down and destroying humanity in its own decay.[1] This then is to be the end of our Homers and Dantes, our Newtons and our Shakespeares, not to speak of One whose name we shrink from mentioning in the same breath with the names of ordinary men! Then surely the epitaph of humanity ought to be written by some evil god, or at best by some Puck or Robin Goodfellow void of conscience and compassion, who has been making his sport, through the ages, out of the miseries and aspirations of mankind, and now throws his toy away. Talk of the upward progress of mankind through countless centuries, what is it all worth if, just when they have struggled up to the surface, a relentless hand is to thrust them down again to darkness and death? This is torture, not progress. To play thus with humanity, as a wicked child plays with a drowning animal, what are we to call it, whether it be the work of a god, or of chance,

---

[1] It is of course *possible* that developed humanity may, by that time, be suited to its environment or enabled to transport itself to another residence. But I have not yet seen that suggestion seriously put forward.

or of fate ? In any case what could we do but curse the author of it, and laugh in despair over humanity its victim ? No, if in this world only we have hope of progress, if our dreams of eternal life are inextricably bound up with the continuity and eternity of progress in this world, and if science distinctly warns us that in this world progress is not eternal but finite, then, as it seems to me, Science must destroy our Religion of Humanity. The noblest picture that I know of heaven has been drawn by one who has realised to the fullest how the life of human beings may be treasured up into a life beyond a life in the hearts of others, and who has expressed in undying language the aspiration to join " the choir invisible" of those immortal dead who remain after death the diffused guardians of mankind. But if science predicts truly the inevitable decay of this present world, and if future world there is none, then surely our dream of the choir invisible and immortal vanishes at once ; then the greatest spirits of all the ages have been so many performers in a transitory pageant made for nobody's amusement; then all the prayers and tears, and sorrows, and sacrifices of suffering mortality are no more than " such stuff as dreams are made of." If this be so, what can we do, we who have no higher object for our worship than Humanity, but turn our eyes from the fading vision of the choir invisible, and soberly take our places in the theatre with Pliny and Swift and other amused spectators, suppressing insanity and mental revolt in the determination to be interested and cynically curious, and calmly looking forward to the last act when the epilogue shall be pronounced—to Silence as sole auditor—in the words of the Enchanter :—

> "Be cheerful, sir,
> Our revels now are ended. These our actors,
> As I foretold you, were all spirits, and
> Are melted into air, into thin air.'

To this objection, if it be replied that the many ages which must elapse before such a consummation as science predicts afford scope enough for the prevision and action of any, even the most ambitious man, much more for ordinary specimens of men, I answer that even the most ordinary imagination has the power of realising the difference between limitless and limited life. We may none of us be able to grasp the notion of a million or, perhaps, even of a thousand years: but we can all grasp with perfect ease the notion of a life with a definite end, beyond which there is no life. This thought will be perpetually recurring to us, dwarfing our thoughts and our actions. True, men can place anything unpleasant (death, for example) at a distance, and can disregard it when it terrifies them and interferes with the pleasures and objects of a selfish life. But the misfortune would be that the death of the human race would be brought nearer to men by their very selfishness. Their own death they would ignore, but the future death of humanity would serve as a convenient pretext for neglecting duty. Thus, to many men of gross natures, with a strong sense of their own interest and a weak sense of the interests of humanity and of the means by which they can further those interests, the end of all things will always be at hand whenever the prospect of it can excuse their selfishness. To such men the ultimate good that they may do will always seem slight and petty, while the pleasure that they must immediately give up in the attempt to do good will seem proportionately great: and though "to-morrow" may be a million years hence, yet they will excuse their selfish sensuality after the old fashion, "Let us eat and drink, for to-morrow humanity perishes."

Besides, if a man's sole trust is in the progress of humanity, and his sole motive to action is the hope that he may contribute to that progress, there must be many occasions when this motive will fail us. In an isolated position, with death in prospect, and no hope of benefiting anybody by our conduct, in an open sea for example, clinging with the last remnants of strength to some floating spar, what motive has a man to help him to fortitude or resignation? It may be a pleasure to us in so agonizing a moment to think that others will be happy when we are gone; but nothing that we can do or think can now contribute to their happiness. The object of our religion fails us in our hour of need; the comfort of worship in our dying moment, is denied to us; for worship in the shape of action is impossible, and worship in words, of what avail is it? How can the progress of humanity receive our dying aspirations? Only if the thought of the happiness and progress of others stirs in us something of a trust or hope that our sufferings and death are not being wasted, but must surely be in some way stored up and utilised for the common good of our fellow-sufferers; only when we find in ourselves a trust, however vaguely implying that there is a Will behind the fantastic pageant of life, and that Will a righteous one, only then can we find motive for right thought and action in an isolated death.

These later objections of course do not show that there *is* a higher object of worship than humanity; but they seem at least to shew that humanity does not satisfy the aspirations of worship. The simplicity of the religion of humanity is, that it appears to take little or nothing for granted, basing itself upon acknowledged facts and ordinary experience. But this simplicity is dearly bought if we find ourselves at some moments in life deserted by our religion and destitute of worship. There is much, very much, that is attractive in the religion of humanity : but it will retain its attractiveness and be made far more productive of trust and awe if one can feel that a higher Will, human yet superhuman, is guiding humanity towards an Ideal, which is one with that guiding Will. In any case, all who adopt our definition of worship must admit that humanity, dwindling into destruction on a worn-out planet, cannot be worshipped, because it cannot excite in us trust or awe. The advocates of that religion may hope that so pitiable a consummation may never come to pass. But if they do they will hope against scientific certainties. They will hope, because their mind revolts against so inartistic a close of the great human drama. Does not this revolt in itself imply some recognition of a divine Author of the Drama ? I cannot but think that it does. It seems to me that, just as those who marched to victory under the Roman eagles were more powerfully moved by the sense of the Fortune of Rome than by any other deity of the Pantheon, so those who enroll themselves as worshippers of humanity, in their sense of the high mission of the human race, of the destiny still in store for it, and of the impossibility that its story should be cut short or come to a lame and impotent conclusion—do virtually, though unconsciously, recognize, and genuinely though faintly worship, a Sender of our race, a Providence that watches over its progress, and a Word of God that breathes through men and nations, whispering a Story without an End.

But I must end with a protest against the title assumed by this religion. It ought not to call itself the Religion of Humanity, but rather, the *Religion of Humanity always excepting Christ.*

CHAPTER IV.

THE SYMMETRY OF WORSHIP.

UNDETERRED now by the danger that "we never know how anthropomorphic we are," we may go on our way intent on receiving into our hearts that conception of Himself which God reveals to us through humanity. But we shall not on this account feel justified in closing our eyes against other revelation. If God reveals Himself to us through all His works, then, in order that our revelation of Him may not be one-sided and disproportioned, we must grow in the knowledge of all His works, and of all parts and sides of them, and not of one side more than another. Now the means of revelation are two, human Nature and Nature other than human, which last we have ventured to call non-human Nature. In order therefore that Worship may retain its proportions, the human and the non-human sources of it ought to increase simultaneously and symmetrically. The true attitude of man has been beautifully described as "looking up and lifting up."[1] Roughly speaking, we may say that the revelation of Nature teaches us to "look up," the revelation of

---

[1] *Endeavours after the Christian Life*, by James Martineau. Sixth Edition. (London: Longmans, Green, and Co., 1876.)

mankind, to "lift up." But in truth it is impossible to "look up" without "lifting up," and impossible to "lift up" without "looking up." In other words, we cannot adequately contemplate without hypocrisy a divine Ideal, unless we strive to act up to that Ideal in our relations with humanity, and it is impossible to act rightly in our relations with humanity without a divine Ideal to regulate our conduct. Neither source of Worship can be neglected, but the other in the end will suffer for it. The knowledge of God grows best when our awe of non-human Nature blends with and purifies our reverence for frail mankind; when our sense of the order of non-human Nature reassures us that there must be an order in human Nature; and lastly, when our love and trust for men helps us to cast out all servility and terror from the awe which we feel for non-human Nature. In other words, we approach non-human Nature best when we personify it, or see a person behind it; and we approach imperfect human Nature best when we feel that our seemingly petty and frail being is part of an admirable system which stretches beyond the reaches of our understanding.[1] It is the combination of feelings derived from these two sources of human and non-human Nature, which enables every human being to feel that aspiration of worship which is to each his revelation—more or less imperfect—of the perfect God.

In old times men had observed both human and non-human Nature, and from both had deduced attributes of God: but, as was natural, they dwelt mainly upon the more striking and superficial qualities of men and

[1] Compare what Wordsworth says about the lesson that may be learned about human Nature from "one impulse from a vernal wood."

things. If they looked at Nature outside them, God was earth, fire, heaven, or sea, or perhaps the sun or moon: if again they looked at themselves, God was war, or sexual love, or wisdom. As in those days men knew nothing of the more subtle elements or forces of Nature which have recently been found to underlie the phenomena of the universe, and which have exploded the four so-called elements, in the same way men in those days ignored, or negligently scanned, those less striking faculties in human Nature which have now come prominently forward. Themis, or Justice, was a divinity, and an ancient one, but in the background; Mercy and Forgiveness were also latent, and there was no name in ancient Grecian poetry to express the Love that includes all mankind. Jesus of Nazareth changed all this, introducing a new type of human heroism, the filial character of voluntary dependence upon a supreme Will, and exalted this type to heaven. The stupendous power of this new revelation caused for a time a reaction against revelation of all other kinds. What, it was asked, could men learn from earth or heaven, what from the life of the nation or the life of the family, comparable with the lesson taught by the Incarnation and Resurrection of the Son of God? Turning their eyes from the revelation of the present, and fixing them solely on the records of the revelation of the past, men began to spin their dogmatic cobwebs around the New Testament as the centre, out of their own untutored and unsubstantial fancies. They fell into the third class of Bacon's searchers after truth, the spiders, who construct their web out of their own intestines, instead of imitating the accumulative ants, or, still better, the bees, who both accumulate and fashion. For many a century mankind has been engaged in recovering from that first excess of Christendom, learning to recognise that there is a symmetry in revelation. The revelation of non-human Nature and the revelation of the Family and the Nation are to be purified, not annihilated, by the revelation of Christ.

In modern times our eyes have been opened to discern new awfulness in non-human Nature. Everywhere is seen simplicity beneath complexity, law unchangeable working through boundless time, and issuing in endless variety. Fossils that were once thought sports of nature are now proved to be the remnants of an antique order; lines in the hills, that once seemed to be nothing but eccentricities of nature's penmanship, are shewn to be old lake-marks or sea-marks formed by the agency of water working through innumerable generations; pillared rocks, and symmetrical structures, called by strange names, recording old beliefs that they were the freaks of some gods or giants, are now proved to be the natural results of decomposing air, or rain, or wind, or frost, all working for ages on the lines of law; down in the bottom of seas, till now unfathomable, is revealed the process of the formation of geological strata; on earth the reign of law is traced in the distribution and form and even in the colours of animals and of flowers; and in the heaven the substance of the sun has been analysed, and the vagaries of the comets are reduced to law. All this has been revealed to us in these later times which was unknown to our ancestors, and all of it swells the revelation of non-human Nature.

Such knowledge is to be welcomed as the gift of God:

but obviously there is a danger that, if we do not increase at the same time in our knowledge of human Nature, we may destroy the symmetry of revelation and the balance of worship. There is a possibility that we may feel too much of awe, too little of trust and love. If therefore this century and the last are distinguished above all others for scientific discoveries, there is all the more need that the history of humanity should just now not fall into neglect. Possibly we may learn something new and certain about the origin and development of mankind, about the implanting and growth of man's intellectual and spiritual faculties, and above all about the limits and the causes of the influence of man upon man. Something of this the earth itself may disclose to us, unfolding the ancient homes and customs of men, their weapons, their utensils, their ways of living, their methods of thought. More perhaps may be disclosed by the comparison of the many different religions of mankind; still more by the examination of ancient thoughts, under diverse shapes, variously imbedded in the words of many different languages; but not a little also may be anticipated from the study of human nature as it *is*, in the researches of physiologists; and something may assuredly be learned from the works of our great dramatist, and of those poets and novelists who have in these days succeeded to the dramatic art.

It was not for nothing, doubtless, that simultaneously with the discovery of new worlds in the heaven above by the telescope of Galileo, Columbus opened up to Europe a new world below. Again, at the very time when the trumpet-tones of the great English philosopher of Induction were summoning mankind to conquer Nature by obeying her, and to become little children for the purpose of entering the Kingdom of Man over Nature, Shakespeare was opening up to us new worlds of human nature, and unconsciously writing one of the best commentaries upon the Bible and the best introductions to theology, by helping men to know themselves and one another. During this century the materials for the study of human nature have rapidly accumulated. The records of history have been ransacked : fresh light has been thrown upon the physiology and pathology of the mind ; the drama has made way for the novel, which, in the hands of its master-writers, analyses character with a subtlety and thoroughness scarcely to be found in former ages, except in the works of Shakespeare : and if the nature of man is best studied when it is put as it were to the question by unusual exigencies, then the modern press teems, amid all the mass of so-called vulgarity, with contemporary tragic deeds of the vilest and noblest kind, noised over whole continents within an hour of their commission, to be the horror or admiration of the unanimous world. With all these materials at our command, we may fairly hope that the rapid progress made by those studies which have, strangely enough, appropriated to themselves the title of Natural Science, may be supplemented by some proportionate development of our knowledge of human nature, so that, applying to Natural Science what Bacon says of "navigation and discoveries," we may say with him, "This proficience in natural science may plant also an expectation of the further proficience and augmentation of all other sciences ; because it may seem they are ordained by God to be coevals, that is, to meet in one age."

But it may be urged that "this sketch of a symmetrical Worship has made no definite mention of science or art. Are they not sources of revelation?" Undoubtedly! Science, in the well-balanced mind, tends to awe and reverence, and exalts our conceptions of the Unsearchable, whose ways are past finding out, though they be ways of order; but this has been implied in what has been said above of the increased sense of the awfulness of non-human Nature. As to the revelation of art, if it means the opening of the eyes to beauty, and the leaping up of the heart at the approach of everything that is beautiful, certainly that is an essential part of the trust and love due to the Maker of the admirable world. Worship, therefore, as defined by us, so far from excluding Art and Science, is incomplete without them, and is perfectly consistent with the maxim of Goethe, that "We are to live resolutely in the Whole, the Beautiful, and the Good"—a maxim which must surely commend itself to all who accept the much older maxim, "Thou shalt love the Lord thy God with all thine heart, and with all thy soul, and with all thy might."

CHAPTER V.

ILLUSIONS.

"THERE are and must be illusions in the Scriptures; therefore let us accept the Scriptures in faith and without reasoning about them, because we never can attain to the truth:" "There are illusions in the Scriptures; therefore, away with the Scriptures:" "There cannot possibly be illusions in the Scriptures; if there were, they would not be from God:"—these are three commonly held opinions; to which it may be lawful to add a fourth: "As by illusions God has trained mankind from its infancy till now, as by illusions He trains every human being from the cradle to the grave, so it is natural that He should train us in His Scriptures by the same means."

Let us take a few examples of illusion, premising that we mean by illusions those deceptions which are, or have been, imposed upon human beings by the natural conditions of a healthy existence. The thoughts and common language of men of the world recognise the blessed power of the illusion of hope. Although they fail to discern the germ of spiritual truth involved in it, they clearly see the benefit of what they call the "lies" and "cheats" of life:

> "When I consider life, 'tis all a cheat:
> Yet fool'd with hope men favour the deceit,
> Trust on, and hope to-morrow will repay:
> To-morrow's falser than the former day,
> Lies worse; and, when it says we shall be blessed
> With some new joys, cuts off what we possessed.
> Strange cozenage! none would live past days again,
> Yet all hope pleasure from what yet remain."

The passionless philosopher may deprecate earthly hope as that "which makes the mind light, frothy, unequal, wandering. Therefore all hope is to be employed upon the life to come in heaven; but here on earth, by how much purer is the sense of things present, without infection or tincture of imagination, by so much wiser and better is the soul." But against the *dictum* of Bacon the common sense and experience of mankind, siding with Dryden, ask with irresistible force, What would life be without hope? If the future lay before us mapped out like the past, who "would live past days again?"

The whole material world is a beneficent illusion to the intellect. As the Parables of our Lord stimulated the spiritual faculty, so does the Parable of the Universe stimulate the intellectual faculty. Those that have patience, discrimination, and reason—to them knowledge shall be added; those that have not, shall lessen the little capacity they had, and become the slaves of the first impressions of their senses. The very air that we breathe and through the medium of which we see, cannot be trusted to present objects correctly to our sight. Even in the purest atmosphere the process of refraction must go on, and the sun must appear each day to rise before its time and with a slightly distorted orb. If then the different layers of our atmosphere, our medium of sight, have been so ordained by God that they shall always reveal to us the truth, yet leave part of the truth distorted or unrevealed, how is it unlikely that God may likewise have so constructed the several strata of the medium of His spiritual Revelation that the truth might be always more or less refracted and concealed, thus mercifully making us ever discontented with our modicum of knowledge, and, as we correct sight by the aid of Reason, so leading us to correct our interpretation of Revelation by the aid of Conscience?

Take now the illusions of children. To every well-trained child the mother in its very earliest years seems the perfection of love, the father of wisdom and power: the mother can never sin, to the father all things are possible; they are as gods to him, and he looks up to them, and loves them, and trusts them as though they were divine. As the child grows older and learns perforce to compare and criticize, he learns—too soon—that his parents are not divine. The illusion vanishes; but it has called forth in the child a faith, an aspiration, which roams about the Universe seeking something to adore, and will not be satisfied till it finds the Universal Father. Again, the exploring instincts and physical constitution of a child placed each day amid a new world, fill his early life with zest, and hopes, and fancies, none of which are ever realised. Each day sees some dream-bubble burst, some illusion vanish; but the spirit of hope which has been fed by these illusions remains. Those dreams of happiness, those infantine passions of hope, do but express proportionately the same conviction with which as an old man he will stand on the verge of the grave: "Verily there is a hope, verily there is a happiness prepared for the children of God." God does not mock little children with delusions. Their childish dreams and illusions are so many angels sent down to lure them toward the Eternal Father and the Eternal Home.

The same philosopher whom we found above deprecating terrestrial hope, deprecates also the illusions of love. "For there was never a proud man thought so absurdly well of himself as the lover doth of the person loved. And, therefore, it was well said, that it is impossible to love and be wise." But once more the common sense and experience even of the more sober part of mankind side with the poet against the philosopher. It is not impossible that Bacon himself would have loved more wisely if he had married at an age when he could have thought more "absurdly well of the person loved." Far better, far happier, far truer than the dry light of the wisdom of the philosopher in his mature marriage, was the illusion of Wordsworth, to whom the "phantom" of his youth became the "angel" of his old age.

The general tendency of the intellectual illusions of mankind has been to make them hopeful. The sun, their philosophers have thought, circles round the earth and was made for no purpose but to give us light; it is perhaps as large as a round table, or, at the largest, as large as Peloponnesus; Arcturus and the Pleiades are smaller tapers made for our convenience, watch-lights for mariners, a nightly calendar for farmers; the earth is a flat square, or perhaps a circle: the ocean runs round it: in the midst is Greece, and in the midst of Greece is Delphi, the centre of the earth. Some evil sprang no doubt from these illusions, but more good. The revelations of modern astronomy, if they had prematurely destroyed the belief in the guardian gods of Rome and the trustful confidence in Roman fortune, might have made civilisation impossible by checking the spread of the Roman empire. For "man, when he resteth and assureth himself upon divine protection and favour, gathereth a force and faith which human nature in itself could not obtain. As it is in particular persons so it is in nations. Never was there such a state for magnanimity as Rome. Of this state hear what Cicero saith, 'Our piety, our religion, and our recognition of the one great truth of the divine government of all mortal things—these are the points wherein all the tribes and nations of the world have been surpassed by us.'" Nor let it be said that these illusions, though politically expedient, were utterly false. The exclusiveness of the illusion was an evil; but the quiet trust in Will (not interfered with by too keen a sense of the vastness of the material universe), the recognition of a Providence above, which worked all things for the benefit of men—this was a blessing, and a truth: this gave the great early nations of the world a sense of mission and of a right to exist, together with a freshness of hope and a joy in the vigour of existence.

Even the moral illusions which have been prevalent among mankind, even those which might be almost called delusions, have generally contained some germ of truth which, after long and painful struggle, has forced its way through the integument of falsehood. Sacrifice, in its earliest form, was probably nothing more than an attempt to feed the hungry dead, or to bribe offended spirits; but as men grew in knowledge and in humanity, this rite became impossible in its original meaning, and came to suggest to the better class of minds the offering up of an innocent or submissive heart to a Higher Will. No doubt Polytheism, involving necessarily the possibility of a difference of will between contending deities, produced many degraded and mischievous forms of worship. But it was at least better that men should thus go wrong than that they should have unnaturally resisted the personifying tendency altogether, and have been content to live in the presence of a sun that was nothing but a piece of gold in the sky, amid woods and streams that were but so many bundles of faggots or so many measures of liquid, wallowing and gorging in their beautiful world, as though heaven and earth closed in between them nothing better than an abundant human stye. Filling the universe with its gods, Polytheism at least taught thus much of truth that the Divine Spirit everywhere sympathizes with men and permeates all space.

All great nations have their illusions, and the most strange, most beneficent, and yet most terrible illusions of all have befallen the greatest nation of the world, that nation which is habitually called the chosen people of God. The Land of Promise! If God could take pleasure in irony, what irony seems to breathe in that name! The land of sin, the land of idolatry, the land of oppression, of discord, of schism, of captivity, of degeneration, of utter ruin! Read over the songs of triumph and prophetic exultation from the triumph-song of Miriam over the Horse and his Rider, down to the latest prophecy or psalm that sang how the future Redeemer of Israel should beat the nations in pieces like a potter's vessel, and how the Saints of the Lord should execute judgment over the Gentiles with a two-edged sword in their hands; and contrast all this with Israel as it is. Yet how glorious has been the mission of this people that is, at present, no people! Spite of all the vicissitudes of fortune, or rather, spite of all the hard consistency of their severe and continuous training, is Abraham ashamed of his offspring? Would he exchange them for the Teutonic or the Latin race? We speak much and justly of the mission of the English people to overspread and colonise the world: but a great part of our influence has arisen from our being the conductors of the influence of Israel, and a great result of our work has been to fulfil the promise made to Abraham and to diffuse his blessing through the nations. The ancient names of the men and women of Israel we even now bestow upon our children; our churches are consecrated to the memories of Jewish peasants; their sacred books are ours and Christendom's; their phrases with all their Oriental strangeness have taken root in our language, and the atmosphere of their thoughts is around us. If to do a great work is the mark of a great nation, was ever nation so great as Israel? And yet no nation has been more perpetually under the influence of illusion.

Yet let it not be said that Jehovah deceived His chosen people. As are the illusions of children, even so pure, so beneficent, so truth-containing were the illusions of Israel. Israel was the child among nations; looking up more than any other; trusting more than any other nation to the power of the Deliverer; thinking little of self and little of Nature, because wrapped up in awe of Jehovah the All-powerful; having no sense of limitation because with Him all things were possible, without sense of art or science to restrain aspirations or to set bounds and proportions to hope. Therefore it was that everything that was seen by the prophets of Israel was surrounded by the same halo with which a child fringes and invests the objects of his fancy. God and the attributes of God, His mercy, His love, His holiness, loomed larger upon Israel than on Greece or Rome. God's acts loomed larger also: God could not give over His people to the oppression of idolaters: sooner or later God must redeem them and place Israel in its right place at the head of the world; at last, far off, there must come again a happier time, better even than the days of Solomon, when every peasant should sit beneath his fig-tree or vine, and silver should be of no account, and gold as plentiful as the sand of the sea: peace should be perfect then, and nation should no more wage war against nation; the very beasts of prey should change their nature; the asp should cease to sting, the lion should lie down with the lamb. Such were the child-like dreams of Israel: and as certainly as any little child has been guided towards the true paradise by its fairy dreams of bliss, so certainly has the nation of Israel, and through Israel the whole world, been led towards Jehovah by these prophetic visions. True for all time, the prophecies of Isaiah still point us forward to a future when they shall be completely fulfilled: they speak of concrete things, beasts and men, cities and nations and the like ; but they mean principles, and then, and then only, will they be fulfilled when all discord is swallowed up in concord. The prophecies of Israel differ from a proposition of modern statesmanship as the laws of nature differ from a conventional rule. Being in harmony with the spiritual order of things, the sayings of the prophets must needs be perpetually fulfilled as long as things exist.

This applies to all the language of the prophets. It is all too vast and grand for the immediate objects to which it often primarily (in the prophet's mind) referred. As the sky includes the earth, so does the aspiring language of prophecy include the narrow meaning of the precise event. They speak of redemption in language that implies a deliverance from more than a mere temporary and visible yoke ; of a rest and Sabbath that shall know no end. In their writings sin and righteousness assume a different aspect from that which they wear in the literature of Greece and Rome : for in Israel sin is an offence against Jehovah, and righteousness is communion with Him. Though they rarely or never speak of a life beyond the grave, yet they link man to the Eternal in ties so close as to lead easily to the inference that man also must share in the Eternal nature. Thus all their language is inspired with a meaning too high for their immediate circumstances. Not that the prophets are like lifeless harps touched with the finger of God. Rather they are children beholding the face of the divine Father, and speaking of things on earth as though they were things in heaven.

ILLUSIONS. 81

If it be said that this training by illusion, however indirectly beneficial to mankind, proved a direct source of calamity to the great majority of the people subjected to it, we cannot indeed deny this. The training of Israel seems to have been adapted rather for the higher than for the lower minds among the people. As compared with Greece and Rome, Israel is like a family of children kept at home rather beyond the usual age, and brought up more than most children in the presence of their parents, taught to look up to their parents as their ideals, and excluded from the outside world. Such a training would make them more intense and earnest, but it would be in danger of making them also more narrow and exclusive. These children who had not penetrated to the spirit of the parental life, but had remained imitators rather than sympathizers, would succumb to this danger of exclusiveness, and would be unprepared to enlarge their conception of the ideal, when at last they were set free from the family circle. They would cling servilely to the parental habits, even where changed circumstances rendered these habits inexpedient or wrong. Only perhaps one or two exceptionally spiritual natures in the circle of the brothers might emancipate themselves from this bondage, and might strive to live in the parental spirit rather than copy the parental habits. But these few chosen spirits when sent into the world would have all the concentrated earnestness of their narrower brothers, together with the duly enlarged conception of the ideal derived from the new world in which they found themselves placed. Such spirits were the Prophets of Israel and the Apostles of our Lord. We mourn over the weaker brethren of Israel as we mourn over infants dead, as we ponder over the problem of death or waste presented by every inch of ground, by every drop of water. We remind ourselves that even the average morality in Israel was, probably, far higher than that of Greece or Rome : but after all we have to fall back upon the faith that the solution of this problem will appear in some one of the many stages awaiting us in the infinite career of the human race. For those who believe that there may be many stages of development for each individual there is no difficulty in admitting that in the spiritual as in the material world there may reign, during each stage, some law corresponding to the " survival of the fittest." If the waste of one generation is the preparation for another, then we may with more calmness acquiesce in the famous saying of Milton, that "God, sure, esteems the growth and completing of one virtuous person more than the restraint of ten vicious."

In any case there remains at least this consolation, that the world, in respect of illusions, is all of a piece, all bearing traces of one consistent handiwork, developing, through illusion, truth. Why it should be so we can no more hope to understand than we can hope to understand why sin has been made necessary to the development of righteousness. Enough for us that it is so. But, if it is so, then a man is not absolved from the responsibility of analysing a piece of truth, even though it may contain some particles of error. Rather he is bound all the more to poise and ponder every mass of truth and to say, "I know that there must be some falsehood here, although I cannot at present discern any ; none the less, I perceive a proportion of truth, and it is my duty to fasten upon that and to appropriate it, so that, in good time, when the false particles fall away, as they certainly will, I may be found to be retaining nothing but what is true. After all, if I should make mistakes, it is the prerogative of humanity to progress by error: beasts make few mistakes and make comparatively little progress. And let me always remember how much more easy and short and dangerous it is to reject *in toto*, than to study and to discriminate."

Take now the illusions of dreams and of night. Any one can now explain at once all the phenomena of dreams on natural principles, and, this explanation given, he thinks the matter is settled. Have you dreamed of an oppressive demon sitting upon your breast? "It is the result of indigestion." Have you been wafted in your dreams upward through the air, or have you been precipitated headlong through space, awaking with a start to find yourself touching something firm? "That is the result of the tension or relaxation of certain muscles, giving to the sleep-bound brain the same result as the tension or relaxation of those same muscles in actual leaping or falling." Have you found yourself reading a sentence that will not read rightly, or solving a problem of which there can be no solution, or toiling up endless hills, or unravelling the mazes of some unthreadable labyrinth? "All this is the natural result of over-exertion during the waking hours, for which night now exacts a natural penalty, compelling you to go over the old toil again, and making you dwell with severest emphasis upon those little points and matters which were slurred and passed over in your waking thoughts for want of leisure. There is nothing new in dreams, it is all nothing but the disproportioned reproduction of parts of your waking life, the disproportion being caused by the fact that the brain in the leisure of repose, uncontrolled by the power that guided it while awake, mechanically plods over those portions of the ground of experience over which it was reluctantly compelled to skim too rapidly during the day, under the strain of an excessive hurry, impelled by the imperious will."

All this may be very true, and, in any case, is very interesting: but does it prove that dreams may do no more for us? To those who believe in Nature, but believe also in a God who rules Nature, will it seem reasonable to neglect thoughts, impressions, and beliefs which have been communicated to men from the earliest times, through dreams, simply because dreams are natural? On the contrary, our belief in their naturalness will surely stimulate us not only to study their causes, but also to trace their effects, and, may be, to recognize in dreams one among many potent levers employed by God to raise mankind nearer to Himself.

But here we are opposed by the sanitary or medical view of dreams. The physician, whose business it is to look after the body, and not after the mind or soul of his patient, naturally dislikes dreams. A dreamless sleep, he says, is the best. Dreams come from a morbid state, and he declines to suppose that anything worth learning could ever have been learned from them, any more than from the ravings of fever or delirium. But we are not now disputing this position of the physician. We are not encouraging men in these modern days to dream dreams, although we may be of opinion that in certain circumstances dreams are not necessarily morbid. We are not even maintaining that much *direct* spiritual truth has ever, even in past times, been conveyed to individuals through the medium of dreams. All that we shall urge is, that mankind, as a whole, is said by men of science and students unbiased by theological leanings to have received the revelation of the immortality of the soul indirectly through the illusions arising from the dreamful tendency, so that the visions of the night, whether true in themselves or false in themselves individually, have collectively led mankind to a very definite and historically important belief. Even those who deny the truth of this belief will not deny the importance of it, but Christians, together with a vast number of others professing other religions, believe in the truth of it. For us therefore the derivation of the belief in the immortality of the soul from illusion (supposing it to be proved) would be a very strong argument indeed that men ought not, without examination, to reject all past illusions as being necessarily destitute of all truth, or truthful tendency.

According to this theory, God has given us the nighttime not only for refreshing the tired limbs and the weary brain, but also as a season when the life of the day may be unconsciously summed up and concentrated into an influence upon the heart. Sometimes we can remember the process, and can trace how the little gaps of the day's thought are supplied by the roving phantoms of the night: more often we cannot remember the process, and are only conscious of the resultant strength and moral freshness. During this period, though the reasoning power is fettered and the will seems numb, yet the affection of love is as strong as ever, or at least much stronger relatively than our other faculties. It is indeed a time when the instincts which we share with animals, being free from the will, are liable to break out if they have not been habitually controlled during our waking moments : but if the day has been marked by self-control, the night is free from danger, and brings nothing but revelations of peace. The love that had no time and no right to brood over the fresh loss of a friend during the stir of work and pressure of duty, finds leisure during the night. In the day we realised the absence of the friend : if we forgot it for a moment, we looked around, and sense, memory, and reason made loss conspicuous. We recalled an image in thought, but we knew that we were but thinking, and therefore the image was but an image. But when the darkness of night fell upon us then came a darkness of the senses also, and an oblivion of all that was not habitual, all that was not part of our daily thoughts. Now the self-same great Nature that prompts the wearied hound to hunt the prey over again as he whines and stirs before the fire in his sleep, prompts the race of men to receive their several revelations of good or evil from the night : the man of action is at his work, buying, or selling, or scheming, the mathematician at his problems, the poet at his fancies ; and the mourner for the dead takes up again the thread of sorrow. Now memory and sense are fettered ; distinctions of time are lost : now we no longer recall the words or looks of yesterday as being yesterday's, irrevocably yesterday's ; now we no longer see the empty seat, or the horrible black garb of mourning, the unopened books, or the toys unused : but we still recall the image of the beloved one, and being without the discriminating test of reason, we know not that it is an image. What in the day was imagination, by night becomes vision or sight, and we see, not an image, but our very friend.

If in these modern and artificial times such reappearances, accepted as mere recollections, have some influence upon us, much greater must have been that influence in earlier ages. In the stir and bustle of these later days, mere multiplicity drives out force and singleness of motive: the reading of books supplants the knowing of books; society excludes intercourse; acquaintance drives out friendship; and the crowded variety of the day makes a medley of the visions of our nights. Yet if, even now, we find ourselves sometimes in the darkness disentangling from a host of petty, grotesque, obtrusive phantoms some fitful glimpses of the old familiar face, how much more vivid must such visions have been in the old times when men and nations alike were men and nations of one idea! For us the use of dreams is past. To us, after the most startling visions of the night, science and experience come at once with their probing touch, and, at their approach, vanishes not only the phantom, but the influence of it. But in the old times it was not so. They had not attained a science or even a theory of dreams; they had not labelled off with names imagination, sense, reason, and will. What they saw, they saw. True, some things seen dwelt in a world where they could not be touched; other things seen dwelt in a world where they could be touched: but both were equally real. When, therefore, the sleeping savage started from converse with the father whom he had buried a week ago, well might he say to himself, "So then my father's shadow still lives. I could not touch it, but

I saw it this night and the night before; and when I embraced it, it slipped from me like a shadow. The shape changed and varied like a mist, and it vanishes in the morning as the breath vanishes in the air. It was my father's shadow or spirit, which cannot be buried in the tomb." At first this belief may have been both vague and cheerless. The spirit was deemed to be in need of food or clothing; he haunted the dreamer, because his armour had not been placed by his side in the tomb, or because his dogs or slaves had not been slaughtered at his funeral to accompany their master in the chase or warfare beyond the grave. Dreary and desolate was the world of shadows in former days: the greatest hero of the Grecian host down below would have endured all hardship, and stooped to be the meanest serf on earth if only he might have purchased a return to the warmth and brightness of the familiar world above. A similar sense of dreariness speaks in the old northern verse:—

> "Bones among stones
> Lieth full cauld,
> While the soul wandereth
> Whither God wold."

To admit this origin of the belief in immortality is only to recognize one more among many instances of a common phenomenon, that a high and noble result often grows by very slow degrees from a very low origin. Grant that men reasoned wrongly in old times about their dreams; suppose that in the course of many centuries, under the influence of nightly visions seen in the hours when men surrender their faculties to God, the hearts of the better, the more active and less selfish sort of men, were led by the guidance of love to believe in the existence of a shade or spirit of the departed after death. What then ? Because God led men to the belief in immortality by love, and in a natural way, by illusion, do we on that account think ourselves bound to set the belief aside ? But you say, " An illusion never could give birth to so sublime a truth." Well, at least we have seen above that an illusion can, and often does, give birth to most beneficial beliefs : and this may be proved by history, by science, by the experience of your own childhood, and of every child that ever grew to manhood. For sceptics who reject the belief in a divine Fatherhood, and in the immortality of the soul, our argument will have no force : but those who hold fast those beliefs must not despise illusion, which has been our guide to truth. To me it seems a thought full of comfort and hope, and a most wholesome rebuke to intellectual pride, that the hour of bodily and intellectual helplessness should have been chosen by God to sow the seed of one of His highest revelations, as if to shew that the foolishness of God is wiser than the wisdom of men, and the weakness of God stronger than the strength of men.

Moreover, it seems to me that the result of all that has been said—and much more might be said, of which a little will be said hereafter[1]—about the salutary power of illusion, would lead us even beyond that negative conclusion which we laid down above, viz., that we are not justified in rejecting truth because it is involved in illusions. If we find that it is impossible for a child, or lover, or husband, or wife, or for a high-spirited youth or man, or for a great nation, to live the sort of life that should be lived, and do the sort of work that should

[1] See Chapters XXI. and XXII.

be done, without hoping and trusting, then does not a positive conclusion seem to follow, that Nature thereby sets her seal on hope and trust as virtues? Now the essence of hope and trust is that they incline the mind to believe somewhat more than can be logically proved upon mere evidence. If, therefore, we are bound to believe, upon the basis of the intuitions of affection, something more of good about our wives, and children, and parents than is warranted by mere evidence, and if Nature inculcates this rule upon us and punishes the violation of it, does it not follow that Nature *may be* training us to practise a similar hope and trust towards herself? And if the want of hope and of trust is a ruinous sin in the children of human parents, may it not be that there is also such a sin as hopeless incredulity in the righteous tendency of things and untrustfulness in the ultimate kindness of Nature? But if this be so, then, since one cannot trust a machine, it would seem that Nature herself is leading us to regard Nature as something higher than a machine, and in some sense as a Person.

PART II.

THE WORSHIP OF NATURE.

CHAPTER VI.

THE ILLUSIONS OF NON-HUMAN NATURE.

WE have agreed that worship means love, trust, and awe, and consequently that we are not to be ashamed of anthropomorphism. We have also agreed that we are to preserve a certain symmetry in worship, so as to include in its scope all provinces of healthy life, such as science and art, in addition to morality. Lastly, we have agreed that the revelations that reveal to us the due objects of worship, are generally contained in illusions, yet are not on that account necessarily to be rejected. Our natural course would now seem to be to point out that the worship of Jesus is best qualified to engender and develop love, trust, and awe, that it includes all conduct within its scope, and lastly that we ought not to be deterred from it by the fear of anthropomorphism and illusion.

But we must not move on quite so fast as this. For I have often heard it objected by sceptics who have been told that we regard Jesus as the fit centre of human worship, "How then did the world manage to rub on for so many years pretty well without Jesus of Nazareth? If worship, as you say, is universal and necessary, what was the world doing for so many hundred, or thousands of years without its 'fit centre,' as you please to call it? You are prepared to admit that Jesus was a man, and that His work was human and not supernatural; why not be sensibly consistent and take the inevitable plunge which you must take sooner or later away from orthodoxy, and say boldly that Jesus was well enough suited to His time, but not to all time nor to all nations, and consequently that the worship of Jesus was simply a temporary phase in the development of humanity." My reply is this. It is certain, indeed, that Jesus was human, and I am ready to admit that His work was human, and not supernatural, except so far as His humanity was superior to ours; but it does not follow that the worship of Jesus is necessarily to be transient. If it can be said, even in hyperbole, of our greatest poet, that he was "for all time," surely it deserves consideration, whether in a much more real way Jesus of Nazareth may not have been, and be destined to be, "for all time." My own belief is that Jesus was "for all time." What other people call evolution, or the spirit of progress, or Chance, or Nothing, or the Unknowable, that I call the Word of God. This Word of God I discern in the old days of Rome and Greece, and the still older days of Israel and of Egypt, and going back still further, I discern it in the very dawn of human thought, leading men towards love and trust and awe, or, in other words, shaping the souls of men for worship with the same spiritual tools which were employed with supreme effect by Jesus of Nazareth. Again, looking to the results of the work of Jesus hitherto, I discern the traces of the same evolution, or progress, or Word of God.

Lastly, looking forward to the future of humanity, I discern the only prospect of salvation for our race in the continued operation of the same Word of God. What then must I inevitably do? What but worship Jesus of Nazareth as the supreme expression of that Divine Word, recognizing that He is, and was, and will be for all eternity the Son of the Father in Heaven, the only Name under heaven by which salvation is given unto men, and that of Him alone of men it may be said without hyperbole,

"He was not of an age, but for all time."

But this we shall not be able to realize, unless we first realize the manner in which, for ages before the coming of Christ, the Word of God, acting through human and non-human Nature, led men by illusions towards love and trust and awe, and so prepared the way for the Incarnate Word. It is the object of the Second Part of this book to sketch the influence of the illusions of Nature upon man in producing worship before the coming of Christ. Accordingly this chapter will be devoted to the influence of the illusions of non-human Nature, first upon childhood in each generation, next upon the childhood of mankind, and lastly upon Greece, Rome, and Israel.

We have said that the revelation of non-human Nature blends with and purifies, without necessarily destroying, the revelation of human Nature. God is Love, human love; yet His love is to our love as the sky is to a hand's-breadth. God is Power, human power; yet His power is to our power as the Alps or Andes to the child's sand-castle on the sea-beach. God is human, yet He is also "not ourselves." Were it not for this revelation of non-human Nature, were we surrounded with nothing but imperfect human beings, or cooped up for ever within some small environment of which every boundary could be reached by human senses, so that we had not the ideas of the illimitable and eternal, it might have been impossible that the feeling of awe should have been generated among us. But as it is, from our earliest years external Nature presses in upon us with material objects beyond the measurement of our senses, thereby suggesting also thoughts beyond the reaches of our souls. Roughly speaking, we may describe her revelation as producing first Wonder, then Servility, but lastly Wonder purified into Admiration and Awe, and Servility exalted to willing Self-surrender.[1] The first is paradise; the second is paradise lost; the third would be paradise regained. Through the two first stages every child passes, and should approximate to the third; and the same is true of the human race.

The first impression produced on a very young child by the sensible world around it appears to be a blank wonderment, without memory or reflection. The glance of an infant has been described by a great novelist as "semi-conscious," and it might also be described, if there were such a word, as "semi-scious," for the child seems so divided between what he is and what he sees, that he can scarcely as yet distinguish between the two, and can neither know himself nor nature. Even later on, partly no doubt through the analogy of language, but partly also through the want of experience and discrimination, he

---

[1] Of course Nature also produces other feelings, such as pleasure, admiration, &c.; but I am here speaking merely of the different shapes assumed by the growing revelation of awe.

speaks of himself in the third person, and personifies inanimate things.[1] He may feel pain or pleasure; but either feeling comes to him, he knows not how, why, or whence, and he cannot at present distinguish between his pain and the dazzling sun or scorching flame, between his pleasure and the fountain sparkling in the sun, or the kitten playing with a ball of string. In such a state he can have no strife with Nature. He knows neither good nor evil. Nature is his god, and he converses with her daily, hearing her voice and seeing her beauty, and is at peace with her. Sin has not entered paradise.

But with the power of distinguishing between himself and external nature comes the sense of individuality, and with the sense of individuality comes the sense of opposition or compliance, defeat or victory. Still the child has as yet no sense of sin, only of mistakes and delusions and defeats. The reflection in a mirror is not the same as the object out of the mirror; fire is not a pretty toy to be handled—these and other little childish inferences he begins to draw from the experiences of past errors: but, so far, his errors are mere errors of the mind. If it were possible that a little child could grow up to manhood without intercourse with his fellow-creatures, it is conceivable, if not certain, that he would remain in this condition, having perhaps some notion of the violation of the laws of health and pleasure as constituting grave and shocking errors, but

[1] It would be interesting to ascertain how far young children *bonâ fide* personify. So many stories of what children say or do are slightly distorted or exaggerated for the purpose of effect, that it is not easy to get at the truth. The following story might have served as a theme for Wordsworth. A child sitting at table with its parents had been forbidden to ask for fruit. For a time the child sat silently staring at what he wanted: but at last he burst out, " Mother, the currants do look at Bob."

not having any notion of what we call sin. He has fears, hostilities, the sense of a conflict of wills, but not the sense of a conflict with a will higher than his own. But now enters the new experience described hereafter,[1] the consciousness of will and the sense of collision between his own will and the will of a higher power. The manner of this collision, being a part of the revelation of humanity, does not belong to the subject we are now treating: but the result of it is utterly to change the attitude of the child towards Nature.

Imputing some lingering remnant of personality, as he does, to the inanimate objects individually or collectively around him, he suddenly finds all Nature hostile. On every side he is capriciously and unkindly checked and punished. Look at Landseer's picture of the "Child in Disgrace," and you comprehend at once the unreasoning and undiscriminating irritation which makes him include all Nature in the circle of his enmity. Like the child of Coriolanus setting his teeth and "mammocking" the gilded butterfly because he had fallen in the chase of it, so every child naturally imputes his own irritation and hostility to everything around him. And when he has passed from the stage of error to the stage of fault, this sense of hostility deepens. When he is under the cloud of sin, the whole world seems dark. His sports no longer give joy; the morning withholds its wonted brightness: the sky rains spitefully; the sun sets with malignant speed; the clouds frown upon him; the night brings new and strange thoughts that make darkness terrible. Nature must be obeyed, for her penalties are terrible and sure; but the child obeys unwillingly. He

[1] See the chapter on the Illusions of the Family.

has lost his old sense of union and peace with Nature. He is at war with her now : and where he must obey, he will obey with the unwillingness of a slave. At other times, when the child is not under the cloud, Nature is his friend ; mere existence is a pleasure, a passionate delight ; every day and hour brings its novel experiences and joys, more vivid now than they will ever be in after life ; Fancy gilds every thought, and enlarges every image ; the present may sometimes pall, but he can always turn to the better future which the next hour, he thinks, is sure to bring. Not what he sees, but what he dreams of fills his mind ; a few bits of tin make up whole armies, a floating fragment of wood is an iron-clad or a fleet ; not being troubled, as Hamlet was, with bad dreams, he can be happy in a nut-shell, and count it infinite space. During such happier moments the child is journeying toward the land of Promise.

As he grows older his attitude towards Nature will depend greatly upon the knowledge of Nature possessed by the society in which he moves : but for the most part we shall be right in saying that Nature will have lost for him the aspect of Personality, and will have assumed the aspect of Law. The thunder no longer terrifies him as if it were the very voice of an offended god, nor the lightning as if it were the missile of a heaven-sent anger. He learns how to predict the coming storm and to watch the approaching clouds ; he is taught to count the seconds between the sight and sound of the lightning, in order roughly to estimate the distance. Or, even though he may not have reached so far—for this is rather science than the mere observation of Nature—yet he knows at all events that the lightning always precedes the thunder, and that neither comes by accident. But is he necessarily the better for all this knowledge? He may be, or he may not be. He is delivered at least from the servile fear of capricious beings ruling the universe; but, unless he sees some other Being, not capricious, behind the newly-discovered order of the world, he is not greatly raised by his discoveries. If he gives up the habit of wondering and admiring, he has lost a faculty almost essential to the freshness and sweetness of existence, the very salt of human life. A certain deadness and torpor falls on the mind of one who has brought himself to regard the universe as a great machine, moving with the regularity of a pendulum, and serving none but certain obvious purposes of utility. Not many men perhaps quite succeed in bringing themselves into this condition of mind. As though expressly to save us from it, Nature teems with puzzles and perplexities, inconveniences and terrors. The mystery of life and death, illimitable space, implying illimitable time, the motions of the planets, the growth and blossoming of the flowers, all tend to keep us from taking what may be called the pig-stye view of creation, and constrain us to look outwards and upwards to something " not ourselves." But, though we may be preserved from the wrong view, few of us take the right one. We still remain under the law; rebels or slaves, it matters not. We cannot so far combine love and trust with awe as to enter the kingdom that is "not ourselves," like little children, believing that the King is with us. The true and right result of our increased knowledge of Nature would be to bring back again, as the result of knowledge, that peace and harmony which we enjoyed in our earliest childhood, when we moved in the paradise of ignorance. The time ought to come when we ought not to see anything so very ridiculous in the spirit of St. Francis of Assisi, who looked on all Nature as the choir of God's angelic ministers, so many brothers and sisters and helpmates to men. For this, or something like this was the spirit introduced by Jesus of Nazareth into the world; the dependent filial spirit which looks alike for the protection of mankind, for the adornment of the flowers, for the feeding of the birds, to the common Father of all beings. This childlike trustful entrance into the realm of Nature, accepting things as they are, not shutting the eyes against facts, but lovingly welcoming them as the Father's facts, probing them, grouping them, and playing with them as a child plays with his toys, would be found in the end to be the path, not only to peace, but to supremacy over Nature. If we but trust her, she reveals to us her secrets and gives us power to produce her results. But now, before we describe the Western and the Eastern attitude towards Nature in the times before Christ let us spare a word or two for Nature's influence upon the childhood of mankind.

If we may trust the evidence of the early language and religions of our remote ancestors, they also, the whole race together, passed through the same stages of Personification and Enmity to Nature which we have described as characteristic of the childhood of the individual. Partly, perhaps, through the same inability to distinguish between the "I" and the "Not I," partly, perhaps, through the tyrannical tendency of language to impose on thought the bonds of its own limitations, the early races of mankind came first to speak, and then to think, of natural forces as persons. At first, perhaps (though we have little evidence of it beyond the suggestions of the hitherto undemonstrated theory of evolution), mankind may have occupied a position little higher than mere animalism. Placed as the sport of the elements and prey of wild beasts, man as he was in those days appears to man as he is in these days, the most wretched and forlorn of animals. Probably, however, he had not realised his wretchedness, and was therefore happy except in moments of actual pain and terror. At all events he had not yet learned sin, and, in virtue of that exemption, may be said to have been dwelling in an inferior paradise. But as soon as man passed out of this first Eden of instinct, driven from his old ignorant harmony with Nature by the sense of a will within him bringing him into collision with a Will without him, mankind straightway entered into a state of war. Nature and man are henceforth at variance. Conscious of his newly-acquired faculty of will, he attributes the same faculty to the natural forces around him, and immediately they become gods to be feared, or gods to be propitiated, or demons to be bound down by the force of cunning rites and charms. In the old times, before this cloud of trouble had passed over his soul, he had known want and failure and pain, but not this new malignity of Nature, not the cruel opposition and vengeance of invisible forces. Before, he had been unsuccessful in the chase, or overtaken by night in the forest, or his cave had been inundated by the rising floods; but all this had been a part of the environment of his life, bringing with it no sense of hostility, scarcely of hardship. But now all was changed. Nature had turned against him. If he was unsuccessful now in fishing or hunting, it was because the rough South Wind had sent a storm, or the mischievous Zephyr had given the alarm to the prey, or the all-seeing Sun had betrayed his secret, or the unkind Moon had veiled her face in clouds. The very air that he breathed now rebelled against him, sending pinching cold, and fog, and rain; the very ground on which he trod turned traitor, and brought forth thorns and thistles instead of fruits. Verily the earth was cursed for his sake.

Now comes religion into the field—religion, the art of bribing spirits, for thus it must be regarded in its lower aspect—the knowledge of charms and incantations, of the caprices of beings evil or only partly good, and of the sacrifices necessary to appease and conciliate them;— religion, so forcibly described by the great Latin poet as trampling human life beneath the weight of its foul oppression, the mother of wicked and impious deeds. To some it might seem that, rather than be cursed with such a parody of true religion, it would have been better to have no religion at all. But it was not so: man was not retrograding. The notion of an external and more powerful Will than that of man was a gain. The mischief was that mankind seemed at present to discern many wills, thereby making it impossible for men to attempt to conform themselves to Nature, and leading them into attempts to bribe or bind Nature into conformity with themselves.

Natural selection prepared the way for a truer theology by discouraging the lower types of religion. In the conflict for existence the race or tribe that was hampered by the lower religion contended at a disadvantage with the race or tribe that had attained to the higher religion. Other things being equal in the combatants, superstition was a disadvantage, paralysing the intellect and imbuing the heart with hopelessness and lethargy. Superstition made itself felt as a disadvantage, not only in the war of race against race, but also in the struggle against the inclemency of nature. The man that could believe in a good spirit was, other things being equal, likely to be superior in hopefulness and in energy to the man that could believe in none but evil spirits. Again, the arts of life prepared the way for a truer theology. Improved weapons raised men above the state in which they had been contending with beasts on equal or inferior terms, and delivered them from some of the temptations to deify brute force and savage cruelty. Metals being discovered and utilised, the art of agriculture became a novelty, a custom, a necessity; and with the patient expectation of the harvest came first, a temporary sacrifice of the hunter's wandering life, then the toleration and at last the love, of a fixed home. The sound of music began to be heard among the villages, suggesting other and higher harmonics than those of sound; and when the labour of the harvest was over, the husbandman, enfranchised from precarious dependence upon the daily chase, and led by settled life toward thoughts more deep and connected than the unstable and isolated fancies of a hunter's wanderings, found leisure to sit down and ask himself, "Whence come these fixed habits and customs of things that add delights to life? Whence come seed-time and harvest? Who sends the sun to ripen our corn? Who banishes him to his evening darkness, and calls him back each morning? What Being is it that commands the blade to spring up, and the green ear to become golden, and gives the ripe corn to men? Who sends the sweet sounds into the stretched harp-string, and fits sound to sound in harmony as mysterious as the harmony of the host of heaven? Whatever beings these may be, they must needs be good and kind." Thus Nature, teaching the arts of life, prepared the way for a truer theology.[1]

In the Grecian cities of the west a cheerful theology, and still more, perhaps, a national tendency to observe and speculate, led to a closer study of Nature. Nature having been separated from personality (at least for a small circle of philosophic observers), and having been resolved into causes and effects, the great question that occupied the early Greek philosophers was, What was the First Cause of the world? A certain self-possession and due recognition of the excellence of human nature enabled the early Greek philosophers to contemplate non-human nature in a more calm and philosophic spirit than was possible in the east. They were not frightened at it, and did not crouch before it, but examined it from a position of superiority. Almost all their early systems of philosophy indicate a desire to find the cause of creation in some one sensible object—fire, water, earth, or air. This necessarily led to error; but being keen observers, they offered theories and suggestions which have been found useful and suggestive even by modern scientific writers. But though they had the keenness and subtlety,

---

[1] With some modifications, this passage is extracted from my *Cambridge Sermons*.

they had not the simplicity and patience necessary to unlock the secrets of Nature. Partly perhaps the existence of slavery interfered with the progress of natural philosophy. It is in the practice of mechanical arts and in the routine of manual labour, that Nature has often revealed herself to those who have their eyes open to observe her secrets. From all such sources of observation the free-born philosophers of Greece were debarred; and deliberate experiment, for its own sake, had not yet come into vogue. A long course of casual and fortuitous observation and experience would be required to make up for this deficiency, and to supply the basis for a sound introduction. In mathematics and in astronomy (where experiment was impossible) the Greeks made progress; but not equally in other branches of natural science.

Foiled in their first efforts, they were diverted from the study of Nature by the perception that the origin of things, instead of being one of the elements, must be a Mind. If Mind, and not any part of sensible Nature, originated Nature, then it seemed to them that the Mind of the Universe might be best studied, not in the universe, but in the mind of man. A great discovery, if only it had not been so one-sided, excluding the old investigation of non-human nature! But the new method seemed to promise a shorter road to truth, and besides, it was no less attractive for its seeming nobleness than for its ease. Hence the study of material objects sank into insignificance. Mathematics prospered, and, so far as they depended on mere description, other branches of natural history made some progress. But no advance was made in science corresponding to the advance in literature and art. With something of unfair prejudice, but with some truth too, Bacon deplores "the old times before the Greeks, when natural science was, perhaps, more flourishing, though it made less noise, not having yet passed into the pipes and trumpets of the Greeks," and declares that "the wisdom which we have derived principally from the Greeks is but like the boyhood of Knowledge; it can talk, but it cannot generate; for it is fruitful of controversies and barren of works."

The feeling of the Greek and Roman philosophers towards Nature may be illustrated by their inability, as far as we can judge from the absence of mention, to appreciate the beauties of natural scenery. Many passages might be quoted to exhibit the keenness of their observation and the aptness with which they could turn natural objects to account in explaining and giving vividness to unfamiliar actions by pictures borrowed from what is familiar in nature. The similes of Homer and Virgil have been the stock-in-trade of the poets of posterity. But the apt application of pictures from nature does not in the least imply appreciation of the beauty of the pictures themselves: indeed many of the pictures are evidently selected with no eye to beauty, but merely to vivid explanation. On the whole it may be said, without any exaggeration, that whereas the modern tendency is to look upon a landscape as a thing of beauty, the ancient tendency was to look on it as a thing of use. The exquisite lines in which Virgil describes the pleasures of the country, however rhythmical and suggestive of rural ecstasy, differ but little in spirit from the more sober lines in which Horace sketches the happiness of the well-to-do man who, far from business, tills his ancestral farm with oxen of his own. It is farming, not landscape that excites their poetic enthusiasm. It would not be fair to take Shakespeare or Wordsworth, or even the more sensuous and classical Milton; but take an unknown inferior author of the sixteenth century, and see with what passion modern thought describes a sunrise in the country :—

> "The sunne when he had spred his raies,
> And shewde his face ten thousand waies,
> Ten thousand things do then begin
> To shew the life that they are in.
> The heaven shews lively art and hue,
> Of sundry shapes and colours new,
> And laughs upon the earth anon.
> The earth, as cold as any stone,
> Wet in the tears of her own kinde,
> 'Gins then to take a joyful minde,
> For well she feels that out and out,
> The sunne doth warme her round about,
> And dries her children tenderly,
> And shewes them forth full orderly,
> And even for joy thus of this heate
> She sheweth forth her pleasures great." [1]

Now if these lines, with all their rough uncouthness, their forced rhymes, and almost bald simplicity, are compared with Virgil's masterpiece at the end of the Second Georgic, the uncouth poet's superior appreciation of Nature will be manifest. Virgil's ecstasy dwells upon the plenty of prompt food sent up by the just earth, the sweet leisure in cool grottoes, the townsman's unaccustomed freedom in the spacious fields, his delight in the untainted water of natural springs, the pleasant lowing of the oxen, the beneficent phenomena of the

[1] *Tottel's Miscellany*, 1557, Arber's Reprint, p. 231.

circling seasons, and all the placid comforts of the rich and prosperous homestead. We in modern times turn with relief from populous cities to the wildest, gloomiest scenery of forest and crag. To the ancients such an exchange would have been exile; their delight was in the crowded market-place and the busy streets. Cicero mentions it as a wonder and anomaly in human nature that men in time, through force of habit, grow reconciled even to forests and to mountains.[1]

As, therefore, the Greek philosophers saw little to admire and revere in rocks and forests and visible nature, so also they found nothing to inspire awe in the invisible laws of nature. Having disentangled themselves from the popular error of those who saw a Dryad in every tree and a Naiad or River-god in every fountain or stream, they scarcely dreamed of looking for a higher Will behind the complex machine to which the banishment of polytheism had reduced the order of the universe. "Happy," says Virgil, "is the man who had power to ascertain the causes of things." But why? Not for the

[1] I have heard it ingeniously maintained that the Greek mythology is as it were a residuum of a past intense worship of Nature. But is this so? If we say, with Professor Max Müller, that "to call Erse the daughter of Selene was no more than if we, in our more matter-of-fact language, say that there is dew after a moonlight night," it would seem that the old Greeks, when they said, "Selene *brings forth* Erse," meant no more than our country people now mean when they say, "The moon *breeds* dew." Where, in all this, is the proof of the more intense pleasure in past times? As for the subsequent personification, that is no evidence of more intense pleasure, but indicates rather a restless intellectual craving to explain every natural phenomenon, and to suppose a Causer, wherever the observers could not discern a cause. Yet I should admit that the Greek mythology proves that the processes of Nature imprinted themselves forcibly on the Greek mind, and arrested their attention. Probably also they had an intense *pleasure* in Nature; but had they anything like the *worship* of Nature which we find in Wordsworth?

mere pleasure of knowing; not to obtain insight into the mysteries of a divine Will; not even to obtain command over the operations of Nature, but simply to deliver mankind from the fears of the vulgar, "to trample under foot all fear and inexorable fate, and the roar of greedy Acheron." The same motive is seen still more clearly in the vehemence with which Lucretius protests that true piety consists not in worship and sacrifice, "but rather in being able to behold all things with a peaceful mind." A horror seizes him lest his proselytes to atheism may relapse into the darkness of religion when they look upon the motions of the stars:

> "Nam cum suspicimus magni cœlestia mundi
> Templa, super stellisque micantibus æthera fixum,
> Et venit in mentem solis lunæque viarum,
> Tunc aliis oppressa malis in pectora cura
> Illa quoque expergefactum caput erigere infit,
> Nequæ forte deum nobis immensa potestas
> Sit vario motu quæ candida sidera verset."

Against such a relapse the mere quiet and leisurely study of natural phenomena severally in their different departments would furnish no sufficient remedy. The poet felt that he must attempt nothing short of a solution of the *whole* problem, a revelation "of the most high system of nature and the Gods, and the first beginnings of things;" and the first great philosopher of Nature is described by him as the champion of mankind against the gods, the hero who broke through the flaming walls of the world and returned, "as a conqueror, to tell us what can, what cannot come into being." But it was not in this prejudiced, self-reliant, aggressive way that Nature was to be conquered. Lynx-eyed observation and a busy brain were some, but not the only, nor the highest, qualifications for entering into the kingdom of man over nature. Patience and docility, lowliness and trustful obedience, these were still higher qualifications, without which even the Greek mind could never understand the language of Nature, " that sound and language which went forth into all lands and did not incur the confusion of Babel. Thus should men study to be perfection, and becoming again as little children, condescend to take the alphabet of it into their hands."

Precisely opposite to the Greek complacency was the feeling towards Nature in the East. Among several Eastern nations the old religious feeling that Nature or God was an enemy, had not died out so soon as in the West. Moloch and Baal were harder masters, and exacted more savage sacrifices, than Jupiter and Apollo. Even among the men of Israel, though they had the support of a higher, calmer Trust, there was a disposition to fear Nature, perhaps to excess. If they did not crouch before it, at least they regarded it with feelings incompatible with dispassionate scientific inquiry. In almost every case the Psalms treat Nature either as the robe and vesture of God, or else as the symbol of the frailty of dependent, transitory man. The hills standing round about Jerusalem represent Jehovah compassing round about those that fear Him ; the sky uplifted above the earth proclaims the height of His mercy ; the rock speaks of His unchanging nature ; the heavens proclaim the glory of God, and the firmament telleth His handiwork. That most beautiful of the Psalms which describes the " natural history of a day," begins and ends with the praises of Jehovah. The utilitarian view is not forgotten; place is found for " wine, that maketh glad the heart of man, and oil to make his face to shine, and bread which strengtheneth man's heart;" but all the goodly frame of the universe is to the psalmist nothing but the vesture of Him who covereth Himself with light as with a garment, and stretcheth out the heavens like a curtain, who layeth the beams of His chambers in the waters, who maketh the clouds His chariot, who walketh upon the wings of the wind.

Such a view of Nature undoubtedly leads to true worship, by tending to awe; but carried to excess, it defeats itself. Reverence might seem to forbid a scientific investigation of anything that could be called the garment of God. Why inquire into the causes of unusual natural phenomena when the agency of the Supreme was always at hand to furnish the solution to every problem? Floods, earthquakes, volcanic eruptions, what were they but the tokens of His immediate presence, the hill smoking at His touch, the earth melting at His approach, the waters seeing Him and being afraid? Now, carefully analysed, this sort of non-investigating acquiescent wonder is often found to be less reverent and less conducive to reverence than the subdued and controlled wonder which is not allowed to prevent the mind from thought, contemplation, and inquiry. To the man who is content always to stare at the stars in otiose astonishment, the heavens will always remain a dark vault lighted with fixed and moving tapers, or he may call it perhaps the spangled floor of the palace of the Supreme: but how can such a conception be compared for a moment, in respect of awfulness and reverence, with the conceptions of illimitable space, mass, force, and order, revealed to modern minds by the patient researches of astronomy? Although therefore we are bound to admit that Israel approximated more closely than Greece to the dependent spirit that is needful for the right study of nature, yet we cannot fail to feel also that in another respect Greece had the advantage. Greece, if it had less awe of God, had somewhat more of trust in the divine faculties and destiny of man. If Lucretius was unscientifically prejudiced and terror-stricken at the possibility that his proselytes, looking up to the star-lit sky, might be unable to resist the belief that "perchance we may find after all that there is some power of the Gods immeasurable, able to wheel the bright stars in their varied motions," yet on the other hand there are traces in the Psalms of an unscientific prejudice, that Nature is an enemy from whom one must seek refuge with Jehovah. Even in the Psalmist's most peaceful expression of thankfulness to Jehovah, the moon and the stars suggest a suppressed thought that the son of man might have seemed too insignificant for the notice of God; and the sense of the hostility of Nature is almost always perceptible in every mention of the sea made by the singers of Israel.[1] The sea is almost always an enemy, kept in and controlled by Jehovah, who "rules the raging of the waves." At the rebuke of Jehovah the waters flee, at the voice of His thunder they are afraid. The ocean is as a wild beast which would burst out to devour the world, if Jehovah had not set bounds which it shall not pass, neither turn again to cover the earth: "the waves of

[1] This terror of the sea finds a curious expression in the book of the Apocalypse, "and there shall be no more sea:" but the spirit of these words is a prediction that all *fear of Nature* shall be removed in the New Jerusalem.

the sea are mighty, and rage horribly, but yet the Lord who dwelleth on high is mightier." Israel, though dependent, was scarcely trustful and fearless enough to be called entirely child-like. Still under the law, in science as in morality, she required the coming of Him whose mission it was to unite the revelation of human and non-human nature; to shew that the perfect Man was perfectly in accordance with Nature; to exhibit mankind, in Himself, commanding Nature by obeying her; to exalt truth and to cast down conventionalism and hypocrisy; to stimulate the love of knowledge and to cast out all fear of it; and to enable all the human race to enter at once the Kingdom of Man over Nature and the Kingdom of God over man, by one and the same means—being born again, and becoming little children.

CHAPTER VII.

THE ILLUSIONS OF SACRIFICE.

UNTIL law came into the world there was no sin. But soon the fear of beasts and men, forcing families into a tribe, necessitated union. Union in war implied obedience and discipline; union in peace implied custom. At first custom did not extend beyond the limits of one's tribe; whatever helped the tribe was right, whatever harmed the tribe was contrary to custom, and (so to speak by anticipation) wrong or sinful. To pity an enemy was weak and contemptible, to slay or rob an enemy was strong and useful to the tribe, and therefore right. On the other hand, to slay or rob a fellow-tribesman was obviously harmful to the tribe, and against custom, and wrong. By degrees, as custom hardened into law, all violations of law, independently of their public harmfulness (which sometimes, as in the murder of a suppliant, might not be obvious) came to seem shocking. Even in a strong man these actions began to create repulsion. His fellow-tribesmen shunned the offender, or perhaps banished him from their camp. Condemned by the judgment of society and by his own conscience, which recognized what was due to custom, the hasty homicide would fain have undone the past, and brought back into the limbs of the murdered man the blood that the earth had drunk. But this could not be done. What could he do to propitiate custom, and to make himself right with the averted world?

Here Religion came in to help and harm mankind. It found the offender shunned as though he had a plague upon him, bringing ill luck to the neighbourhood: and it suggested that the dread of infection might be removed if the body of the offender were cleansed and purified with lustrations made efficacious with rites and charms. But of what nature should be these accompanying rites? There were rites already in existence. Before now, the living had been haunted by the spectres of the dead. Even in the darkness of the night, the closed eye of the chief of the tribe had sometimes refused to shut out the reproachful face of some buried elder or hero, coming out of the grave to complain that he had not been honoured on his passage from this world, as he should have been, with gifts of sheep and oxen for food, or captives, or wives to attend him, or hounds, or horses, or bow and arrows to aid him in the chase. At such times Religion had long ago revealed what was to be done. Gifts were to be offered to the dead, such as his soul desired. Yet you could hardly call them gifts, for they were gifts that *must* be given. If the gifts were denied, evil had followed; the tribe had been defeated in war or foiled in the chase, or pestilence or flood had come upon them. All these evils Religion had averted by teaching men the art of giving seasonable gifts. Nor had it been the freshly-buried dead alone who had thus been propitiated by Religion. Sometimes evil had come from remote ancestors of the tribe, whose memories, celebrated by annual gifts for many generations, had been of late neglected and dishonoured. Their spirits had brought the plagues which Religion had driven away with sacrifice. It was the duty of the wise men of Religion, or priests, to discern Spirit from Spirit, and to tell the tribe which Spirit had brought the evil, and what was the appropriate gift by which the offended Spirit might be appeased. The problem was sometimes complicated, because there were some older and more remote Spirits who did not haunt them in nightly visions, and with whom the tribe was only connected by the most distant ties of descent, Spirits that dwelt in the sky or flood, the sun or night : and these, too, had to be propitiated by continual and costly gifts. These did not appear in visions ; but they were visibly working for or against the tribe in open day or in the waking hours of the night. All these Spirits had to be discriminated by the priests, their caprices understood, their wishes satisfied, and their anger averted. This was the business of Religion.

No gift seemed more impressive and appropriate than the sacrifices of the lives of living things. In the first place they were food : and the Spirits, dwelling perhaps in a land where there was no food, might need them, and be angered for the want of them. In the second place, gifts of this kind seemed to go directly and immediately to the Spirit in a way in which no other gifts went : fruits and loaves seemed to spoil beneath the touch of the Spirits, and to linger on their way to the other world ; arms and armour might seem to early rationalists not to go at all, but to remain in the grave by the side of the recumbent bones. But an ox or sheep could be sent by a straight path, so that it would never come back again: a single blow dismissed the gift to its destination. True, the body remained, but something went out of the body that never returned, and as for the mere flesh, that could be sent up afterwards in the ascending smoke of fire. What could be more direct than a gift like this, transferred, as it were visibly, from the hands of the living to the invisible hand of the exacting Spirit?

Special circumstances sometimes demanded more awful sacrifices. Sometimes a Spirit had sent a cloud of infatuation into the heart of a chief, so that he had slain a suppliant in a fit of folly; or in the woods an axe had slipped from the hand of a tribesman and had been turned by some offended Spirit against a brother or a father, so that an unholy death had followed, bringing pestilence and the wrath of all the Spirits upon the tribe. When blood had thus been spilt so as to anger the Spirits, there seemed at first no remedy, but the guilty man must perish. What could the Spirits take less than the blood of the man who had angered them? They had lost their suppliant; must not the murderer be given to them in fair exchange? It must be so: life must be given for life, and blood for blood; and hence it came to pass that not only sheep and oxen, but human lives were also offered up as sacrifices to the offended gods.

But was there no escape from this? Could not Religion, which had helped them so often in their need, help the tribe once again to discover some remedy by which they might at once remove a pestilence and conciliate the Spirits, and yet retain the precious life of their chief who had incurred the wrath of the Spirits by some foolish spilling of blood—their chief, foremost in war and in council, the safety and life of the tribe? Mere resistance to the demands of the Spirits was not to be thought of; for, even if the tribe refused to sacrifice their chief, besides the ruin such foolhardiness entailed on the whole tribe, the chief himself was not safe from the wrath of the Avengers. With snake-like locks, hissing their vengeance and darting their fangs into his soul, the Furies would haunt him by night and by day, and would drain away his life's blood, dogging him over land and sea, and hunting him like a wild beast. Was there no escape from these avenging Deities?

Once again Religion stepped in, and suggested that some other life might be given as a substitute for the life of the offender to appease the angry Spirits. Some captive of distinguished beauty, or, if that was not enough, a score of captives, might be given: surely this would satisfy the demand for blood. Or, if this would not suffice, then let the chief offer up for himself what was most precious in his eyes, his first-born son, and thus make propitiation for his sin. For their part the tribe would not be idle, but with lacerations of their own flesh, as they danced around the altar of the god, they would make up the quota of pain and blood. Accepting this as a ransom, the god would avert his wrath, and would be at peace with the tribe. Thus in savage tribes, before sin was known and forgiveness possible, sprang up the first rudimentary notions of Atonement.

By degrees, as the influence of the universe became more and more responded to and morality advanced, human sacrifices became unusual and repulsive. Strong proof came to be required among the more civilised nations before men would believe that the gods insisted on so terrible a sacrifice. Once again Religion came to men's aid, and suggested that perhaps the semblance of a sacrifice might please the spirits as well. The shape of the guilty man might be counterfeited in clay, or a wicker image of him might serve the purpose, or costly hecatombs of unblemished sheep or cattle might buy off human life. Slowly and cautiously had Religion to tread its path of tentative humanity. If, after one of these humane innovations, there suddenly fell on the tribe a pestilence, or famine, or defeat, this was a clear proof that the new-fangled and niggardly sacrifices were less efficacious than the old liberal gifts of the blood of men. In that case the nation was at once thrown back upon the old conservative worship. Even in civilised Rome we are startled at finding, during seasons of extreme panic, remnants of the old system of human sacrifice.

A great stride upwards was made when Moses, as a natural part of his Revelation, assigned the same merit to the turtle-dove of the poor man as to the bullock or lamb of the rich, and silently discouraged the offering of whole herds or hecatombs at a time. In the West too, as men were freed from many of the sore servitudes and superstitions of earlier ages, taking a more cheerful view of the Spirits who rule the world, having attained a higher standard of human justice and applying that standard to the doings of the gods, they came to take a different view of sacrifice. Gratitude, more often than fear, seemed now to be the natural motive for it. The gods were, in the main, good: they gave light and joy, harvests and fruits, the grape and the olive to mankind: it was but natural that men should recognize these favours with grateful offerings. In the West this notion of thank-offering almost superseded the old notion of sin-offering: in Israel the two sacrifices were kept distinct, but though thank-offerings were recognized in the law, sin-offerings seem to occupy the more prominent place in the Prophets and Psalms.

The marked distinction between sin-offerings and thank-offerings—so natural in Israel, where the idea of sin, if I may so say, was first invented—must have had a great influence in leading the Prophets of Israel to the true conception of the ideal sacrifice. A lamb or bullock offered up as thank-offering—that was one thing: a lamb or bullock offered up as sin-offering, that was quite another. Whence and what the difference? In the former case part of the flesh was eaten by the sacrificer; in the latter, it was not. But could that be all the difference? Clearly not: it could not be that one sacrifice had more or less effect with Jehovah than another simply because in the one case He received the whole, in the other only a share, of the flesh. There must be some deeper and inner difference of meaning between the sacrifices. What was it?

To begin with the name, the one was a sin-offering; and what could the offerer wish for his sins except that they might be utterly destroyed and slain within him? Yet, on the other hand, it was an offering of a sinner, and what could he wish for his sinful self except that he might not be destroyed, but wholly given up to the Lord? The offering on the great day of Atonement expressed very clearly for Israel this double object and meaning of sacrifice. On that day, of two goats precisely similar, one was sacrificed and the other set free; thus typifying the destruction of sin and the liberty of purified life. The two goats seem to have represented, the one the principle of the sin-offering, the other that of the peace-offering. But something of the same double meaning appears, though less clearly, in the single act of every sin-offering. For in the sin-offering the victim is entirely given up by the offerer; *for him* it is utterly destroyed: this represents the guilty self utterly renounced. On the other hand, the sacrifice, if not consumed "outside the camp," was eaten by the priest "in the Holy Place:" that is to say, the purified self of the offerer either went up to Jehovah in the flames of the sacrifice, or was appropriated by Him in the Holy Temple of His presence.

It would be difficult to suggest any rite by which a thoughtful heart might be more stirred up to self-searchings and questionings than the spectacle of a sacrifice. Once certain that he was not offering up a mere bribe, the offerer must have felt at once a strange impressiveness and a strange powerlessness in the purifying rite. That his sin could not be forgiven without pain and death, this in itself must have intensified, in a reflecting mind, the sense of the fatal power of sin. Yet again, even in peace-offerings and thank-offerings the same sad element was present. It seemed impossible to approach Jehovah save through the medium of death. Whether to obtain forgiveness or to express gratitude, it was necessary to offer up a life. Did it not therefore seem that the two sacrifices, though different in form, were really the same in essence? In order to appease the wrath of Jehovah one must give up one's guilty self entirely to Him to be destroyed, as was just; but in order to be at peace with Jehovah one must also give oneself up entirely to Him. In either case, then, was not the object the same, to devote oneself entirely to Jehovah, and to be made one with Him by submission to His will? In proportion as the human will was guilty or innocent, the destructive element or the purifying element would predominate: but in either case the meaning of sacrifice was willing submission, devotion, "Lo! I come to do Thy will, O God."

Yet even to those few chosen spirits in Israel who reasoned out, or rather felt out, the true meaning of sacrifice, how inadequate, in spite of all its suggestiveness, must the rite have appeared! Perfect submission, complete devotion of every human faculty to Jehovah—how could that possibly be expressed by the slaughter of a bullock or ram, struggling against the sacrificial cords, or at best, dumb and passive through ignorance of the impending knife? A type so imperfect suggested much by means of its very imperfection: but after a certain advance of knowledge had been gained, it rather suggested what the Ideal could not be, than what it must be. Thus much the prophets clearly discerned, that the true sacrifice could not be the mere superficial thing that it appeared to be in the minds of the common people of Israel. It must be some invisible offering of the heart. The Almighty could not be bribed with the flesh of bulls and goats: "Thinkest thou that I will eat bull's flesh, and drink the blood of goats? Offer unto God thanksgiving, and pay thy vows unto the Most Highest;" and the same psalm implies that the highest sacrifice is that of a pious life: "Whoso offereth Me thanks and praise, he honoureth Me, and to him that ordereth his conversation right will I shew the salvation of God." Prophets and psalmists alike inveighed against the popular fancy that there was security in the multitude of sacrifices, and that external purifications sufficed. Sacrifice offered in the spirit of a bribe was declared by Isaiah to be an "abomination" to the Lord: "cease to do evil; learn to do well; seek judgment, relieve the oppressed, judge the fatherless, plead for the widow,"—that was the true purification. Still deeper goes the Psalmist down to the very root of the matter, when he declares that "the sacrifice of God is a troubled spirit; a broken and contrite heart, O God, shalt thou not despise." Not merely must a man "order his conversation aright," but the heart, the source of action, must be changed, and only God can change it: "Make me a clean heart, O God, and renew a right spirit within me." The same thought is expressed still more strongly by Ezekiel, who declares that not a "renewal," but a re-creation of the heart is needed; the "stony heart" must be taken out, and a "heart of flesh" must be given by Jehovah. The fundamental principle in all these statements is the same: the meaning of sacrifice is doing the will of God. The old heathen sacrifices were bribes to bend the will of the gods to the will of men; the sacrifices of Israel were expressions of the wish to conform the human will to the divine.

When this great truth had been discovered, the rite of sacrifice might almost seem to have answered its purpose and to have become superfluous. As a suggestive rite it had been useful: but when its suggestions had been once accepted, it might sustain and impress, but did not exalt or purify them. The blood of bulls and goats could not take away sin; it dragged down some sacrificers to the level of the imperfect type; it could hardly raise any except the most thoughtless and gross, who might possibly be impressed by the spectacle of the sacrificial death. In the ordinary course of things, perhaps the abuse of sacrifice and the protests of the prophets might have done away with the rite sooner: but the captivity of Israel and Judah, throwing the people back upon the law, and substituting legalism for the spirit of prophecy, naturally perpetuated sacrifice among other institutions. Yet at least the sect of the Essenes, noted for its piety and for its ascetic purity, is said to have given up all sacrifice of living things. Among some of the Western poets philosophy had engendered something of the same feeling. In Greece and Rome the idea of sin had scarcely taken root as yet, and consequently the necessity of a complete change, a complete surrender and destruction of the lower self, in other words the necessity of a death, as a condition of regeneration, was hardly recognized. "If a guiltless hand hath touched the altar," writes Horace, "it is as potent to soothe the averted Penates with a handful of meal and salt, as with the costliest victim."[1] Lucretius is even more vehement in denying that there can possibly be any piety in the sacrifice of beasts. Instead of "offer unto God thanksgiving," we have

[1] However this passage may be rendered (and it is well known that it has different renderings), the spiritual tendency of it is the same.

only to write "behold the Universe with peace," and we shall find Lucretius and Isaiah expressing almost identical thoughts:

> "Nec pietas ullast velatum sæpe videri
> Vertier ad lapidem atque omnis accedere ad aras,
> Nec procumbere humi prostratum et pandere palmas
> Ante deum delubra, nec aras sanguine multo
> Spargere quadrupedum, nec votis nectecs vota,
> Sed mage *pacata posse omnia mente tueri.*"

Yes, but how to gain the "guiltless hand" thus eulogized by Horace? How to "look upon all things" with the "peaceful mind" recommended by Lucretius—that was the question to which no satisfactory answer had as yet been given in the West. And hence among the masses of Greece and Italy, as well as in Israel, the old unspiritual sacrifice still went on, in the West as a service of gratitude often degenerating into a bribe—in the East as a legal and ordained means of purifying the sacrificer from sin and defilement.

There was no reason why sacrifice, having once reached this stage, might not have continued for centuries (in spite of the remonstrances and protests of the spiritual thinkers in the East and the West) a lifeless form, harming those whom it had once helped, as meaningless and as debasing as the prayer-mills of the Buddhists. Something of the same kind we may notice in art. A nation rises to a certain stage of conception and imitative skill, and then, having arrived at certain conventional falsities in perspective and imitation, it stops short and hardens. For the next century or two Nature may display her pictures, and strive to impress the laws of imitative art; but in vain. What is wanted at such a crisis is not Nature, but some great interpreter of Nature, some artist who shall be a mediator between Nature and the dulled eyes of his countrymen blunted against the truth by long habituation to conventional errors. In the same way was it with the art of sacrificing in Israel and Rome. They had reached—the higher minds among them—a certain level of thought, but no higher than, or not so high as, the level of the Psalmists and Prophets of seven hundred years ago : and higher they could not go. What was there to raise them higher ? They needed the spectacle of some ideal sacrifice, some human will conformed with perfect willingness and complete surrender to the divine Will. Such a sacrifice must combine two things, in their nature apparently incompatible, the absolute self-surrender for destruction implied in the sin-offering, and the absolute self-surrender for absorption implied in the peace-offering. Yet how could a man offer a perfect peace-offering to Jehovah unless he enjoyed the perfect peace of sinlessness ? How, on the other hand, could he offer the sin-offering unless he were a sinner, laden with every sin that had ever entered into the heart of man ? If a man could in his single self offer up these two ideal sacrifices, he, and only he, might be a mediator alike for East and West, exhibiting to all nations, once for all, an ideal self-surrender that might bring home to the West the revelation of the death of sin, and to the East the revelation of the life of the children of God. The sight of such an offering, instead of dragging the spectator down, might raise him up. Like a lamp shining in a dark place, and drawing towards itself the birds and insects that hate the day, even so the old institution of sacrifice, not powerful enough to dispel the darkness, had at least succeeded in drawing all mankind, even those who most loved the night, out of their own selfish existences into the dangerous proximity of its destructive brightness. Now it was time that the Sun should arise, bringing light and life to all things, and surpassing the petty tapers of man's device, not only in the glory of its splendour, but also in the safe unapproachableness of its life-giving flame.

"But all this," it may be urged, "is a mere contention about words. You have whittled down sacrifice to nothing at all. You described at first an angry god wanting blood, then a greedy god wanting food, then a good god wanting devotion. Of the old notion nothing remains but the word. Give it up." Why give it up? What will become of human language if we give up all words that, in the course of ages, have changed their meaning? Take "love." The evolutionists will tell us, I suppose, that love was once a mere physical thrill, having little or nothing in common with the word in the highest sense which we now attach to it: but what then? Are we prepared to give up the word love? The same reasoning applies to the word sacrifice. We have not whittled it down, but have purified it by stripping off the integument of illusion. The old illusion of sacrifice was, that peace with God could be purchased by the gift of a bribe: the truth latent in the illusion was that peace with God can be procured by gift indeed, but the gift must be the free gift of one's heart and will. Why give up the word sacrifice because of this discovery? As well give up the fruit, because the shell which inclosed and preserved it for our use has in due time decayed and fallen away!

CHAPTER VIII.

THE ILLUSIONS OF SEERS.

MANY instances of visions might be collected by a careful study of the literature of different nations and of the history of the Christian Church; but the nation of Israel stands pre-eminent as a nation of Seers. In other nations, in Greece and Rome more especially, the sense of the presence of the Eternal has not been strong enough to subordinate the will of the Seer. The visions or myths in the pages of Plato are no true visions; they display the will and plastic power of the Seer too clearly. The visions that best deserve the name in the history of Greece and Rome, where they are not fictions or legends, exhibit the intensity of patriotism rather than of religion, and come from the gods rather as national tutelary deities than from One all-controlling Righteousness: hence these also fail to awe and subordinate sufficiently the human will of the Seer. But among the people of Israel, the Word of the Lord has been always more powerful in subduing the word of man. Sometimes, it is true, among the later prophets, there are traces of ordinary human imagination and of unconscious, perhaps even of conscious, combinations and modifications of past prophecies. The vision seen by Zechariah of the woman seated in the midst of the ephah, the vision seen by Amos of the Lord upon a wall made by a plumb-line, and the vision of the basket of summer fruit, seem rather to be striking images, or no more than actual sights which had suggested certain spiritual similitudes. But the great majority of the Old Testament visions seem to indicate a complete subordination of the will of the seer. Many are preceded by bodily prostration, during which the mind is made a passive recipient of the divine revelation. Yet even in the visions of Israel there is to be noticed not only a progress in the character of revelation from generation to generation, but also a correspondence between the vision and the Seer which shows that, even in the visions of Israel, human nature is not excluded. Grant that, at the moment when the sight flashes on the mind or when the Word of the Lord is borne in upon the heart, the will is passive; yet the nature of the sight and the meaning of the message is suited to the past life and habits and thoughts of the seer. The prophet was no automaton, nor yet a lifeless harp vibrated by the finger of God, but a living man with all his individual characteristics pre-ordained, developed, and consecrated to the prophetic work. The royal prophet Isaiah, the herdsman Amos, and the priestly Ezekiel proclaim the same principles, but under shapes in which one may clearly recognize the individual characteristics.

It may be well rapidly to glance at some of these different embodiments of the same truth. First then there was the vision of Abraham, "a smoking furnace and a burning lamp;" then that of Moses, "the angel of the Lord in a flame of fire out of the midst of a bush : and behold the bush burned with fire, and the bush was not consumed." Then it is recorded that Moses and Aaron, with the elders, "saw the Lord God of Israel; and there was under His feet as it were a paved work of a sapphire stone, and as it were the body of heaven in His clearness;" and "the sight of the Lord was like devouring fire on the top of the mount in the eyes of the Children of Israel." Then to the royal prophet Isaiah, living in the royal period of Judah, while the temple and its worship were still intact, the "King" and "Lord of Hosts" revealed Himself, encompassed by attendant seraphim, crying "Holy, holy, holy is the Lord of Hosts; and the house was filled with smoke." To the priest Ezekiel, in the land of Babylon, whose sculptures have made the winged bull familiar to us, a more complicated vision appears. He sees four living creatures, having the likeness of a man, yet each with four faces, mysteriously connected together with a system of "wheels," whose appearance was "like burning coals of fire, like the appearance of lamps:" the noise of their wings was "like the noise of great waters." Thus, instead of the narrower notion of the temple, we find substituted the broader notion of the universe with all its subtle organization, revolving in regular course, and instinct with vital spirit. Above the "living creatures" was "the likeness of a throne, as the appearance of a sapphire stone, and upon the likeness of the throne was the likeness as the appearance of a man above it." The whole vision is preceded by a whirlwind, a cloud, a fire, and a brightness as the colour of amber. Here note how the visions, as they go on, reveal more and more the personal, and what may almost be called the social nature of God, that is, the impossibility of knowing Him apart from His relations with the beings that He has created. The earliest vision reveals God simply as fire, a revelation that pervades almost all the subsequent visions; we then learn that He is a fire that sometimes devours, but sometimes purifies without consuming; then that He is a King in splendour; next, that He is a King attended by adoring seraphim; and lastly, that the universe is His throne, and His figure is revealed as " the appearance of a man above it." In the later visions of the Book of Daniel this development is still more striking. The Ancient of Days is revealed sitting on a throne of flame, supported by wheels of fire; and a fiery stream issues from before Him. So far we recognize the imagery of the earlier visions: but now enters an entirely new element: "Thousand thousands ministered unto Him, and ten thousand times ten thousand stood before Him." Thus are we step by step led up to the revelation of God in the likeness of man, and, in conjunction with man, a revelation of the Divine nature implying the immortality of the human soul.

" But what is the practical utility of all these visions and voices? What have they done for men?" On the answer to this question much depends. For if we admit the historical accuracy of ever so many narratives of visions, but deny their utility, they would cease to have claims on our attention, at least as revelations, and indeed would become so many stumbling-blocks in the way of faith in God. In that case the visions of the seer might be classed with those of the maniac, the lover, and the poet, and might all be contemptuously put aside as they are put aside—not by the dramatist, for it is not Shakespeare, but Theseus, the strong man of action, who is speaking—in the well-known words, which reject all such unsubstantial things as being " of imagination all compact." I think the answer to the question, " Have visions done any good ?" would be, that they have done much good and some harm, but that the good has greatly predominated. The visions of holy minds have benefited both the seers and mankind at large by being remembered ; the visions of diseased and perturbed minds have served as punishments and deterrents from sin, and by mankind they have been forgotten so that thay have done little general mischief. Take in particular, as being of the commonest class, the visions of departed friends which have been manifested to survivors.[1] They have no doubt caused pain, sorrow, solicitude, fear, superstition: but they have probably often aroused in the living wholesome memories that were in danger of being too soon erased ; and in any case they have kept up both in those who have witnessed these visions, and in others to whom they have been imparted, the sense of the presence of an invisible world acting upon the visible, and of possibilities of things in heaven and things on earth more than are dreamed of in our philosophy.

[1] I assume that every educated person believes that there have been, and are, such visions ; and that many of them are not the mere effect of material external objects converted by pre-occupied imagination into some other appearance, as a sheet or coat may be hurriedly mistaken for a human form. Years ago, a physician, who had no religious belief of any kind, and who was one of the most truthful of men, assured me that he had seen his mother's face stooping over his bed at night, shortly after her death. " I was as much awake as you are now ; and I saw her as clearly as I see you. But of course I knew it was a mere optical delusion."

But the question will be asked, "Are visions objective?" I answer, what is meant by "objective"? If "objective" means "tangible" or "perceptible to all persons, no matter what their state of mind," then certainly they were not real any more than God is real. But if by "objective" is meant "in accordance with the laws of Nature," or "eternal in good results," or "in accordance with the will of God," or "fraught with spiritual truth," then unquestionably I say the Vision of Isaiah was objective, quite as objective as any ordinary sight.[1] But it is still further urged, " the whole thing was an illusion ; the Seer believed his vision to be tangible." I answer probably he did so believe, and probably, so far, he was under an illusion : but we have proved, or attempted to prove, that no man is justified in rejecting spiritual truth, simply because it is conveyed through illusion. But some sceptics will be ready to admit this ; only they will say that the vision detracts from the force of the spiritual truth, " Insight into higher things is always impressive, even when conveyed in false forms." I do not assent to this detraction from the vision of Isaiah for example, nor should I assent to the justice of the expression, " false forms." It is true that visions seen now by educated Englishmen should be regarded with suspicion. Our knowledge of the nature of such optical phenomena as visions, our national self-control or stolidity, and the whole atmosphere of

[1] If "objective" means that which exists independently of the perception or consciousness of persons perceiving or conscious of it, then I should say, in that sense, the vision of Isaiah, and many other visions of the prophets, *are* objective. Whether we perceive it or not, God *is* a King, holy and exalted ; whether we perceive it or not, God *is* a consuming and a purifying fire. If anyone replies " These are but metaphors," I answer " All language and all thought, applied to God, is necessarily metaphorical."

modern thought, tend to prevent the state of mind in which alone visions would be possible. But in Israel during past ages it was not so. A Seer was then expected to see visions, and they were to him little more than what unusually vivid thoughts would be to Englishmen. We claim therefore for visions the same kind of attention that we claim for impressive spiritual thoughts; and we claim the more attention, not the less, for the fact of their assuming the shape of visions. For we maintain that the seeing of a vision was a proof not only that the thought was deeply stamped upon the mind of the Seer, but also that he was in that state of surrender to external influences, and in that state of freedom from narrow, individual, and self-regarding thoughts, in which state Seers (no less than Poets) are most likely to see things consonant to the laws of the Universe.

But what, it may be asked, is to be the test of a vision, and why do you call one true and another false? Let us answer that question by asking another. In pictures, and sculptures, and poems, why have some succeeded, while others have failed? Is it not because some have been in accordance with Nature—I mean human as well as non-human Nature—and others have not?[1] So it is with visions. Thousands of visions were seen, no doubt, by the priests of the Grecian and Roman deities, in which little if any divine truth was expressed. Many of the visions of the middle ages seen by the saints of the Church are in the highest degree unnatural; some even grotesque; none, as for as

[1] I admit that some are preserved for a very long time by what we call accident. But the general rule holds.

I know, to be compared with Fox's vision of the ocean of light and love flowing over the ocean of sin and darkness. Of many thousands of visions only some few in the course of ages have so arrested the attention of men that they have escaped the general well-merited oblivion, and have permanently influenced the religious faith of mankind. Where the will has been predominant; or subordinated, but not sufficiently; or where the life and habits of the seer have been warped or artificial, there the vision will be defective. The blemish in the mould will repeat itself in the blemished vase. Opinion blending itself with insight, the image is found combining clay with gold. But where a simple-minded man, who has drunk in one or two great truths with his mother's milk, who sums up in himself, perhaps unconsciously, the meditations and devotions, or may be the mute longings and dumb aspirations of many generations of ancestors, and who has breathed the atmosphere of grand national traditions hailing God as the Father and Saviour of the people—where such a man finds himself and his nation placed in a furnace of trial, in times when wrong seems uppermost and right seems trampled down, while the comfortable classes sit dumb and the respectable are abashed, while those who should teach have nothing to teach, and those who should guide have nowhere to guide to, and the whole nation is like a flock of sheep without a shepherd—then, at such a crisis or day of judgment (in accordance with the laws of the progress of humanity, which I call the Word of God), a Visible or Audible Righteousness has sometimes revealed itself to the protesting and prophetic heart of the fore-ordained servant of the Lord. At such periods in different nations arise Seers like Isaiah and Ezekiel; or poets like Dante and Milton; or half-seers, half-prophets, like Fox; or half-prophets, half-poets, like Bunyan.

Of all these men it may be said that their spirits have been at discord with their immediate, visible, and disorderly surroundings, but in tune with the invisible and harmonious environment of the spiritual world, and with the impending will of God. Their visions have not only been the necessary results of their lives and the natural expression of their thoughts, beneath the divine influence: they have also been an eternal treasure for posterity. To the Seer himself visions have given force and faith, intensifying pre-existing knowledge, or drawing into vital existence what was before a mere latent germ of truth: they have also aided him in communicating his revelation more intensely and vitally to others. Suppose George Fox had merely recorded in his journal a conviction which had possessed him, that " good would ultimately triumph over evil:" would such a conviction, so recorded in general terms, have impressed an incredulous world as deeply as the vision of the overwhelming " ocean of light and life"? That is a vision which will yet run through mankind, doing a great work for us all: the other is a mere thought which is useful or useless according as it is expressed with much or little of the vitality necessary to rouse faith. In fine, there have been bad visions as well as good, barren visions as well as fruitful, artificial visions as well as natural. The latter have contended with the former, and the survival of the fittest decides which are most in harmony with the invisible environment of eternal spiritual truth, and assigns to these the victory.

Discord with visible environment seems almost an essential condition of prophecy, that is, of proclaiming the specially-revealed will of God. "Things move," says Bacon, "violently to their place, and easily in their place." Now the prophet is emphatically not "in his place." Looking round on the visible world, he finds that all things are out of joint, and it seems his cruel destiny to make things first wrong, that they may afterwards be made right, and to make men miserable, if perchance he may, through misery, lead them to happiness. The Seer or prophet often deprecates his task. It is no pleasure to Amos to be taken from his herds and sycamores to prophesy evil against Israel and the house of Jeroboam. Jonah flees from the presence of the Lord. The first impulse of Isaiah in that Presence is to cry "Woe is me!" Fox had bitter preparation for his prophetic work, "Great troubles and temptations came many times upon me, so that when it was day I wished for night, and when it was night I wished for day. I fasted much, walked abroad in solitary places many days, and often took my Bible and sat in hollow trees and lonesome places till night came on, and frequently in the night walked mournfully about by myself; for I was a man of sorrows in the time of the first workings of the Lord in me." In the same way speaks the Epistle to the Hebrews of the prophets as men banished from the society of their fellows, and from the joys of life, "of whom the world was not worthy; they wandered in deserts and in mountains, and in dens and caves of the earth." By such a discord with the jarring strains of mortal melodies the prophets are led to look upward, and fashion their souls for the reception of a heaven-sent harmony. Then, the instrument being thus prepared, when at last, in the shape of some great calamity or trouble, the breath or spirit of the Lord comes down upon the nation sweeping across the heart-strings of all alike in the universal perturbation, while the hearts of the unprepared masses are dumb, tuneless, and irresponsive, the Spirit finds one or two chosen and prepared harps of the Lord, who give forth sounds in accordance with the laws of the spiritual music, that is, with the everlasting laws of God, and Man, and Nature. Is it not true that, even in these days, some of us in the making of a sudden resolution have once or twice in a life-time felt something like a voice within us not only summing up and giving fit expression to our past lives, but also saying for us something that we were not deliberately and consciously prepared to say for ourselves, but which we accept, when said, as being our own and yet not our own, something that shapes perhaps a new and better future for us? Our will has been momentarily dormant, and we have been irresistibly guided in the right direction by something that cannot be explained as mere habit. Here we have for each and all of us " inspiration," upon a small scale. But, upon a large scale, this inspiration has been a powerful influence in the history of the human race, making the martyrs and enthusiasts of the world, and feeding the flame of the purest worship.

Of the visions recorded in the New Testament this is not the place to speak. It is sufficient to remark that it is reasonable to expect that they would exhibit something of the same continuity and correspondence to the character of the seer which we found in the visions of the

Old Testament. Moreover, the human or social character of God would, so we might anticipate, be still further illustrated by them. During times of crisis, and change, and trouble, we might conjecture there would be visions; in peace and general good-will there would be few. Further, if a new reign of peace and truth should be introduced, so that men were bound together by love, we might expect that the new diffused revelation of God's nature might altogether supersede the necessity of isolated visions. Lastly, if some new Prophet, greater than any of the former prophets, should come to bring an ampler revelation from God, then in proportion to the new Prophet's closer relations with God, we might conjecture that his visions, if he had any, would be freed from the prostrating circumstances which we noted in the visions of the Old Testament seers. Nay, it might be that his whole life would be one communion with the invisible Lord, so close and so natural, and so inextricably interweaving for him things visible with invisible, that it might be hard to say for such a Prophet where sight would end and vision begin. Of Him it might be said from one point of view, that He had few visions; but, from another, that His whole life was one continuous vision.

CHAPTER IX.

THE ILLUSIONS OF DEATH.

WHAT lesson has God's institution of death taught to mankind? It might have been thought indeed that death would have been beneficial to man as God's last warning, impending ever on his declining years, that he was not sent here to do his own will, but the will of Him that sent him. More than any terrors of nature, death, it might have been supposed, would have the power of rousing the dullest heart from apathy, and of exciting the most irreverent to awe. Old age teaches this lesson in part, and death might seem to sum up the teaching of old age. Age brings a gradual detachment from earthly ties; sets the old man below those on whom he once himself looked down; deprives him of bodily pleasures; increases his bodily pains; weakens his memory and intellect; dulls his senses; leaves him no pleasure but that of receiving gratitude, no faculty but that of loving. To sum up the lesson comes Death, and takes all away. Could nature give us a more effective demonstration that we were not sent merely for our own pleasure?

Yet, as we know, the great majority of men have not

read this lesson in death. More than this, it may be said that very seldom has the prospect either of death or of old age reformed a selfish man. Death is rather the last perfecting lesson for the good and faithful, than the first step in reformation for the bad and faithless. If men have been previously prepared to worship, then the prospect of death has made them better worshippers, by adding a fresh tinge of awe, and by exercising to the utmost their powers of trust. But if they have not been thus prepared, the lesson has been thrown away upon them. What should have been awe has been in the bad, servility, what should have been faith, has been reckless presumption. The servile have crouched before death; the bold have mocked at it or welcomed it.

It is hard to say how much good and how much evil has been blended in the fear of death; how far this fear has improved, or how far it has lowered, morality. On the one hand it has no doubt had a sobering and levelling effect in many minds disposed to insolence and pride. To the strongest and haughtiest it has appealed as the one common fate of all mortals alike, from which no human greatness can preserve the greatest. The conqueror, rejecting a captive's petition, can always lightly put aside all other claims to sympathy, " Poverty, bonds, scorn, degradation—these things I shall never live to endure; but death—" that is different: there conqueror and captive meet. Even with the fear of death before them, men have been cruel, but without it we can scarcely doubt that they would have been more cruel. On the other hand, death has lowered morality by making men servile. The author of the Epistle to the Hebrews speaks of mankind as being, before the coming of Christ, " all their life long in bondage" through the fear of death; and this exactly describes the pernicious effect of that fear, not manifesting itself in any particular crime, but in a general lowering and degrading of motive and morality, an introduction of self-interest into every department of life, self-interest, I mean, not in the hope of reward, but in the dread of punishment. Travellers in the Polynesian Islands describe the gloom cast over the life of the natives in those delightful climates by the sacerdotal influence which sets its veto now on this object, now on that, closing up with the barriers of religious horror all sorts of innocent paths to happiness. Just this kind of gloom is shed over the beauty of life by the irrational and superstitious fears of death. No other term can describe it than "bondage."

The man who always has self-interest in mind is in some sense a servant; for instead of giving the willing obedience of a child to a father, he is always working for pay, and this is what distinguishes servants from children. But the man who not only has self-interest at heart, but also that kind of self-interest which consists in the escape from arbitrary penalty of which one does not recognize the justice—he is worse than a servant, he is a slave who works merely to avoid the lash. Such a state of mind is the veriest bondage, and the aptness of death to produce such bondage affords our best reason for calling death a curse.

To avoid the slavery of death, the bolder sort of men of action have rushed into the slavery of the present. That was not the right refuge. They ought to have faced the thought of death, instead of bandaging their eyes against it. If they had had leisure enough for reflection, and insight enough into the nature of their own selves and of things around them, they might have trusted that whatever death might bring, being, as it was, not an accident, but the "all-common harbour" of mankind, it could not bring cruelty, or injustice, or caprice. Probably some such mute thought inspired many brave men in the times before Christ who gladly gave up their lives for their country. As we have found good side by side with evil in the fear of death, so let us acknowledge, and with much more willingness, that in the pagan contempt of death there was good as well as evil. It is to the credit of human nature, and it is a testimony to the solid foundation, deep down in many hearts, of a belief in a supreme Righteousness, that so many among mankind have avoided the "bondage" of the fear of death even by despising it. But we must not close our eyes to the evil. The contempt for death was sometimes a kind of cowardice, like the shutting of the eyes in danger. "Let us eat and drink, for to-morrow we die"—there is no bravery or freedom in that. Moreover such a contempt for death implied a negation of existence after death: and, say what men will in these days to the contrary, that must have dwarfed the affections and taken away much of the sweetness of life. A lump of clay moulded by the Maker's fancy to be a puppet in a doll's theatre, shaped by the versatile Maker to play now one part now another in the several acts of the comedy, baby and school-boy, lover and soldier, counsellor, grey-beard, decrepit, dotard, and then—to the worms with it! If this was man, what man could feel respect for himself or worship for the Maker of men? Lastly, the contempt for death sometimes sprang from an evil hope. Men of strong wills and wicked lives could not bear to believe in a future after death. A future would not be likely to give them the licence they now enjoy; it might possibly give them something very different. Like Macbeth, they were prepared to "jump the life to come," if they could but attain success in this present life; but their hopes were parents to their disbelief. Continuity of existence promised them nothing but terror: annihilation was not a terror, but a hope.

Roughly speaking, we might say that Greece and Rome felt too much contempt for death, and Israel too much dread. The Israelite, even though he had before him no pictures of Elysian fields or cells of Pluto awaiting the souls of the departed, nevertheless seems to have dreaded death more than the Western people. "The fear of death hath encompassed me," cries the psalmist. "The dead praise Thee not," says the King Hezekiah, praying to God for deliverance from his disease; "the living, the living, they shall praise Thee." On the other hand the Romans, at their worst period under the early emperors, exulted in the butchery of gladiators in the arena, and put themselves to death as calmly as if they were but taking a bath. Both excesses were to be avoided, if death was to be restored to its right place, and to be made no more a curse unto men. For that purpose there was a need that some Man should deliver the too timid from the fear of death, and the too bold from the hope or contempt of death. To pass through the dark shadow and to appear in the sight of all mankind on the other side triumphant—this might destroy fear in the hearts of all who would trust in the mighty Passenger; but if He also revealed the continuity of existence, bridging the

L

old gulf between life and death, if He shewed in the soul after death the marks and imprints of what the soul had been before death, and if He brought home to the hearts of men a sense of eternal results depending upon earthly actions, and of judgment following upon sin as thunder follows upon lightning, then the self-same Passenger who destroyed fear in the minds of the faithful would inspire in the minds of the faithless a wholesome and purifying awe. He would deliver the West from servility to the present, from the bondage of life; He would deliver the East from the bondage of death.

We pass from the influence of death, that is, the prospect of our own death, to the influence of the dead upon the living. There is something, we scarcely know what, in the fleshly presence of a friend, which builds up and cements the structure of a friendship, and yet at the same time prevents the structure from attaining its full perfection: much like a scaffolding, which hides the building that it has helped to raise. Not till the man is dead do we see brought out in due relief all the good that was in him. While a man lives, very often his superficial faults obtrude themselves upon us: he is talkative perhaps, or conceited, or a little parsimonious, and we never think of him without thinking of these faults. But when he is dead, these matters seem too petty to take up the foreground of the past. Our mind goes further back and deeper down to the constancy, the affection, the unselfishness, which in old days we scarcely noted taking them perhaps as matter of course, but which we now recognize as constituting the man's true character.

Are we unfairly partial in thus exaggerating a man's virtues after death, and extenuating his faults? May not a man have deeply-seated vices as well as deeply-seated virtues, and may not the vices as well as virtues escape notice during life and be revealed after death? Is it not true that *bonhommie* and a turn for humour often cover, during life, a multitude of sins which are never judged with due severity till after a man has ceased to be humorous. Yes, sometimes. It cannot be denied that death may sometimes compel us to judge more instead of less unfavourably: yet, even in that case, it might well be maintained that the judgment after death is more just than the judgment during life. But as a rule, the busy stir and competition of life prevents us from looking at men with fairness, and, when it is over, death enables us to regard them, not only more calmly and dispassionately, but also more favourably. Not till we have ceased to look on men as rivals are we in a position to be their judges. We gain nothing by flattering the dead: why then, for no reason except the lies of ostentatious epitaphs, suspect the justice of that calmer judgment with which, judging a dead man at the quiet sessions of our own souls, we seem to see in him more of good and less of evil than we discerned in the same man when living?

Rightly or wrongly, we do idealize the dead. The orator's assertion that the evil that men do lives after them, while the good is buried with them, was a mere rhetorician's falsehood. On the contrary, it would be perhaps truer to say that the evil perishes, the good remains with us. The memory of a dead friend often impresses us more than his living presence. Especially is this the case with those on whom our affections have been long and firmly fixed. Just as when a lamp at which we have been long and steadily gazing is suddenly extinguished, we see against the background of the darkness a corresponding image vividly floating before our eyes, so the sudden gap made by a departing friend is filled by a form that supplies his place. The fleshly presence is gone; the face cannot be even mentally recalled with such exactness as to satisfy our requirements. A stranger's face we can recall, as we can the face of an animal or a mask, because it is devoid of expression to us: but a friend's face suggests transient shadows and changing hues of thought and feeling, gladness or sorrow speaking in the merest motion of a feature or glance of the eye, all sorts of recollections and associations which crowd in upon the mind when we try to paint the countenance of the dead, and prevent us from painting it as we could wish. Driven thus to have recourse to a thought picture, because we cannot have the picture painted by mere memory, we set to work unconsciously to build up, out of the materials of the memory, shaped and fashioned by the inferences of affection, a new ideal friend, to be our companion through life, dwelling in our hearts through love. We have no longer the presence of our friend to tell us precisely what he would wish, or how he would have us act in this or that emergency; but though his precepts and rules are absent, the *tendency* of his life is present with us. He is no longer a law to us, but we have the compensation of the presence of his spirit.

Next to the revelation of Christ the revelation of the dead has perhaps been, and ought to be, the most powerful of all God's revelations to mankind. All the more pity that so many, even among Christians, neglect it as they do! Religious selfishness and superstitious gloom have been the great barriers in the way of receiving this revelation. A servile dread of the possibilities of hell, and a suspicion that God may be more arbitrary, unjust, and cruel than a moderately good man, have caused some persons to put aside all thought of dead friends, because the thought suggests infernal horrors on which no man of feeling can suffer his mind to dwell, on penalty of losing sanity. If we thus shrink from even mentioning the dead, because their mention reminds us that we may soon be called to join them, or because we have given up the hope of ever meeting them again, then indeed we must go through the wilderness of the world without the help and presence of the dead; then every time another friend is torn from our side our hearts become harder and colder; the pores of faith are closed in us as we incase ourselves in a crust of sullen worldliness, determined to make the best of this wretched unsatisfying existence, by disregarding ties that may be snapped at any moment, and by taking as our watchword "Each for himself." At what a disadvantage stands the friendless schemer for the next world's salvation, or the friendless schemer for this world's delight, as compared with the man, foolish and weak though he may be, who has grown up from childhood amid a protecting circle of kind spirits, fostering all good within him, and driving far away all that is evil and base!

Parents, in the natural course of things, first take their place in this invisible guardian circle. Their influence may furnish the best illustration of what the dead may do for the living, and of the manner in which the living rightly and naturally idealize the dead. Too often old age works its will too ruthlessly upon those whom we loved most when we were children, not only bowing down the back, making the cheek hollow, and the utterance thin and dry, but also weakening memory, intellect, almost affection. But blessed death undoes this evil, carrying to the grave the worn-out, decrepit machinery of the flesh, and restoring to our recollection the image as we recall it at its best and brightest. Then straightway rises up the vivid picture of long years of devoted kindness, unwearied watchfulness—heightened, perhaps, by the thought of our inadequate, if not ungrateful response—the memory of parental patience, wisdom, justice, love at all events, manifested in a thousand shapes: and as we turn and shift the old scenes in our minds, associating them with our daily and our nightly prayers, there is shaped in our hearts a second image of the departed, reminding us of all his wishes, and instigating us to perform them, an image not of the fancy, but of the spirit, and instinct with such spiritual activity and comforting energy that we might almost say that we find in it a comforter to supply the place of him whom we have lost.

Goodness, kindness, gentleness, wisdom, all the attractive qualities of human nature help us to recall the memory of the dead; but there are special circumstances which increase their reminding power. One of these is, the memory of some unfulfilled wish of the departed. Not merely affection, but the sense of incompleteness, of a life truncated and maimed, appeals powerfully to the survivors, leaving them restless till what is missing is supplied. Especially if the wish be a noble and natural one, it haunts the friends of the deceased, like the notes of a noble but incomplete harmony, leaving on the ear a sense of pain at the delay of the completing note. Very naturally has the popular imagination devised among the causes that have presented visible phantoms of the dead to the eyes of the living, the existence of some unsatisfied wish of the restless dead. That popular fancy represents a spiritual truth. A great and good man dying, with a great and good wish not yet performed, rises from the grave into the hearts of his surviving friends and followers, and in them his spirit works its will.

There is a second circumstance that sometimes intensifies the influence of the dead upon the living. It is our consciousness of past ingratitude, or at least of misappreciation; the memory of wise words significantly uttered, and the effect of which was anxiously watched, but they fell idly on dull and inattentive ears; the memory of loving deeds, by us roughly rejected or sullenly tolerated, of which now for the first time the full tenderness is opened up to us under the enlightenment of death; the memory of mighty sorrows, too great and pure for us to share in or even comprehend; the memory of silent but wistful petitions for sympathy addressed in vain to hearts preoccupied by selfishness; all these recollections, coming in a flood upon our souls, rouse in us an irrepressible longing for the touch of the vanished hand, for one last look upon the face of the buried dead. Our remorse would fain summon from the grave the very image of the departed, that we might receive express absolution from his lips. Failing that, our sense of the wasted past creates a vacuum in our souls which nothing can fill except the consciousness that we are still working for him and in his spirit.

A third intensifying circumstance will be the participation of sorrow with a large number of fellow-mourners. The sweetness of sympathy may make sorrow less bitter, but does not make it more superficial. On the contrary, as every feeling is swelled and exalted by being shared with others, so is the feeling of affection for the dead. Moreover a community of mourning induces a community of feeling generally. Brothers and sisters, are linked closer together over the graves of parents, soldiers by the death of a general ; schisms and parties vanish when a nation becomes a family mourning for the loss of some hero or king, who, while he lived, was the father of his people. When such a hero goes down to his grave with the purposes of his life effected, there is room for nothing but unmixed sorrow ; but where he lived hampered, and checked, and thwarted, there his death raises up a host of followers instinct with his spirit, and in their work he rises again, and in their success he is exalted, and triumphs over the grave.

Not always, however, does unmixed happiness come from the idea or spirit of a dead friend to the mind of the survivors. However good and great he may be, and however certain we may be that it is well with him wherever he is, we cannot always feel easy at the thought of him. While we long for, we shrink from, his presence, at least in our less noble and faithful moments. His spirit seems to convict ours of sin, and we cry to it, as St. Peter did, "Depart from me, for I am a sinful man." Perhaps even before, while our friend was living, we sometimes felt abashed as being in the presence of a superior frankness, honesty, or affection. But now, by the side of his ideal image revealed in death, the image of our own life seems more than ever poor, mean, and contemptible. By the side of his idealized unselfishness and single-heartedness our life seems selfish and double-minded; his sincerity and trustfulness rebuke our circuitous ways and hesitating doubts. If it be the part of an ideal judge not to pronounce an arbitrary and unaccepted verdict, nor to inflict an arbitrary and external punishment, but rather to force the offender to see and acknowledge his own fault, to pronounce his own condemnation, and to inflict upon himself his own fittest and most salutary punishment, then, in the truest sense, the spirit of our best friend may be said to sit in judgment upon our life, convincing us of sin, and inflicting on us the penalty of a purifying sorrow.

"But all this is nothing but influence, a mere matter of every-day observation." Its every day occurrence is just the important element in it, the very point on which I desire to lay stress: as to the name of it, no great importance attaches to names unless we allow ourselves to be made slaves by them. The name of "influence" represents an exploded notion that man acted upon man by an invisible stream of matter, "flowing," from one to the other, mostly through the eyes. There is no evidence, there is no need, for the truth of such a theory, and it exists no longer. In like manner the name of "spirit" represents another exploded notion that this "something" of a man, which still is present with his surviving friends, sometimes in dreams, more rarely in waking visions, most commonly in thoughts, was a "breath." This too has vanished; but what then? Some name for this "something" is an absolute necessity. Discarding the word influence, as representing an artificial and baseless theory, we accept the word spirit or breath as at least representing one truth vividly, namely, that this "something" comes from the dead man's life and blends with our life as breath does. This "something," this spirit, we believe to have a separate existence of its own when the body is lifeless; but none the less, though separate from that putrifying mass which we once called its home, it need not be separate from us. Is it absolutely impossible that a spirit should move us, save through the medium of living flesh, or else—if we are to believe in ghosts—through the medium of gauze-like transparencies such as we see in stage-plays? If there be spirits, can the spirit of a dead man be shut in the coffin with him, or is it separable from us by any interval of immeasurable space? Where is the *locale* of the spirit of any living man? Surely we do not know it. Your body and mine may at this moment be governed by spirits residing—if we are to speak of such absurdities as residence and space in relation to spirits—in Saturn, or the sun! As then we know nothing whatever about the position of the spirits of the living, so neither do we know anything about the spirits of the dead. If, therefore, we believe in spirits, there is no obstacle in the way of our believing that death need bring no diminution in the action of a friend's spirit upon us, provided we have faith to realise its presence.

Let no one accuse us of credulity in believing that the spirits of the dead continually accompany us. By such a faith we are not pledged to suppose that invisible beings of a certain shape, and with the exactly limited faculties of living men, beings occupying so many cubic feet of space, are hovering within so many feet from our bodies. All that we mean is that our friends had bodies, but that they also had something more, real, and, as we believe, immortal. That "something more" we find now in our hearts, and very close to our dearest thoughts, invisible, intangible, but none the less present in effect, as real and present as the ground in which their bodies lie buried and on which we tread. For want of a better name we call this "something more" a spirit, and we say that though our friend's body is rotting in the ground, his spirit still abides. In our thoughts, in our words, in our actions, we feel his spirit acting in us with all or more than all the vitality of his vanished life. Word it how we may, we feel this to be a fact: and it is a fact which, ever since the first man died, has been raising each succeeding member of the human race nearer and nearer to the divine ideal.

But I may be told I am confusing two distinct things. One is the memory of the dead, which is undoubtedly a powerful influence, and is scientifically verifiable: the other is the separate existence of the dead, which is not scientifically verifiable. But I am not using the influence of the dead to establish the belief in their separate existence. That belief rests upon very different grounds, partly, no doubt, upon the belief in an eternal Father, who would not have implanted in the hearts of His children aspirations which He did not intend to be in some way satisfied, but partly, and perhaps mainly, upon the life and teaching of Christ. But I am trying to meet the objections of those philosophers who tell us that Christ is "nothing but the real or ideal Founder of Christianity," and that He did nothing, while His disciples did everything. I maintain, on the contrary, that Christ did everything, and that, without Him, the disciples would have done nothing. These philosophers will not try to explain the conduct of Christ's disciples after His death in a natural scientific way, because a scientific explanation would force them to recognise the presence of a Personality unusually grand and powerful in its influence, if not unique in the history of the world; and this they have made up their minds not to do. My object therefore is, not to prove that the dead have an independent existence (though I believe that they have), but to shew that in the purified influence of the dead upon the living there is something, on a small scale, analogous to the intense influence said to have been exerted by Jesus after death upon His surviving disciples. When this is once admitted, we shall ask the philosophers not to put aside, in the old unscientific way, the records of Christ's influence after His death, but to subject them to a searching and scientific investigation, impartially disentangling the kernel of truth from its integument of miracle and illusion. When they have done this, we shall then say, what do you think of the Personality whence sprang the wonderful influence which, in a natural way, founded the Christian Church and regenerated the Roman Empire?

This is what we shall say to Sceptics. But to those who believe in a God and in the immortality of the soul, we shall appeal with greater cogency. To them we shall say, Can you imagine any way in which the Word of God, which has since the Creation influenced the living through the dead, could better sum up that influence than by the death of a Saviour who should die as Christ died, and rise again as Christ rose, in the hearts of His disciples? Suppose for a moment that Christ had not yet died and risen. Then, in order that this precious discipline of the dead upon the living might be made current for all mankind, would it not be well that for every human being some Friend should die, who should represent, at the highest, that idea of Fatherhood which does not cease to attract us from the other side of the grave? Goodness, wisdom, and love He must possess more than any other being that we know. Towering above mankind in the altitude of an inimitable humility and devotion to others, He must strike us all with a consciousness of misappreciation and ingratitude; designing infinite plans of inconceivable grandeur and nobleness for the good of mankind, He must leave those plans unfulfilled, and this life painfully incomplete; impressing those friends who lived around Him more than any mortal ever yet impressed other mortals, He must nevertheless bequeath us no definite memorials of His fleshly life, no painting or sculpture in colours or stone, in the words of precepts or in any code of laws, nothing but His spirit knitting men for ever together in the fellowship of a common sorrow and a common allegiance, nothing but His presence dwelling in our hearts by faith.

CHAPTER X.

THE ILLUSIONS OF THE FAMILY.

" EXCEPT a man be born again he cannot see the kingdom of God," is a doctrine more easily intelligible than the development of it in the words, " Whosoever shall not receive the kingdom of God as a little child shall in nowise enter therein." To be born again into some nobler, more intellectual, more highly-developed and endowed condition, might well seem a natural requisite for entrance into the Kingdom of God. Such a second birth has been insisted on by many sects of philosophers and mystics. But to become a little child, to exchange a developed for a half-developed state, to receive ignorance for knowledge, dependence for independence, how retrograde seems such a movement! The new birth, as a passage into higher immediate manhood, is conceivable; but permanent childhood seems a strange boon to offer to those who have tasted what manhood means.

Yet it will appear that Nature, no less than Christ, aims at making at least some of the feelings of childhood permanent among men. For what is the main characteristic of childhood? It is loving, trustful, and reverent dependence upon a father. Childhood has of course many other characteristics; it is ignorant, impulsive, thoughtless, forgetful, hopeful, inquisitive; but the principal characteristic of a child is loving and almost instinctive obedience, not unwilling obedience, like that of a slave or hireling, nor the merely rational, intelligent obedience of a reasonable subordinate who understands the general utility of subordination, and appreciates the claims to command of the man whom he obeys; but willing, trustful self-surrender. Now if the influence of Nature—we are now speaking, not of non-human, but of human Nature—be duly considered, it will be found that one great difference between the training of beasts and the training of men is, that the former are allowed to forget their impressions of dependence upon parental help, while the latter are encouraged to remember them. Beasts are trained to self-reliance, men to dependence; beasts are permitted to act after their own instincts, men are endowed with the terrible responsibility of a will, in order that they may surrender that will to One above them. Nature herself might have appropriated and applied to her training of mankind the very words used by our Lord to describe the purpose of His life, " I sent you into the world not to do your own will, but to do the will of One above you." But everything depends upon the manner of doing that will. The ideal child does the will of the father with love, trust, and reverence, and his acts are the expression of those feelings, or, in other words, are worship expressed in action. We may therefore say that Nature trains men in childhood to worship, and that Christ warns us that we cannot enter the kingdom of God unless we can learn to worship in the spirit of little children.

Whatever objections therefore may apply to Christian theology, that it is artificial, complex and, circuitous, will apply equally to the complex and circuitous training given by Nature in the family. If it is strange that God, instead of drawing us irresistibly towards Himself, without permitting deviation or retrogression, rather permits us to go wrong that we may love to go right, and to go backward that we may love to go forward, this is nothing but what meets us every day in the training of every little child. If the mind revolts at the theological conception that this long life forsooth, this mere span's breadth of fourscore years or so, may be a period of probation and inferior tutelage, a preparation for a higher manhood in a higher region, so may the mind not unnaturally revolt at the thought that in the training of Nature man of all creatures, man, whose time is so precious, and whose works so wonderful, should be subjected to a period of probation and helpless inaction longer than that imposed upon the lowest or the highest of the irrational animals. Lastly, if we are repelled by a superficial glance at the doctrine of the Incarnation and the Atonement, because we cannot help believing that God might have redeemed and re-adopted His straying children by some other and shorter method; if it seems inexplicable that the Son of God should have descended to earth to take unto Himself not the mere integument of mortal flesh, but a real human will, and all for the purpose of giving back this will unto the Father; if we are shocked by a painful sense of waste in trying to believe that all those sorrows and tears, those temptations and agonies, and that most mysterious agony of all which forced Him to cry that He was deserted, were all endured that He might simply give back again what He had received—let us turn to the very similar spectacle, in miniature, of a little child gradually receiving from Nature, first the terrible gift of a conscious will, then the consciousness of collision with a higher Will, and only at last the power of resisting or obeying it; let us think of all the struggles and failures, the painful temptations and repentances, and all the lasting miseries that rise out of this life-long conflict, and let us remember that in the Incarnation and Atonement Christ is but doing the work that He Himself has imposed upon every little child, and every full-grown man that ever breathed. He is but taking a will, that He may render it up again. He is leading us to worship by making His life the supreme expression of worship.

To come then to God's revelation in the family. No doubt there are many savage tribes (and some degraded spots even in civilised nations) where this divine revelation is so entirely obscured that the parental tie is scarcely stronger among men than among beasts. But for the most part the difference between men and beasts in this respect is striking. In men the tie of fatherhood is a permanence, a possession from the cradle to the grave; in beasts it is a transitory convenience. The permanence of the human tie arises from two causes, both of them beautifully suggestive; they are intellectual strength and bodily weakness. When I say intellectual strength, I mean strength relatively to the condition of animals. It is in virtue of the habit of classifying and comparing that man rose above the beasts of the field. From this faculty of comparing came the very names of "man" and "mind." "Man" is the comparing creature, and "mind" means the comparing power. But this power of comparing implies the retention of the past; for, in the greater number of cases, one can only compare present acts with past acts. To the lower creatures incidents present themselves as isolated incidents; the past is forgotten, or only indefinitely retained in the residuum of an instinctive habit; but to man has been communicated by nature the power of retaining the past so as to group it with the future. From this retentive intellectual faculty which we call memory, sprang filial affection. Without memory, without the recollection of those incidents on which is based the permanent gratitude of the child to the parents, filial love could hardly have risen to anything higher than the transitory instinct that appears to unite parents and offspring in the majority of animals. Again, without prolonged period of bodily helplessness, Memory, the "mother of all things" would have had no time to drop her seed of something better than herself. If children at the instant of birth were so completely adapted to their material environment, that, like fish or insects, they were impelled to move out at once into their place in the wide world, quitting the parental care, filial affection could have no existence, for it would have no basis of parental action; or if the period of dependence had been prolonged to three or four years, a period longer than that of the dependence of any other animal, even that would have been insufficient for the beneficent seed-time of memory. But occupying as it does more than a sixth part of a long life, the period of bodily helplessness combines effectually with the human prerogative of memory to sow the divine seed of that affection by which we approach most closely to Him whose name is Love.

At first a child has no sense of will, or even individuality, but is a mere helpless mass of tentative instincts. Even the faculties of pleasure and pain are not developed in earlier as they are in later years; but to compensate for this, the inducements to motion and experimental activity are greater. At first the child is a part of Nature, at union with all around him. Wrapped in his mother's arms, he feels, for a brief space, no ungratified desires, no collision with his environment. If the sun flashes upon his eyes, he shuts them; if the cold nips his tender limbs, he shivers. But it is the mere bodily and instinctive response to the material influences around him. He has no sense of opposition or enmity with Nature, but is one with it all. He is in the paradise of animalism, in the primitive Garden of Eden.

But as he enlarges his little world, he finds that it contracts itself around him. As he extends the circle of his experiences and desires, the walls of necessity compass him more closely about. The infant impulse to activity and exploration brings him continually into collision with his environment. He wills and strives to touch and taste all sorts of things that he may and may not. Here he touches and meets with compliance, and he associates pleasure with the sense of mastery: here again he touches and meets with resistance, and he learns to associate pain with the sense of opposition and defeat. But sometimes Nature marks her veto with a more emphatic penalty. The child strives to walk, and violates the laws of motion, and the hard earth straightway inflicts the inevitable penalty for the offence: the child touches fire, or handles the sharp steel, and a still more cruel punishment is immediately inflicted. Thus amidst the pains and penalties of infancy the little one learns his first notions of "may," and "must," and "must not:" he begins to distinguish himself from things around him; he realises opposition outside him, and in himself something for which he has no name, but which we call a will. Yet still, although cruel Nature herself dashes him as it were against the walls in which she herself has imprisoned him, and forces him to break her laws as though for the pleasure of punishing him, the child has no grudge against her. If she seems capricious, at least she seems less capricious day by day; if she gives pain, she gives pleasure also. The world is full of joy for a child, and each morning brings forth new joys. All that the child knows, or begins to know, as yet, is, that he has a will of his own, and that he is often prevented from accomplishing that will by strange, unlooked-for obstacles.

But side by side with the growing consciousness of an internal will, and the recognition of an external, unvarying opposition or unvarying compliance, there has been growing up another feeling. Another and a Higher Nature, corrective of the seeming caprices and harshnesses of the lower or material Nature, has been long quietly working for the child, and is now beginning to be perceived by him. With a halo of bright recollections this Higher Nature is now borne in upon the child's mind, associated with genial thoughts of food, the touch of soft caresses, pleasant sounds, and bright and loving looks. When the Lower Nature has inflicted pain, how often has the Higher Nature stepped in to relieve it, or still more

THE ILLUSIONS OF THE FAMILY.

wonderfully to prevent the infliction! Miracles of help, miracles of beauty and of brightness, all issuing from this Higher Nature, have wondrously suspended the Lower Nature's rigid laws, and seem to point up to this better and higher Being, as a superhuman combination of strength and love, attracting the child's love and trust and admiration. Thus the child is entering upon its first lesson in theology, and is beginning to be trained to worship God in heaven by first rising to the worship of his father and mother upon earth.

Yet this better Nature, generally so compliant or helpful, and so suggestive of happiness, sometimes opposes or controls the child's dawning will, not indeed by harsh, unexpected penalties after the manner of the Lower Nature, nor yet by mere prescribed punishments inflicted in case of disobedience, but rather by the manifestation of a new will, higher than the child's will. It is in the shock or collision between the lower will and the higher will, between the child and the child's Ideal, that there first arises for mankind the terrible germ of sin. Here, as everywhere, the highest gifts go hand in hand with the deepest pains. As memory sowed the seed of pain as well as of love, so the sense of fatherhood begets sin as well as faith. If indeed it were possible that the recognition of the higher will could be so symmetrically accompanied by the surrender of the child's own lower will that the child could find no too severe struggle, no over-mastering temptation, no break or dislocation in experience, but could pass smoothly and imperceptibly from that first instinctive and unconscious union with Nature which he enjoyed when he had no will, to the second conscious, reasonable, and loving union with

Nature which consists in giving up one's own will to a higher Will, then indeed for such a child there would be no fall, no loss of paradise. Eden would be Eden still, lit with a brighter sunlight, and there would be no forbidden tree within its woods.

But this has never yet been possible, except, we think, for One. Nature herself, the lower nature, gifting the child with an inquisitive, exploring spirit, and with a restless tentativeness disproportionately greater than the nascent faculties of love and trust and reverence, forces the child into opposition with the newly-revealed will. When the child obeys the will, he finds joy and peace in obeying; but he sometimes disobeys, and disobedience brings with it a new and painful uneasiness. What this uneasiness is he does not know; but it is something quite new in his experience, something quite different from the old consciousness of mere *mistake*. When he touched the candle-flame and was scorched, the penalty was painful, far more painful than the new, vague, undefined feeling which for the present he can easily shake off, but which makes him uneasy when the face of his parents is clouded against him. The new feeling cannot be called pain: it is only uneasiness; but he does not like it. It seems a kind of burden, an oppression, which passes from himself to his mother or his father. They share it with him. It takes the smile from their face, the brightness from their eyes, and brings into their features quite a new expression, such as he had never noted before. From their faces the darkness passes back to him. The mirth goes out of his sports, the brightness passes out of the sunshine; his toys seem dull and dead, until he can shake off this vague and strange uneasiness, for which, at present, he has no name, but which he will learn, if he lives, to call by the name of Sin. But Eden has vanished now, and never more shall he see it in its old beauty, till he returns to it in a second and purified childhood, finding his Paradise regained.

Yet upon the altar-steps of this stumbling-block of sin the child is ascending to the altar of a higher worship. For to the Higher Nature, to which he has already assigned so many divine attributes, he now learns to add one more, the highest of all. The same will that produced the consciousness of sin has also the power of destroying sin. That same face, which by its darkness produced the feeling of oppression, can relieve him of the burden, if it will but look brightly again upon him. No matter against whom the fault may have been committed, whether against brother or sister or friend or stranger, every fault is an offence against the parental will, and none but the parents have the absolving power. Whatever others may say or do, the uneasy sense remains; but when the father accepts the child's sorrow, and welcomes him back into the old familiar intercourse making him feel that all is forgiven, then, and not till then, the uneasiness vanishes and all is peace again. Such power has been given by the Word of God to parents upon earth to forgive sins.

But a great part of the child's life is often spent, not in open or direct rebellion, nor in complete surrender to the will of the father, but in a neutral state. He submits, but he submits unwillingly. The unwillingness may be in different degrees, and may arise from different causes. Submission may be tendered, not always through fear of punishment, but often through hope of reward, or in the certainty that refusal will prove eventually useless. Such submission is in many respects better than rebellion; the child often learns, by submitting, the wisdom and duty of submission; he recognises the wisdom of the law, and learns to trust the lawgiver, and to distrust himself. But, whatever the ultimate results may be, this state of submission is not the true child-like state, but rather the condition of a servant; the child is not under faith, but under the law. In that condition he does what he is obliged, but no more. He carries out the letter of his father's precepts, but not the spirit of them. He has no strong affection prompting him to probe the depths of the parental words and wishes, no passionate trust in the parental wisdom, no powerful attraction towards the parental example. Taken at its worst, such a state has nothing good in it: all the child's acts are what St. Paul calls "works," that is to say, actions performed through interested motives, and all the child's life is a commercial investment. But such a state is never perhaps quite at its worst. Always in the domestic life there are forms and signs of higher relations than those of master and servant, command and submission. In words, and salutations, and forms of intercourse, and in a thousand indirect ways, there are suggestions, types, and shadows of the true family tie, the child-like dependence, the sacrifice of the will of the son to the father. Every act of submission unwillingly performed suggests to the child how much better such an act might be performed, and points, like one of the old Mosaic sacrifices, to the ideal sacrifice of love. Thus even for children in a family, as well as for Israel of old, the law is the guide to conduct them to a higher childhood, depending upon a higher conception of fatherhood.

But some children are, it may be, not under the law, but under grace. That is to say, they give a willing and ungrudging obedience, not out of desire of reward, nor from fear of punishment, but out of affection. Parental love, filial trust and reverence, both are free gifts or acts of "grace." Where this is the case, the father has a wonderful power of inspiring his children with his own virtues. This parental influence cannot be explained as the mere result of the imitative tendencies of human nature; it is principally the result of the filial trust, or, as St. Paul would call it, "faith," by which the child, looking up to the ideal which he recognises in his father, is unconsciously raised up to a higher level by force of sympathy. Partly the sense of reciprocated trust, the feeling of parental support encourages and stimulates him in following on his father's path. The influence of faith has been illustrated from the instance of a dog. "Take an example of a dog, and mark what a generosity and courage he will put on when he finds himself maintained by a man, who to him is instead of a god or *Melior Natura:* which courage is manifestly such as that creature, without that confidence of a better nature than his own, could never attain." How much more is this true of every little child who, "when he resteth and assureth himself" upon parental protection or favour, gathereth a force and faith which childish nature in itself could not obtain! Thus it is true no more of Israel than of each of the endless generations of little children that have sprung into being since first men learned how to love and trust one another, that "the just shall live by faith."

The filial love, faith, and reverence thus created Nature herself makes it her business to foster and develop. Parents, in the ordinary course, must pass away, and long, often very long before they have passed, there has departed the old childish faith in the parental power and goodness; but it has prepared the way for a faith equally childlike, but pointing to a higher power and a higher goodness. The Better Nature, as Bacon calls it, who could do no wrong, whose word was truth, whose presence was strength or beauty, whose will was power —this sublime ideal the mature man returning to the old home can discern no longer in the decrepit shapes that come forth to welcome him. But from the old perishing seed of faith there has arisen a new faith in truth, and righteousness, and power all combined; and this faith and love will never perish. From the cradle to the grave there is scope for the exercise and growth of these childlike feelings, which never grow ridiculous or antiquated. The child passes into the man, but the principle of childhood, the spirit of love and faith, should abide for ever. For herein love, and faith, and hope, differ from other affections; and love excels even its two companions. All three "abide," St. Paul tells us; but love is the greatest of the three. Our own experience proves the greater permanence of love, in that one may look back and laugh at one's early hopes and childish forms of faith, but the *love* of infants and of children never suggests a smile. Our childish hopes of a material heaven after the model of a well-filled nursery or park, our faith in a God with a kind human face looking through an open window in the skies, how grotesque, how disproportioned does all this appear to our maturer judgment! How infinitely wiser and nobler appears our present faith! Perhaps we are mistaken; perhaps our childish hope and faith, under whatever grotesque masks and integuments, may not be so inferior, perhaps they may be even superior, to our present calmer notions; but in any case it is noteworthy that we never imagine in the same way that we can laugh at our former love for our parents. We may hope that our present love is more thoughtful, more appreciative, more consciously grateful: still we are too well aware of our deficiencies to boast of any great improvement. However lovingly we may dwell upon the good points of those whom we reverence, we cannot now help comparing and judging; a larger experience of human nature has made us critical. But a child critical of parents we feel to be an abomination. Conscious of the critical spirit, most grown-up sons will find the laugh at their childish theology die away when their thoughts turn to their old, childish affection. The illusion has vanished, but we can never mock at our belief in it. On the contrary, we know it was not a deception, but rather a truth proportioned to our powers of receiving truth; not a mere dry, unsatisfying mirage, but rather a tiny rivulet dancing down cliffs just out of reach, freshening our outstretched faces now and then with its cool spray, but serving us best by being our guide as we climb up towards the great still water whence it flows, and whither we go. No, the man who can laugh at his childish love for his mother and father —it were better for him that a millstone were hung about his neck, and that he were drowned in the bottom of the sea. When the secret thoughts, and motives, and springs of action come to be revealed at that last Day of Judgment, who knows how many of us will then for the first time acknowledge that a mother's love led us to the love of God?

But by this time the child we are considering has become a man, and has stepped out into the world. His parents, the former objects of his love and faith, are no longer able to concentrate upon themselves all the worship that he is capable of giving. Their work being done, they pass into the back-ground. Where now must he turn to find the Higher Will? How keep alive the filial habit of dependence? Where is the Father, entering whose family he may become a second time "a little child" still offering up the worship of his love, trust, and reverence? Or what is the next illusion that must guide him upwards as he ascends from the Illusions of the Family on his way to the Worship of the Truth?

CHAPTER XI.

THE ILLUSIONS OF SOCIETY.

Society is the next means appointed by Nature for taking up and continuing the work left incomplete by the parents. Obviously it is a critical time when the youth moves out of the family circle at last to "depend upon himself," as the phrase goes. He is apt to confound the duty of thinking and toiling for his daily bread, with the supposed privilege of thinking and toiling for none but himself. No longer being under the roof of his parents, he thinks that the habit of "honouring" or reverencing is obsolete. Not yet having measured himself with others, he is now, more than at any other time, in danger of laying aside the former standard of conduct, and of falling into selfishness of some kind, manifesting itself in shyness, uppishness, vanity, self-conceit, or some other form of the unfilial and non-dependent spirit. Here then society ought to step in to sustain and elevate the ideal taught by Fatherhood, and to train the youth still further in the duty of righteous worship.

The influence of society is twofold, being exerted partly indirectly through its approved leaders who derive authority from the social approval, but partly directly through the mass acting upon the individual: The latter seems to be the more entitled to the name of social influence. Each member of a society when merging his individuality in the common and social feeling is, to some extent, benefited and ennobled. He is at all events made for the time less selfish, less self-conscious, less conceited, less insolent; and in such a condition, he is more open than before to all the better kind of thoughts. The feeling that may animate the crowd or society may be unreasonable, mad, bloodthirsty; in that case the individual may possibly receive more harm than good from the social influence; his moral standard may be lowered, not raised; the demon of selfishness may have been exorcised only to make room for others worse than itself. But in most cases the feeling of the crowd will but represent, in a larger and less selfish form, the feelings of his own heart, his own unreasonableness, madness, and cruelty. It is better, or rather less evil, that a man should be even wicked with others and for others, than by himself and for his own mere advantage. And this is taking society at its very worst, in the shape of a merely disorderly rabble, a casual crowd. In its higher shape as an army, a city, a state, or a church, society has shown itself a worthy mediator between God and man, fit to take up the sublime task of continuing the revelation of the family by training maturer mankind to recognise that they were not sent into the world to do their own will, but to offer up the worship of their lives to a higher being than themselves.

The influence of religion would come in naturally, just

when the child is learning to compare and to become critical. Just when the disillusion of the child's belief in the parental ideal is impending, the belief in another higher Nature would step in to supply the place, else likely to be left dangerously vacant. Most happy, in that dangerous crisis, is the child who has been in some way prepared beforehand by the human father to believe that there is One above who is a higher Father than any father on earth; most happy the son, who, while kneeling by his mother's side, has caught something of the spirit of her worship, and has realised that she whom he regarded as perfect, herself looked up to a higher perfection. But happy also, in less privileged times and nations, have been those children who, when gradually drifting from the old anchorage of the harbour of their home, have found themselves surrounded by a society which will still keep up in them the wholesome habit of " looking up." One of the Romans of the imperial times, Pliny, I think, or Seneca, insisting on the need of some ideal of life, advises his friend to " take Lælius or take Cato, by the rule of whose righteous life you may straighten the crooked line of your own." But it was not the Lælius' or the Catos of Rome, it was the spirit of Rome as a whole, that constituted the saving influence, giving to every youthful Roman at that critical period when he assumed the manly dress, a sense of looking up to a Being higher than himself, to a destiny, a fortune of Rome, to a mighty providence, which imposed on every citizen of that great country a feeling of mission, of being sent into the world to scorn delights and to do great deeds. In Rome and elsewhere in the great cities of Greece, this " looking up " was often a not altogether noble feeling; a co-operative selfishness of an enlightened kind, only a little less selfish than ordinary selfishness; a patriotism which placed the country above self, it is true, but placed the good of one's own country in the injury of other countries. The fortune and glory of Rome to which the youthful Roman looked up was a hard and cruel fortune to other nations; the Athenian looked up to nothing more than a bright flash of freedom and exuberant art, the transient efflorescence from an unscrupulous and despotic empire; the citizen of Sparta had no higher aspiration than the maintenance of the stern, forbidding, military supremacy of his city; but even such "looking up" as this was infinitely better than looking down to one's own interest and gain. It is better, if need be, to imagine that heaven has destined the earth and the nations of the earth to be the spoil and prey of one's own peculiar city or country, than to take the view of the solitary beast of prey, which, whether in the mouth of a great conqueror or a bragging cut-throat, is almost equally ignoble: "This world, it is mine oyster, which I with sword will open." Contrast with this base and sordid feeling the famous epitaph on the three hundred Spartans of Thermopylæ, "We lie here obeying orders." Christians though we are, we can never afford to put aside the sublime lessons of patriotism in which the great heroes of Greece and Rome have bequeathed to us an undying revelation that every man was sent into the world to obey a Being higher than oneself, and to obey lovingly, trustfully, and reverently, that is, to worship.

But before we speak in detail of the revelation of the nation, we must say a word on another kind of revelation. The influence of the love of wife and children might seem to fall more naturally into the last chapter, which treated of family ties. But the dependent relation of children which was then discussed, differs altogether from the independent and protecting relation of a husband and a father. The former was "looking up," the latter is "lifting up." The former developed awe and trust; the latter rather develops love. The love of man for woman, as soon as it emerges from the mere animal stage, comes as a kind of repetition and inculcation from nature, warning us that, although we have quitted the parental roof, we are not to consider ourselves free from all ties of affection. At that most critical time in manhood, when all the self-reliant passions are at their highest, when our area of action is suddenly enlarged, without any corresponding enlargement of deterrent experience, love steps in like a guardian angel for those who have learnt the filial lesson of reverence, teaching us a new reverence, a new sacrifice, not the dependence of weak childhood, but the passionate devotion of the strength of manhood. The great philosopher who reckoned wife and children among "impediments," would persuade us that love is the child of folly; and so indeed it often is. But it is so for those who have not learned to love or reverence anyone more than themselves, for those who—in the peculiar meaning of the word common in our Bible—are "fools," whom nature answers according to their folly. Far better has Wordsworth described the illusion of marriage as no mere folly, but rather as a fair phantom of delight, vanishing to disclose a higher reality, the apparition that seemed at first sent to be the ornament of the moment revealing itself at last as a permanent help-mate for man upon earth, but none the less as—

> " —a spirit still, and bright
> With something of angelic light."

But in case a man may still have closed his heart to the voices which on all sides suggest some other than self-worship, God brings up against our selfishness, as His last reserve, the appeal of helpless children. Certainly if anything could break through the triple armour of selfishness encasing the man who has passed through childhood, youth, and early manhood, loving nothing better than himself and looking no further than the immediate present, it would be the loving trust of innocent children looking up to him as to a god, and lavishing upon him the affection that he himself has never given to others. The free love of children, scattered, like God's blessed sunshine and rain, upon just and unjust parents, given without conditions or reserves, expecting no return—how often has it proved twice blessed, blessing the child that gives it and the father who receives! How many a sin-laden, profligate, vicious father has been stung to remorse, or even to a fruitful repentance, by having held up to him, in the exaggerated ideal which his children have formed of his character, the mirror showing the image of what he might and should have been side by side with the image of what he is!

"Freely ye have received, freely give"—so Christ exhorts His disciples, ordering them to lay aside suspicion and hostility, and to meet the whole hostile world disarmed. If they will do this, He promises them a liberal return, "good measure pressed down and running over shall men give into your bosom." This is Christ's exhortation; but how few of us are capable of acting on it! We cannot disarm, we cannot lay aside our doubts, our suspicions; we sow the seed of a half-hearted love, and we naturally reap the niggard harvest of a poor and doubtful gratitude. Children, and none else, are the true ungrudging missionaries of Christ: they alone faithfully follow Christ's method and "freely give" their love; and because they follow Christ's spiritual law, they obtain its natural result, "good measure pressed down and running over."

Great also is the influence of children as heralds of a future. The grossest and most sense-bound of men, who refuses to think of the morrow for his own sake, must, unless he regards his children as mere playthings for an idle hour, sometimes cast a thought forward into a time where he may be absent and they may be left alone. But this is nothing as compared with the child's influence in inspiring that best and most useful kind of self-reproach which comes to us joined with self-respect, when we blame ourselves the more because we contrast our pitiable facts with our glorious possibilities. For let it not be said that children do no more than call out our power of loving. Little children come to us fresh from the brightness of an ideal which we Christians have been taught to call the face of the Father. "They do always behold it," says Christ, and their innocent trust reveals to us something of it. For whoever realises a child's love realises something of the fatherhood which should correspond to it. When a weak, erring, sinful man finds himself looked up to by a little child as a god two courses are open to him. He may amuse himself with the delusion, as the drunken Stephano played on the devotion of poor Caliban; or, instead of amusement, he will find himself possessed with a terrible awe, awe-struck at his own new and solemn responsibilities, awe-struck also at the vision of the Fatherhood of God revealed in the illusion of his innocent child. Verily the Latin poet was right in more ways than one when he said, "*Maxima debetur pueris reverentia!*" The face of a little child is one of the last warnings sent by God to selfish men; and a man had better neglect all the warnings of Scripture, and make light even of the distorted conception that he has formed of Christ Himself, rather than neglect that last most solemn appeal of the Divine Father, or make light of those little ones whom Christ selects as His most sacred and effectual messengers.

For a man who has learned to "look up," the love of wife and children, supplementing the past lesson of "looking up" with the new habit of "lifting up" is an admirable discipline of righteousness. But the mischief has been that the habit presupposes the lesson, and too often the lesson has not been learned But where the lesson of reverence has not been learned, the faculty of true love is not yet developed. To the selfish man, wife and children are either mere instruments of pleasure and amusement, if he leads a life of luxury; or, if his life is one of toil and hardship, then they are mere servants and drudges. Again, where force and violence are the objects of general worship, the love of the helpless falls naturally into a low place. Hence it has come to pass that in many races the influence of domestic ties upon mature manhood has been, to all outward appearance, slight as compared with the influence of patriotism. In Sparta, as we know, the Family was entirely subordinated to the State. In a less degree the same subordination may be traced in the other States of Greece, and also in Rome. Let us therefore now pass to the lessons of worship taught by the State, taking for our examples the States of Greece, Rome, and Israel.

The bright side of Grecian and Roman patriotism has been before touched on. It brought out some of the most conspicuous instances of unselfishness to which history has borne testimony. Not merely in the battle-field, but in the market-place and at home, the citizen in those states subordinated himself to his country. He was content to be lowly that his country might be proud; private incomes and houses were modest, public treasuries and temples ample and magnificent. The citizen's time and money, life and children were always at the disposal of the city. Patriotism was the religion of those days. It was true they had a religion, and worshipped gods; but the gods were not the gods of the whole world, but the guardians of their own peculiar nation, and men fought rather for their country than for their country's gods. Polytheism prevented the Greek or Roman from feeling towards any one of their gods the concentrated allegiance felt by the Israelite for Jehovah, or by the Christian for Christ. They had many gods, but one city; and they transferred to the City something of the devotion that might be paid to a person, " beholding," as Pericles said to the Athenians, " the power of the city, and becoming *enamoured* of it."

Thus their patriotism gave them something to look up to and to love, and, in a certain sense, to trust. Their country, surrounded by enemies, depended upon their efforts and sacrifices. The work of their forefathers in building up so glorious a State they must not let drop. It was their mission to live for her, and if necessary to die for her. The fortunes of their country accompanied them to the battle-field, and they fought as though they trusted it was a god and might accompany them even beyond an honourable grave.

So noble an illusion naturally produced much true worship, much high morality : but the sphere of its action was limited, and its duration curtailed by this great defect— it was essentially exclusive. The heroic deeds of the ancient patriots were almost all extorted by the pressure of a contest felt to be for life or death. The very notion of patriotism implied the desire to lower other countries that one's own might be exalted. Now this being the case, as long as the nation was fighting an up-hill battle, patriotism implied endurance, suffering, fortitude, patience, trust against appearances in the nation's destiny, and much other passive virtue ; but as soon as the nation gained the ascendant, there was no scope left for all these passive virtues, and patriotism now began to imply oppression, cruelty, unscrupulousness, and insolence. It was now no longer unselfish to be a patriot. Patriotism was profitable, and paid : and it was quite possible to be now a patriot and think of one's self at the same time. Thus the State lost its old chastening influence on the hearts of its citizens, and no longer helped men to worship.

Even at their best, the Western States had never

thoroughly taught the lesson of awe. Non-human nature, as we have seen, had not revealed it to them; and human nature had not made up for the deficiency. They had, it is true, laid stress upon the parental authority, Rome more especially ; and the spirit of obedience and discipline, extended from the family to the state and to the army, had, in Rome, the natural result of producing stability in the state and success in the field. But this spirit, like the spirit of patriotism, sensibly declined when the period of danger and struggle for the state was definitely passed. If each province, absorbed by the conquering empire, could have been so completely identified with the empire that the citizen might have enlarged the circle of those whom he called fellow-citizens till it excluded none, then indeed the enthusiasm of the State might have ripened into an enthusiasm of humanity, and patriotism might have originated general benevolence. But this was in no way possible where patriotism, by its very nature, excluded general benevolence, and implied the duty of injuring other states in order to benefit one's own. Hence, when at last the Roman empire came to include the whole civilised world, it had come to be felt, in spite of satirists and poets, that old Roman patriotism was an obstructive, obsolete, and inhuman passion, interfering with the progress of the empire, and setting the interests of a single city above the exigencies of the world. What Bacon (to the disgrace of the Christianity of his time) says about the State in his day, that a healthy State requires the exercise of war, was far truer and less discreditably true of the states of Greece and Rome. All the virtues of their citizens breathed the atmosphere of war : in peace they sickened and decayed. The whole meaning and object of life seemed to have passed away when once the world had been conquered. Military arts and self-control and courage having now no scope, men turned all their faculties to the passionate pursuit of enjoyment. It was as though an athlete, after long training and many preparatory contests, engaging at last in the final struggle in the Olympian games, with mind and muscles on the stretch, in the full heat and excitement of the conflict, suddenly found himself without an adversary, and yet compelled by some mysterious instinct still to beat the air and go through the idle motions of the struggle, but with the increasing sense that it was all a mere delusion, and that he was struggling without a motive. Such was the fate of the whole of the higher life in Rome. Languid and listless, it searched the world in vain to find again the almost forgotten pleasure of a motive. It was felt by all that the old world, with the old motives, had passed away, and that some new motive was required, some new bond and tie between men and nations to keep mankind together. Some strove to find this in religion. In the general stagnation of peace, national religion had passed away; yet some religion seemed to be needed more than ever. Rejecting or supplementing the old worship of Jupiter and Vesta, the Romans began to import the worship of new Eastern gods, unknown or despicable to their ancestors. On the other hand the conquered nations turned from their conquered gods, looking for a religion to victorious Rome. In their craving for some common centre of union, for some god who should be a just, impartial, protecting deity alike to Greeks and Italians, Spaniards and Syrians, they turned at last to the man who sat on the imperial throne as the true lord and god of mankind, the saviour of the erring world. In the decrepitude of his old age, and almost in his dying moments, the Emperor Augustus was beset in the harbour of Baiæ by the importunate worship of the sailors freshly arriving from a prosperous voyage in the Egyptian corn-fleets. Whom else, they all exclaimed, could they more fitly worship than the source and centre of the world's peace and blessing? Jupiter might thunder in heaven, and was a god to be believed in also, but Augustus—quelling with his terrestrial thunders the enemies of order and of the Empire, the Britons and mischief-working Parthians—was lord on earth. "He shall be esteemed," says Horace, "a very present god." The imperial poet was not expressing in these words the courtly flatteries of a knot of flatterers, but the temporarily satisfied longings of a yearning world. Elsewhere he uses even more explicit language. The old gods, he complains, were selfish and cruel; Vesta was deaf to entreaty; Venus made sport of her neglected offspring; Mars exulted in their savage internecine conflicts; to Cæsar, sent from above, must be assigned the task of expiating the crimes of the past; "Late mayest thou return to heaven!"

Patriotism was making way for a new feeling not yet quite defined, including all nations in its scope. For the present it assumed the shape of a craving for peace and order. All the nations of the earth were to be as one under the common heavens: and between heaven and earth the emperor was the appointed mediator. To this the Roman world had been driven as its last hope of salvation. A minority of purer and more philosophic spirits might hold aloof from the new debased religion: but the great mass of the population of the civilised world rushed into a spontaneous and passionate adoration of an incarnate godhead, deifying in the emperor the divinely restraining and coercing power that held the world at peace. The new belief did not spring from the virtues of the ruler, nor did it select the memory of the greatest or the wisest of the emperors. This year the imperial incarnation might produce an Augustus, the next year a Tiberius or a Caligula or a Nero: it mattered not to the indiscriminating adoration of the myriads of the Roman world. To be emperor was to be a "present god," and worthy of worship. Such seemed to all appearance the outcome of five centuries of western patriotism.

We turn to the history of patriotism in Israel. Here, indeed, it is not so easy to separate patriotism from religion. The diffused feelings of the Western nations towards their many gods were, in the Israelite, concentrated on Jehovah alone. He, too, was not only the Friend of their great ancestor Abraham, but the Guide and Deliverer of their nation from the first, and their laws were made by Him. Consequently very much of the passionate feeling which in the West displayed itself in patriotism was diverted in Israel towards Jehovah, or at least towards the nation regarded only as the Chosen People of Jehovah. The men of Israel lived with the constant sense of the presence of a God not worshipped with statues or temples—for even when the temple was built there was but one, whereas in Greece or Rome every little town had its visible objects of worship—but nevertheless dictating weekly and monthly cessations from labour, regulating their customs, and imposing on them minute daily recognitions of the purity which was to be expected from His worshippers. No wonder if this feeling, however obscured at times by deviations into idol-worship, drew to itself very much of the devotion bestowed elsewhere upon the nation. Nevertheless the patriotism of the Israelites, modifying their conceptions of Jehovah, can be shown to have indirectly influenced their notions of worship and the lessons they had to communicate to mankind.

Certainly if the object of the State is to teach the citizen that he must subordinate his will to a Higher Will, that lesson was effectually taught to the citizens of Israel. The ordinary modern objects of life, the different means of "bettering oneself," or "getting on," were almost all denied to him. The accumulation of wealth was positively discouraged, commerce forbidden, art hampered, if not rendered impossible; and as the result of all these restrictions and of the insulation of the nation, science was at least indirectly checked. The object of the state of Israel was to train up a people of agriculturists, like one family, knit together by the common worship of their national Deliverer, the One God, Jehovah. The pushing spirit, the competitive spirit, the inquiring spirit, were all alike discouraged. The object was to produce a spirit of reverent obedience.

But it may be urged that the purpose of Sparta and Rome was to produce the same spirit of reverent obedience. True—but the object of obedience, being different for Israel, changed the nature of the obedience.

In Rome and Sparta the object was the good and honour of the state; in Israel the good and honour of the people of the Lord, or rather the honour of the Lord Himself. It was the reproach against Sparta that their statesmen deemed things profitable to be honourable; and even in Rome, during its declining period, there was the taint of the same immoral and debased patriotism which may be glossed and made to look excusable in an Aristides, but finds its true expression in the sentiment of the footman: "Though I never scruple to tell a lie to serve my master, yet it hurts my conscience to be found out." Now in Israel it was felt, at least by the master-minds of the nation, that Jehovah could not be served by lies: lying and evil-doing would bring dishonour upon the Name of the Lord, and cause Him to be blasphemed among the Gentiles. Jehovah was not a man that He should lie or repent; He was not one among many gods that He should change His will. His word was truth, His will was righteousness, and neither He nor His chosen people could be served by unrighteousness. To reverence such a Being as this was a far higher kind of reverence than to reverence Rome or Sparta.

The dependent spirit, rather than the self-reliant spirit, was naturally encouraged in the state which recognized the supremacy of Jehovah. Far more than the soldiers of Greece and Rome did the soldiers of Israel put their trust in the God of their fathers. Doubtless the Western nations also relied to some extent on the help of the gods in battle. It was to the twin sons of Jupiter that the Romans assigned the honours of Regillus, and at Marathon the gods of Greece were not wanting; but, for the most part, the trust of the Western soldiers was rather in their weapons than in their gods. Not that they imitated the atheism of Mezentius, who recognized no god but his spear: so far from this, the whole warfare of the Roman soldier was tinged with religion. But on what did their trust in the gods depend? On the feeding of chickens, or a flight of vultures, or the look of the entrails of an ox! Such superstition as this cannot be mentioned (as a moral influence) in the same breath with the trust of the Israelite in Jehovah, nor did it encourage the true dependent spirit. When Cæsar stepped up into his chariot he never omitted, they say, to mutter a charm: yet Cæsar was the type of self-reliance, counting his fortune a match for the stormiest sea. The trust of the Romans in their gods, if analysed, would be found to be a trust in the Roman name, coupled with a perpetual *distrust* lest any rite or ceremony omitted should have irritated the gods. But the trust of the men of Israel could not depend entirely, though it did in part, on rites or ceremonies. It was the worship of a righteous people that Jehovah required; so their best teachers taught them. If they were faithful to the Eternal Righteousness, then the world in arms against them could not withstand the shock of their onset: if they were unfaithful, a thousand of Israel would turn their backs in flight before ten pursuers. No chariots of iron or squadrons of cavalry could win the day for them: victory depended upon Jehovah alone.

As the self-reliant spirit of later Rome was stimulated by conquest, so the dependent spirit in Israel was fostered by defeat. Instead of turning round to examine the efficient causes of their disasters, their minds were always fixed upon the original cause, the displeasure of Jehovah. Their disunion and discord, their want of military training and their deficiencies in the equipments of war might possibly have served to explain many of their defeats : but the improvement of such details did not suggest itself to them as the remedy of their evils. Always it was unfaithfulness to Jehovah, always some shape of unrighteousness, that had seduced them to ruin. To Him all the good and evil of the nation was referred. What in other states were offences against the State, or *crimes*, became in Israel offences against Jehovah, or *sins*. Their hatred of idolaters, as enemies and oppressors of their country, was merged in the hatred of them as enemies and blasphemers of Jehovah. "Do not I hate them that hate Thee ?" cries the Psalmist ; " Yea, I hate them as though they were mine own enemies." Hence it came to pass that many actions of which the Western states did not take cognizance, because their results did not appear to affect the state, were noted and condemned by the legislation of Israel. For who could tell how far a sin against Jehovah might not, by averting His face from His people, prove to be also an injury against the state ? To be holy was to be faithful to Jehovah, and therefore to the state : to be unholy was to be unfaithful to both ; not only sinful, but also unpatriotic. Hence all the passionate fervour of Western patriotism was poured by the singers and prophets of Israel into the praises of holiness and righteousness, the yearning for sinlessness, and the hatred of evil-doing and sin. The sweetness and beauty of the Roman life was to die for one's country : the sweetness and beauty for which the singers of Israel yearned was the beauty of holiness, the presence of the Living God, for which their souls longed as pants the hart for the water brooks.

Why did not this great and noble training lead straight towards some greater and nobler development? It did, in the better spirits of the nation: and the reasons of its failure with the rest are not difficult to discern. The training of Israel was a training in awe rather than in love, and, so far, was incomplete. Love was discouraged, partly perhaps by their attitude towards Jehovah, but still more by their attitude towards foreign nations. Not indeed that they were aggressive, after the manner of Rome; but they were passively repellent. The exclusiveness of Israel was far greater than that of Greece or Rome. Even in their relations with one another one seems to discern less of the social feeling, less loveableness, than in the Western states. The great heroes of Israel are not members of a senate, but kings or judges or prophets sent from the Lord, doing their work mostly by themselves. Often they are prepared for the work by a life of retirement and meditation. We must except David, and be ready to admit other individual differences; but in the general character of the Redeemers of the people of the Lord there seems to be something more solitary and awful than in Socrates, Scipio, and Pericles, although the two last went among their contemporaries as heroes of the solitary type. Towards foreigners, at all events, the attitude of the whole people of Israel was studiously and deliberately repellent. Such an attitude was inconsistent with any full development of the worship of Jehovah, and was only permissible as a temporary expedient, a means for guarding the child

Israel, while still a child, beneath the paternal roof, safe from external temptations.

The prophets perceived the temporary nature of the anti-foreign and other restrictions of the law. The time would come, they said, when Egypt and Assyria should share in the blessings of Jehovah. Taught by a divine inspiration that a righteous God could not be unjust even to Gentiles, they predicted that the Chosen People would be a blessing, and not a mere conquering scourge to the nations of the earth. Penetrating to the meaning of sacrifice and purification and worship, they warned their countrymen that the real sacrifice was the sacrifice of the broken and contrite heart, the real purification was the washing of justice, the real worship was "ceasing to do evil, learning to do good." But the grosser minds of the masses in Israel and among the later Jews could not accept this teaching. Their sufferings and disgraces, instead of making them sympathetic and loving, made them sullen and cold towards other nations. Fastening on the new belief in the immortality of the soul, which they had perhaps borrowed from their captors, they looked forward to that as their compensation for the miseries of their present existence. What had been the cause of their disasters? It had been disobedience, their own and that of their fathers. Henceforth then they would obey. But what were they to obey? The words of the prophets furnished them with no sure, fixed standard: they must recur to the law. Henceforth prophets appear no more, making way for explainers of the law. The law, and not righteousness, was to be the new lamp for their feet and guide of their life. If there was any province in private as public life not covered by the law, the law must be explained, or explained away, so as to afford some definite rule. As in the silver age of Rome we find Seneca exhorting his friend not to live for Rome or in the Roman spirit, but to copy Lælius or Cato, so in the silver age of Israel we find the later psalmist no longer on the spiritual level of the outpourings of David yearning for purity and righteousness, but reduced to a monotone, harping through a hundred verses upon "commandments."[1] The trust in a Righteous Will was thus becoming supplanted by trust in a righteous law. Patriotism had once intensified the worship of Jehovah, and had made it purer by associating it with duties towards fellow-worshippers in Israel. But now the exclusiveness of Jewish patriotism encouraged, and was encouraged by, this apotheosis of the law. If God was indeed the God of the Jews and not of the Gentiles, then the ordinary instincts of mankind and the feelings common to Gentiles as well as Jews were unsafe guides to the knowledge of Him, whose will might be more definitely studied in the law. Mercy and judgment and truth sank into the back-ground: did not even the Gentiles practise these things? But Jewish rites and ceremonies, Jewish sacrifices and feasts, all things small and great contained in the law of Moses, became paramount, overshadowing all broader and more natural obligations. In the Chosen People even during its lowest degradation, there were many whose hearts revolted against this servility to the letter of the law, and who kept up the traditions of prophetic aspiration. But the vast majority degraded the prophecies no less than the law, and as they literally fulfilled the latter, so they

[1] See Ewald's "Dichter des alten Bundes," p. 475.

looked forward to the literal fulfilment of the former. Having exchanged the sense of allegiance to Jehovah for a servile obedience to a law, they had loosened the former bond of national unity. Sects and schisms sprang up among them, and once more the Chosen People, under a foreign yoke, without shepherd, ruler, or guide, was brought to the verge of a second captivity. Thus the dependent spirit encouraged by the state of Israel seemed to have culminated in the enthronement of a book on the seat once filled by Jehovah.

Now, therefore, the illusions of Rome and Israel had played their part and done their great work: but both had been found wanting. The one had developed the powers of self-reliant humanity; the other had begun to train, and had succeeded in training to a certain point, the faith of humanity in a divine Will; the one had taught the love of external order, the other had engendered in its better spirits the love of righteousness; to Rome we owe the social spirit, to Israel the spirit of holiness. But both had stopped short, and indeed appeared to have retrograded. Both had resisted the premonitory tokens and warnings of their own transitory natures, and of a coming change. The philosophers of Greece were to Rome what the prophets were to Israel. As the teaching of the prophets was the solvent of the literal law, so the teaching of the philosophers was rightly felt to be destructive of the old unreasoning, illiterate, aggressive, selfish patriotism. But neither the prophets nor the philosophers had spiritual force sufficient to carry their words into effect. To the prophet Isaiah it seemed as though his mission was rather to "make the heart" of his countrymen " fat and gross "—so void of understanding were they : and the philosophers scarcely expressed a hope that they could convert all mankind to general philanthropy. Thus the later years of Rome and Israel, so far as they benefited mankind at all, seem rather to have benefited it mechanically than morally. The shell of the nut hardening round the fruit protects it from injury till the time shall come when the fruit shall fall ; but then, becoming obstructive rather than preservative, it only hinders the friendly decaying influences of earth and moisture, which are intent on destroying for the purpose of fructifying. In the same way the hard shell of Roman order and administration, keeping the world together, was destined for a time to preserve the new seed of philanthropy : and the hard dry obedience of the Jews had served to preserve, during ages of peril and persecution, records and thoughts of righteousness which have helped to the saving of the world. But, at the time, and looking only to their direct effect in producing worship (that is, love, trust, and awe), it might well have seemed that the training of society both in the East and in the West had been a failure. Other ages might be called the dark ages of the world, but this was the age of death. Reverence and patriotism were dead, art and literature dying. If the world was to be saved, it must be born again, and become a little child, in love, and faith, and awe. To what unspeakable and irretrievable degradation might the empire seem to have fallen when the highest object of Roman and provincial awe was a Tiberius ! Truly there seems to be something more than the mere painstaking accuracy of the chronicler, rather an inspired irony seems to breathe in those familiar words which relate in detail who they were that sat in the high seats of judgment and sovereignty at the time when Christ was born, telling us how in the fifteenth year of the reign of Tiberius Cæsar, Pontius Pilate being Governor of Judæa, and Herod being Tetrarch of Galilee, Annas and Caiaphas being the high priests, the word of God came to John the son of Zachariah in the wilderness, inspiring him to proclaim the advent of a new Emperor, who, in the words of the common prophecy recorded by Tacitus, "setting out from the East should make himself master of the whole world."

This was to be the true Emperor, to whom, and not to Augustus or Tiberius, God had committed the task described by Horace "of expiating past sin," the only Emperor who might be obeyed by the universal world without servility and without superstition, and who would command obedience without the aid of legions, sitting enthroned in the hearts of mankind; this was to be the true pattern and ideal of life, to whom alone, and not to "Cato or Lælius," mankind can look as the Judge and Reformer of our crooked morals; a Man, yet higher than a man, combining the revelation of humanity with the revelation of what is non-human; not a prophet of Israel, nor a philosopher of Greece, nor a soldier or statesman of Rome, but a new force in East and West alike, more human than the philosopher or hero of the West, more divine than the prophet of the East—a Power giving power to the sons of men to become the sons of God.

CHAPTER XII.

THE GAINS OF THE WORSHIP OF NATURE.

"THE Gospel did not *make* God our Father:" this is a truth to be borne in mind if we wish to understand ante-Christian as well as Christian times. It would be a terrible stumbling-block in the way of those who would wish to trust in the goodness of God if we could not believe that from the first He has been our Father, guiding us toward Himself. In morals, then, as well as in literature and art, we shall be prepared to believe, upon evidence, that much was done for mankind (and not only in Israel, but also in Greece and Rome and elsewhere) before the coming of Christ. Before proceeding to describe what the Word of God as Jesus of Nazareth did for mankind, let us briefly sum up what the same Word had previously done for Israel, and Greece, and Rome.

First, then, the whole of the civilised world had gained the idea of law. In the East the law of Jehovah had completely possessed Israel: in the West the love of external order and peace had been manifested by an apotheosis of imperial power. Their idea of law was not a noble one : Israel served the letter of a code, the empire adored an emperor as the attracting centre of the world : it was law regarded in that dreary aspect in which St. Paul describes it as a prison in which expectant Israel was "shut up" for a time awaiting the Redeemer. Nevertheless, even this sense of universal law was perhaps an advance in some respects upon some shapes of the old patriotism, which were really nothing better than systematic brigandage. Of the two laws, the Roman law promised more for mankind than the law of Israel : for the latter, as long as it remained unreformed or undeveloped, involved all the narrowness of the old Western patriotism, while the former had begun to include within its scope the whole of the population of the provinces. Rome had learned to look upon herself rather as supporting, than as trampling on, the empire. What the world wanted was, motive : it had learned the first part of the famous saying of Christ, "I came not to do Mine own will ;" but it had not yet received the revelation of the Higher Will which would enable it to add—" but to do the will of Him that sent Me." Nevertheless, the effete, motiveless condition of the world was a negative gain. St. Paul, who preached without much effect even to the later Athenians, would probably have made even fewer conversions had he preached to the Athenians under Pericles, or to the Romans in the Punic Wars. It was necessary that the two great nations should have their fill of art and conquest, and should "do their own will" to the utmost before they could be made to feel that their own will would never satisfy them. Now they had attained so far in knowledge. The age of Nero, with all its degradation, was an advance (if one could have looked beneath the surface and discerned the germs of the future) on the age of the Scipios and the Catos. It was a gain that the world had lost its freshness, a gain to have been deprived of its illusions, a gain to feel that the gods had flown from earth and heaven, and had left men hopeless and godless, yet yearning for a god who could bring back hope again, and help men to—

> "Have glimpses that would make them less forlorn,
> Have sight of Proteus rising from the sea,
> Or hear old Triton blow his wreathèd horn."

The second gain was that both Israel and Greece, through their prophets and philosophers, had attained a higher standard of individual morality. The teaching of Nature and of Society had not been thrown away upon the philosophers. Many of them had discerned clearly how necessary it is for every human being to be born again. The self-gratifying instincts of a child they felt to be incompatible with the duties and highest pleasures of manhood and with the claims of society. The selfish man was at perpetual war with himself, with his friends, with the laws, with nature, with the gods: whatever he did was wrong; to use their language, "though he but raised a finger, it was a sin." To avoid such selfishness was not only virtuous, but wise, the supreme wisdom: and the unselfish man alone deserved to be called the wise man. The language of St. Paul describing the difference between the regenerate and the unregenerate nature was scarcely stronger than the language of the Stoics in distinguishing between the "wise man" and the fool. The wise man was in harmony with himself, with society, with nature, and with the gods. The wise man had his every wish fulfilled: for he wished for nothing but what was right and possible. If anything became impossible, he ceased to wish for it. The wise man had all possible pleasures, all conceivable happiness, every virtue and every grace. In the truest sense of the word, he was a king. Something of the same conception is embodied in Israel's description of the "righteous man," who, however, less independent than "the wise man," is always waiting on the hand of Jehovah. Jehovah's secret is with the righteous: the righteous shall be delivered out of trouble, he shall be recompensed in the earth, his house shall stand, and he hath hope in his death. Just as it would be a mistake to suppose that the teaching of the prophets of Israel represented the ordinary morality of the nation, so, no doubt, it would be a mistake to suppose that the philosophers represented the ordinary morality of Greece and Rome. They were but solitary instances here and there of exceptional self-denial and moral insight. They had little aggressive power, at least with the common people. Yet they at least stood in the midst of the low morality of the masses, like the spires of unfrequented churches in a crowded city, silently pointing upwards, and bearing witness to the existence of an ideal higher than that of the crowd. As the prophets prepared the Jews, so did the philosophers prepare the upper classes of the Gentiles to welcome an Incarnation of wisdom and righteousness, higher than the wise man of the Stoics, or the righteous man of the Psalms and the Proverbs.

The third gain was the introduction of the belief in the immortality of the soul. Without such a groundwork it would scarcely have been possible to erect such a faith as Christ erected in the universal Fatherhood of God. A Father who exists for all eternity, but who sees each of His children flutter for its little hour of life and then pass into a state where He no longer knows it, may be called a Maker or an Owner, but in no very high sense of the word a Father; or, if He is to be so called, then a Father who is being perpetually robbed of His children, and will be ultimately childless. The belief in immortality lowered to insignificance the distinctions between Roman, Greek, and Jew: it intensified the relations between men as men: it supplied new motive for action by exhibiting the durability of the results of action: it offered scope to new aspirations, and made life a possible duty amid circumstances that would have otherwise rendered life an intolerable burden. The belief was not perhaps of a high order. Among the Jews it may have been exclusive and narrowly national. Among the Gentiles it may often have been rather a fear than a hope; a thorn in the side goading the superstitious to seek for new religions, new mysteries, new initiations into the secrets of the prison-houses of the dead, by which one might secure oneself while still living against ever coming into those places of horror. As of the ante-Christian law and the ante-Christian ideal, so it may be said of the ante-Christian belief in immortality, that it wanted vitality, hope, spiritual force, and vigour.

Life, indeed, and nothing else, was what the world needed at the time of the coming of Christ. The world was like a child that has rapidly outgrown its strength, having the limbs and some of the thoughts and aspirations of a man, but no sufficient store of vital energy to carry them into effect. Men had a law, but no strength to fulfil it; rules and ideals for the few, but no power to live up to them, or to commend them to the whole of mankind; a belief in immortality, but no knowledge of that righteousness which alone could make immortality for all mankind a hope and not a fear. What the world needed was some Man who should concentrate into Himself for the help of men all those beneficent forces by which Nature is bent on regenerating mankind, so that His life might be the natural life of all. He was to do for us the work of the Family by giving us a new and higher consciousness of sin, a new ideal of the fatherhood, and a new ideal of the faith and love of little children. He was to do the work of Society by knitting, not one nation, but all the nations of the world together in the bonds of a brotherly amity. He was to do the work of Nature by exhibiting to us the laws of Nature as identical with the will of God, by triumphing over the weakness of life while submitting to it, by conquering death itself while entering the grave, and thus by manifesting, alike through His life and through His death, that instead of rebelling against Nature, and instead of crouching before Nature, if we will become little children in obedience to the Divine Will working through Nature, we shall find ourselves at once in harmony with Nature and with God. Lastly, He was to do the work of Death by dying that He might triumph over Death, living for ever in the hearts of His mourning friends, and afterwards in the hearts of generation after generation of those who, though they had not seen Him, would none the less be drawn within the scope of His Spirit. But if you ask me *how* was the new Redeemer to do all this ? I should reply, by being a consummate Man, as far superior to ordinary men as the Truth is superior to even the very best of Illusions.

CHAPTER XIII.

THE DEFICIENCY IN THE WORSHIP OF NATURE.

THE great deficiency in Morality before the coming of Christ lay in the weakness or absence of the faculty of forgiving. The forgiveness of the sins of children is a parental prerogative, and it might, therefore, be thought that this faculty would have been developed by the natural training of the family. But it was not so. The art of forgiving was so undeveloped both in Israel and in Rome that we may almost say it was invented and introduced by Christ. Now, forgiveness, being a composite emotion, is capable of more analysis than simpler emotions such as love and faith: and unfortunately the history of Christendom has shown that it requires more analysis. Though the noblest of human acts, it has been treated as one of the most ignoble; though the hardest, it has been thought most easy. There is scarcely any error in our conceptions of God, and Christ, and morality, which may not be traced to erroneous conceptions of forgiveness. Moreover the study of the processes of forgiveness will reveal to us not only the deficiencies of Worship before Christ, but also the manner in which these deficiencies could alone be supplied, and man by Atonement could be brought close to God. If this be true, there needs no further apology for a somewhat minute analysis of the act of forgiving.

What then is meant by forgiveness? Etymologically it means "giving up" something. Giving up *what*, then? Clearly forgiveness means more than merely giving up a penalty. A penalty may be remitted through negligence; or from mere easiness of temper and dislike to inflict pain, no matter how salutary or necessary pain; or from a desire to gain credit or influence, or from a thousand other selfish reasons: and in none of these cases can it be said that a genuine forgiveness has taken place. What is needful for forgiveness is, besides the mere remission of penalty—which is a mere outward sign, not essential, though in most cases practically necessary—a certain state of mind in the forgiver, a certain spiritual attitude toward the person forgiven. In some sense a forgiver must spiritually lift up the person whom he forgives.

Take the case so commonly used as an illustration in the gospels, of a master defrauded by a servant. We will suppose that the servant, feeling that he has sinned, —that is to say that he has not only inconvenienced his employer and brought himself within the grasp of the law, but also that he has done wrong—comes to his master asking for forgiveness. What must be the qualifications and motives that will enable the master truly to forgive?

The first qualification is some degree of unselfishness, some power of putting oneself and one's own interests at least temporarily out of sight. Without this a forgiveness must needs be nugatory. Take the case of a master forgiving, or rather remitting the penalty, because he desires to retain a useful servant, or to prevent disclosures that might injure his business, or to gain a reputation for humanity, or because the loss resulting from the fraud is too trifling to justify in his eyes the loss of time in entering into the details of the matter. Such cases of spurious forgiveness have been touched on and rejected, above: it is obvious that every true forgiveness implies some kind of "giving up," some shape of *sacrifice*.

Take another case. Let us suppose that the master is no longer acting from self-interest. He is, we will say, of a kindly disposition, good-tempered and genial, unwilling to give pain, and fond of seeing happiness around him: but of sin as distinguished from inconvenience, or of sin as distinguished from crime, of sin as *sin*, he has scarcely any sense. Fraud he resents as uncommercial, unlawful, and extremely inconvenient, exposing the sufferer from the fraud to grave annoyances, and the perpetrator of the fraud to legal penalties; but the sickness and weariness of heart from which the sinner suffers, sin as an ever-present and intolerable burden, a wearing and shameful disease, an offence against one's own better self and a still higher Will better than one's best self—all this is quite unintelligible to him. His servant's distress pains him, but seems unintelligibly excessive: he cannot possibly sympathize with it. If he professed to do so he would be a hypocrite. However he may try to go through the usual forms of forgiveness and commonplaces of regret and sympathy, he feels himself out of his depth here. What then can the master do in these straits? Forgiveness and sympathy he has not, but of such as he has he can give; and what he has to give is the remission of the penalty. This then he gives. It is a definite and substantial gift, but it is not what is needed. The servant goes from his master's presence with the penalty remitted, but with no sense of having been "lifted up." A week hence the master will have forgotten the whole business, he will have forgotten, but he will never have forgiven: for not yet having learned the sinfulness of sin, he is not one of those to whom the Son of Man hath given power on earth to forgive sins. We see then that one of the first requisites for the exercise of this mighty power of forgiving sin is to hate sin.

Take yet another case. Let us imagine a master of a different stamp, a man with a deep sense of sin, and strongly marked religious impressions, but disposed to take gloomy views of things. Human nature he regards as essentially sinful. Man is born to sin as the sparks fly upwards. Sin is hateful and horrible, but then all the world habitually sins, and this repentant sinner, now before him promising amendment, he too, thinks the master, will be next week or next month sinning in the same fashion again. He is indeed bound to forgive, for the Scriptures enjoin forgiveness; and indeed he is willing to forgive, for his heart is filled with pity; but it is pity not tinged with hope or trust. "I forgive you, my friend"—such may be his reply to the petition for pardon,—" but I have no hope or expectation that your promises of amendment will be fulfilled. Henceforth I will remove from you those moderate temptations to which you have succumbed, and will place you under such closer supervision as may render it impossible for you to go wrong in the same way again without my immediate knowledge. I remit the penalty, and you have my sincerest pity and sympathy : go, but I cannot say go in peace ; go rather in distrustful sadness, and I will take measures that, if possible, you may sin no more." Is it not obvious that such a forgiveness, though it contains some elements of the genuine act, is nevertheless not of a nature to lift up a sinner's heart to God as the hearts of sinful men and women were lifted up in old times by the forgiving acts of Christ? No, it is not enough to have sympathy and the sense of sin : a man should also have faith [1] in God as the Father of men, and in men as the children of God : and without this faith it is impossible to forgive sins.

To take a last case of spurious forgiveness—we may suppose a master who has the sense of sin and also a theoretical faith in God as the Maker of man. Mankind, he believes, was made by God in His image, and will eventually be conformed to it. Sin is not the law of the world, but a violation of that law of righteousness which will ultimately be established beyond all violation. But unhappily, with all these high views about the ultimate perfectibility of mankind as a class, he has little affection for, and little sympathy with, men as individuals. Towards congenial friends, or persons specially interesting to him, his heart is drawn out in such a manner as to refute the charge that he is incapable of affection. But he has no strong love for man as man, no such a passion for humanity as may be called

[1] Or some other faith corresponding to this ; the same in essence, though different in words.

enthusiasm, no power of discerning the divine, attractive Image in dull, uninteresting, commonplace persons, such as, we will suppose, is the servant who is now standing before him confessing himself guilty of very disgraceful ingratitude and deceit, and anxiously awaiting the master's reply. What is he to do? Himself a man of high spirit and spotless honour, he finds, in spite of conventional religious precepts, that his first emotion is one of contempt: "Had I been in this fellow's place I would have starved sooner than treat my master as he has treated me." Though he gradually allows himself to realise more clearly his servant's position, weakness and temptations, yet his first impulse is rather repellent than attractive to the penitent. This tinge of contempt, or this slight deficiency in sympathy, may not perhaps be expressed in words, but it makes itself immediately perceptible to the sharpened instincts of one who is craving for sympathy: and the result is a quick collapse in the emotions of the sinner, a closing of the avenues of the heart, which a moment ago were open. By the time the master has reasoned himself into the sympathetic state of mind, the moment for the effective action of sympathy has perhaps passed away, and when he is ready to forgive, the sinner is no longer ready to be forgiven. Here, therefore, once more, though there are the elements of the true forgiving act, yet it is not consummated; for, in addition to unselfishness, hatred of sin, and faith in God, the consummation of forgiveness requires an instinctive and fervid love for man.

But now, on the other hand, imagine a case in which there are present all these requisites. In a man endowed with trust in God and passionate love for man, the wickedness and vileness of sin, though felt by him to the utmost, instead of calling forth unmixed anger against the sinner, will suggest the depth of the fall and the misery of the degradation from the high ideal of human nature. Pity for the offender will accompany, without suppressing, resentment against the offence. Believing that man is not born to sin but to righteousness, he regards sin as the accident, not as the law, of human nature in its highest and truest sense. In part sin is an act of the will; but, in part, it is an involuntary or ignorant servitude, and, so far, the sinner may be regarded as distinct from the sin. Without shutting his eyes, therefore, to the enormity of the offence, he may feel not less, but more, compassion for the offender. Never can he bring himself to look on the most repulsive and ferocious of men as a mere brute beast, sinning by instinct, and incapable of any higher existence here or hereafter. Hating sin, he regards it as a loathsome disease of the soul, from which the sinner is by all means to be delivered: trusting in God, he feels assured that He, the Father of all men, Father also of this erring and sinful child, does not intend the sinner to die, but to be healed of his disease; loving men for their own sakes, as being (not by theological fiction, but by nature, in the highest sense of the word "nature"[1]) children of the heavenly Father, loving them not with a reasoned or calculated affection, but with an instinctive enthusiasm, he loves and sympathises habitually with all, and therefore with the sinner before him; and, in proportion to his love and sympathy, he is grieved and distressed by

---

[1] Just as it is the *nature* of a clock to indicate the correct time, though no clock ever does indicate always precisely the correct time.

the sin. He puts himself in the sinner's place, and remembers his own shortcomings. He, too, has been tempted and has sinned, though never perhaps so grievously. Under pressure of greater temptation he also might have succumbed, as his servant has; and, if he had done so, would he have felt himself utterly bad, utterly beyond all reach of pardon? No, he would not have felt himself for ever condemned: he would still have remembered moments of strength as well as weakness, moments when his heart had gone out to God in trial and suffering, in thankfulness and joy, moments when he has felt lifted above the pollutions of earth, and has breathed the air of the very presence of God. All this he remembers of himself: may it not be also true to some extent of this dull, uninteresting-looking man who stands there waiting to be forgiven? May not this man, too, have rejoiced and sorrowed over his firstborn? May not his soul also have been lifted up to God in mourning for the irrevocable dead? No doubt it has been so; no doubt there has been—or if there has not, there yet may be—a divine life within this repentant sinner. Looking at him more earnestly, his heart thus filled with sorrow and sympathy, with trust and love, he may be enabled by the grace of God to perceive, beneath the crust of sin, the latent image of God in the sinner's heart, revealed with such clearness as to make him confident that the confession is not only sincere, but also efficacious, not a mere high-tide of passionate remorse, but a settled turn and drift of changed feeling. Even if the repentance be weak and wavering, the sympathy, the faith, and the spiritual force of the forgiver have power to confirm and strengthen it. By trusting a man we make him worthy of being trusted. By imputing righteousness to him we create righteousness in him. Such power—a power attested by common experience and by common proverbs of men of the world—hath God given to men upon earth. In the strength of this spiritual strength, and aided by that insight which only Christ had perfectly, and which none of us can have except so far as we share in Christ's Spirit, every human being has some power of not only saying, but also acting, forgiveness, some power of lifting up others into a higher righteousness.

"But this," it may be said, "only applies to sins against men, not to sins against God: men may forgive the former, only God can forgive the latter." Is it so? Consider the forgiving power of parents with their children, more especially with very young children. Take such a case as we imagined in the last chapter, the case of a child who has committed some offence, some petty, very petty theft perhaps, very trifling in the world's estimation, but very serious in the father's eyes, as being the possible germ of something worse—against a neighbour. Now who shall say that it is absolutely necessary in such a case that the child should confess his fault to an ordained priest in order to obtain forgiveness, or even that it is needful in all cases and for the pettiest faults that the child should ask forgiveness of the neighbour himself against whom the offence has been committed, who may chance to be an entire stranger? Surely it is clear that the father, knowing the child and all his inmost thoughts and secrets better than any stranger can know them, realising also the child's sin, and grieving over it more than any stranger could, is the person best fitted by Nature, and indeed most truly appointed by

God, to forgive the offence : and when the father accepts the child's contrition and penitence, though it be for a sin not committed directly against himself, and tells the little one that he is forgiven, and that now he will be a good child and sin no more like that again—is the father overstepping the bounds of the duties of fatherhood, or is the child wrong in going its way with its heart at rest and with a sense of burden lightened and peace restored ? Surely we are bound to admit that every human being, so far as he has the powers that naturally go to make up the forgiving act—I mean love, trust, self-subordination, and hatred of sin—must also have the power of forgiving sins, not only in his own name, but also in the name of society, and even in the name of God Himself. And if this be so between fathers and children, then it must be within the experience of all that there are persons so highly endowed with the spiritual gifts of faith and love and the hatred of sin, that they tower above the ordinary average man as much as fathers above their children. Such men must be recognised as specially adapted by Nature, that is by God, for the divine task of forgiving. They are Nature's priests ; and if anyone should appear pre-eminently endowed with these natural powers, he will be Nature's High-Priest.

Where is the remission of penalty in the whole of this transaction of forgiveness ? Not necessarily anywhere. It is quite conceivable that in a genuine forgiveness such as I have attempted to describe above the penalty may actually not be entirely remitted. The servant may feel that it is his duty, and the master without any thought of his own interest may also feel that it is the servant's duty, to pay back the sum of money which has been taken by fraud, and to make also some further reparation. But though this is conceivable, and though there are no record acts of forgiveness in which the full penalty has been exacted, it is extremely rare and difficult. Why difficult? And whence arises the popular feeling that forgiveness implies, and absolutely requires, the remission of penalty, so that, if a man were to say to another, "I forgive you, but I must have my penalty," the world would laugh his cheap forgiveness to scorn, and condemn him as a hypocrite? The answer is, that this is one of the very many cases in which the outward and visible sign of an invisible and spiritual act has been confused with the act itself. There are obvious causes that might lead to this confusion. Forgiveness, when genuine, is one of the most difficult, when spurious one of the easiest, of human actions. No human forgiveness is complete; and even to approach completion it requires in the forgiver the highest and most divine qualities that humanity possesses. Yet this act, so singularly difficult and divine, cannot be tested and distinguished from its easy and ignoble counterfeit. The mere words "I forgive," the shake of the hand, the saying of a few phrases of good-will, the resumption of the old salutations and forms of friendship—how easy is all this, and, very often, how meaningless! On the other hand, it may be full of the divinest meaning. How is the world to tell what to think? How is it to know whether it is witnessing a hollow mask or a divine, spiritual reality? How also can the man who is to be forgiven be convinced of the sincerity of the forgiver? How but by some outward act of sacrifice, representing the inward sacrifice of self-will and vindictiveness?

The world's attitude towards forgiveness is much the same as its attitude towards repentance. The latter has been expressed in the well-known lines :—

> " The world will not believe a man repents,
> And this wise world of ours is mostly right."

In the same way the world " will not believe a man forgives," and its incredulity is mostly justified. Therefore to fortify itself as far as possible against the cheap and obvious deception of a meaningless forgiveness, the incredulous world insists that when a man says "I forgive," he shall *do* something to show his forgiveness. And the same feeling also prompts the forgiver himself, not indeed out of a desire to blazon his inmost thoughts to the world, but because, like David on Araunah's threshing-floor, he cannot bear even to appear to offer up the sacrifice of that which costs him nothing. Now one obstacle in the way of forgiving consists in a certain pleasure or vindictive satisfaction that might have been derived from punishing an offender, not because he has done wrong, but because he has wronged *you*. This pleasure, for which in modern times happily we have not so keen a relish, was, in old times, one of the delights of life : vengeance was as nectar to the heroes of Homer, and even now it is not without its sweetness. But vengeance or vindictiveness is clearly incompatible with forgiveness. Punishment is conceivably in some cases compatible, but vindictiveness never : it must be entirely given up if a man is to forgive. Therefore the best and most natural sign that a man is really constraining his will to unselfishness, and making in his heart the sacrifice of that selfish feeling which we call vindictiveness, seems and always has seemed to be this, that he should give up that material penalty which a selfish and vindictive man would certainly exact. Any other sacrifice might have answered the same purpose; but this has always seemed the most natural. Being so natural an accompaniment and sign of the inward sacrificial act, it has often been mistaken for the act itself. But it is only the sign. The true forgiveness is an invisible sacrifice of the will.

Step by step we have been led up by our analysis of forgiveness to see that it partakes of the nature of a sacrifice or atonement: and so indeed it does, and we shall see hereafter that it affords the best human analogy for the illustration of Christ's Sacrifice for men. But let us first meet a very natural objection. For it will recur to everybody to say, "How rarely is this act of forgiveness in all its completeness exercised or even required in ordinary life! The men who have done us most good, and by whose society we have felt most uplifted, have never forgiven us; for we loved them and never injured them. How then can this power of forgiving be called a great and general uplifting power?" I should reply that there is a forgiving spirit, as well as the forgiving act. In other words, the forgiving faculty in a man, besides the influence it exerts in action upon those who are its direct objects, also exerts a powerful indirect influence upon all who are brought into contact with the man possessed of that power. Does not this follow from our definition of the requisites for forgiveness? In order that a man may forgive we have shown that he must be unselfish, that he must hate sin, that he must look hopefully on the destinies of mankind, and that he must have an instinctive love of men. What follows? Surely that such a man's hopes will be purer and higher, his hatred of selfishness and of meanness will be more intense, his sympathy with the wretched and sinful more powerful, his judgment at once more just and more charitable than in ordinary men. Now such men as these cannot live without lifting up those with whom they live. You go forth from their presence refreshed, with a distinct sense of having been lightened of a burden of selfishness, with better hopes, better aims, with a wholesome self-reproach leading to a wholesome self-respect. A few such men can make a great nation or a great church. But everyone has, or may have, something of this power; and it was this power that Jesus came to give to common men. It might have been described as the power of love, or the power of faith, or the power of hope; but any one of these terms would have been inadequate. Forgiveness presupposes and includes them all, and exhibits them in action. It was in this power of forgiving that the ancient world was most deficient; yet even in these times there were not wanting men who could, however imperfectly, forgive. Such men were Mediators between mankind and the Supreme Goodness, and types, though poor types, of that One Mediator, in comparison with whom all other Mediators are but as Illusions compared to Truth.

PART III.

THE WORSHIP OF CHRIST.

CHAPTER XIV.

THE TRUE METHOD OF CREATING WORSHIP.

PROCEEDING now to describe how Christ summed up all Revelation in Himself, and in a natural way created in mankind Worship, that is love, trust, and awe, we have to show how He did for us the work of the Family, the State, Nature, the Dead, so that in a word He superseded illusions and became a new and true world to mankind. Not that He has enabled us to dispense with the visible world: on the contrary, He has made it more than ever sacred and necessary to us by filling it with meaning, and pervading it and all its institutions with His Presence. Every Christian family, for example, is an institution more real and spiritual than it could have been before the coming of Christ.

Let us begin with the Revelation of the Family. Christ worked, as it were, upon the lines of the family in two ways, first by introducing and diffusing among mankind, in a higher degree than ever before, the uncalculating, disinterested, and instinctive love and trust of a little child for its parents, to be extended to the relation between man and man; and, secondly, by introducing and diffusing, between man and man, the compassionate, forgiving love of a father for his children.

The old attitude in the West and East, of man toward man, had never before been of this loving nature. A general attitude of self-defence had seemed most natural. Among the best the rule—with few exceptions—had been to love one's friend and hate one's enemy, or, as Israel would have expressed it, to love the righteous and to hate sinners. Yet the Revelation of the Family had for ages been appealing to mankind, pointing to the influence exerted upon the most callous and cruel by the unreserved trust of little children. Here then was a Law of Nature, if men had only had eyes to discern it and courage to act upon it, telling us that helpless, absolute, unsuspecting Trust, without possibility of coercing, without reserve, without conditions, has a power to produce righteousness in the persons trusted. Now the trust of little children is based upon ignorance of sin; but it derives its power, not from its ignorance but from its thoroughness. If therefore a new child of God could appear with an unreserved and unsuspecting trust in sinful men, and this trust not based upon ignorance of their sins, but upon a divine knowledge of the underlying capacity for righteousness in all men, even in the most despised and desperate, might not such a trust as this have quite a new power over even the lowest of mankind? Acting on this law, Jesus called on His disciples to lay aside the old aggressive or self-defending attitude and to throw themselves like little children, in perfect love and trust, upon the suspicious and hardened world. They need not fear, He said, that they would be rebuffed. On the contrary, the gratitude of mankind would secure them an abundant reward. "Good measure pressed down and running over" would men give into their bosom. They were to give love for hatred, blessings for curses : so far from resisting injury, they were almost to encourage and court it. As a motive for such self-denial, He set before them the desire to resemble the Father in Heaven, who sends His rain and sunshine on the evil and on the good. But His whole teaching about the Fatherhood of God presupposed the brotherhood of men, and led His disciples to see in every human being a natural friend.

There was therefore, no make-believe in the affection for all men which Jesus enjoined on His disciples. The precept to love one's neighbour as oneself was not dictated by a sense that such love would be in the end profitable to all the world. It was founded upon facts. God being the Father of mankind, and men being made in His image, it was fitting that His children should recognise it and love it fervidly in one another. What that Image was, and how and where they should discern it and how they should love it, Jesus showed them in Himself. He Himself approached all mankind with trust and love as a matter of course, outcasts from the synagogues, fallen women, tax-gathering renegades and traitors. He could see something worth loving in all. He knew what was in the heart of men, and loved them, not in spite of His knowledge, but because of it. With the instinctive love of a child He combined the reasonable and compassionate love of a father : and in this way He created in the hearts of all who knew Him not only love, but also trust. But the cause of success was not mere childlike, indiscriminating affection. With the innocence of the dove He combined and taught His disciples to combine the keen sight of the serpent. He did no violence to His sober judgment. There were some in whom what was worth hating overshadowed, for the time at all events, what was worth loving. Such men He neither forgave nor instructed His disciples to forgive. On the contrary, He taught His apostles to retain sins as well as to forgive sins, and spoke of the Pharisees as a generation of vipers and as children of the Devil. To forgive and to trust were divine acts, but for that reason to be performed in accordance with truth and order, not arbitrarily nor capriciously. What was the nature of the "hypocrisy" of the Pharisees and why Jesus could not forgive them, are questions which cannot be conveniently discussed here. But this marked exception does not disprove the rule. Towards mankind in general, Jesus inculcated on His disciples, and Himself naturally preserved, an attitude of unhesitating and unreserved affection. How he succeeded, and what "good measure running over" was given into His bosom by the gratitude of repentant sinners during His life, and has been given for many centuries since His death, is too well known to need repetition. Every reader of the New Testament knows that the disarming of Jesus was more effective than the arms and armour of Philosophy or of Pharisee.

How does a father create love and trust in the hearts of his little children? Simply by living his natural life in their presence. Not by declarations that he is to be loved and trusted, not by doing definite works of power and kindness to prove that he ought to be loved and trusted. The relation of fatherhood would be felt to be

THE TRUE METHOD OF CREATING WORSHIP. 225

polluted by declarations and demonstrations, and the simplicity of childhood would be at the same time destroyed. The only true education of the child lies in the natural life of the father. In the same way Jesus shrank from declarations and manifestoes of His nature. "If thou be the Christ, tell us plainly," said the formal Jews driven out of their textual and mechanical test by the presence of One who seemed to be a prophet, and yet to violate all the old canons of prophetic conduct. But no: Jesus would not tell them plainly. If they did not feel Him in their consciences to be the Christ, the Redeemer of Israel, He would not try to convince them by declarations: or rather if they did not feel Him to be their Redeemer, then He was not their Redeemer. If in answer to the Pharisees, He had replied, "Yes, I am the Christ," would that have been a "plain" answer? Would it not have confirmed their false impressions, sending them to their homes wrapt in a fatal complacency infinitely worse than the bewilderment of acknowledged ignorance? Here lies our answer to the question so vividly put by Celsus, who assails the silence of Jesus about Himself: "Did anyone ever hear before of a messenger who made it his main object to conceal his message?" Had Celsus looked about him, he might have found hundreds of pagan messengers laden with the divine message of fatherhood and motherhood for their little children, and taught by a divine instinct (which we call the Word of God) that the best way to reveal their Gospel is, not to obtrude it in words, but to convey it through the silent medium of a loving life. *If* therefore the Word of God was made flesh, what was more natural than that He should adopt the old method upon which the Word of God had worked with success before for so many thousands of years, from the time when fatherhood and motherhood were first introduced into the world?

Deliberate demonstration in deeds is no less fatal to true fatherhood than deliberate demonstration in words. The life of a father is one continuous series of acts of protection and fostering love, appearing to the very young child a kind of suspension of the laws of nature by paternal power in the child's behalf. Before the eyes of the child the father stands, averting or healing pain: procuring food, the child knows not where or how; working strange wonders, tokens of strength, or full of beauty; and forgiving sins. But all these acts, to be effectual, must flow naturally from love itself, and only secondarily from a desire to demonstrate love. In the same way the so-called "miracles" of Christ (which should rather be called "mighty works" or "signs") were indeed signs of goodness and of power, but they were not wrought primarily as demonstrations, but as the natural results of His love for men. Good scholars and good Christians may differ widely as to the amount of what is called supernatural agency which would be left to be regarded as based on fact, after full deduction had been made for natural accretions and the misunderstanding of Metaphor: but few, even of the number of decided sceptics, will doubt that Jesus had a power far exceeding anything in ordinary experience of healing some diseases, through an emotional shock. Now to imagine that these miracles were performed, like operations in a hospital, simply with a view to the instruction of spectators, is to lower Christ's work and character below the level of an ordinary man. Scarcely perhaps, even an ordinary physician can so far close his heart to sympathy as not, at times we hope, to feel a primary interest in the sufferer, the relief of whose sufferings he is utilising for the information of his pupils : how much must this be true of one whom we believe to be the Great Physician of body and soul ? Moreover, if Christ had intended His mighty works primarily as demonstrations, surely He would have performed them in public, or at least, if that was impossible, in the presence of the largest possible number of witnesses : He would have proclaimed them and encouraged others to proclaim them : whereas, on the contrary, He performed many in private, some after expressly excluding witnesses ; and, so far from encouraging, He systematically discouraged His disciples from proclaiming them abroad. The miracles of Jesus then must not be regarded as demonstrations. They may have been so regarded in after years. They may have been hence exaggerated and distorted : but they were not so regarded by Jesus Himself. They perhaps entailed some strain and sense of painful effort: but so far from their being mere demonstrations, it would be truer to say that they flowed from Him as naturally as there proceeds from any ordinary father that act of loving forgiveness which is to the little child the "mighty work" and "sign" of fatherhood.[1]

Faith, in itself, is colourless, and takes its colour from its object, whether it be wealth, fame, comfort, art, humanity, or whatsoever else. Of what nature then is the faith or trust a father would desire to implant in his

[1] For a consideration of the acts of healing see Chapter xx.

children? Not merely, I think, trust in his righteousness, and certainly not merely trust in his power, but a kind of inferential trust arising from these two. Believing in his father's righteousness and believing in his power, the child is to be led to believe that righteousness and power go together, and finding that power is subordinated in his father to righteousness, the child is to be led to the inferential belief or trust that in·all cases right makes might, and not might right. This is the fundamental principle of the virtue of faith. It was this principle that Jesus sought by all means to inculcate in His disciples. He stood before them as the Incarnation of Right, and in His life His followers might read that righteousness was mighty. Sins and diseases vanished at a word. From beholding the highest human power steadfastly subordinated to a higher Righteousness, the disciples of Jesus were led up to a belief in One Divine Righteousness, the source and fountain of all human and all natural might, who claimed the obedience of Nature and the trustful devotion of men His children.

Not righteousness, therefore, but faith is the cry of Jesus to His followers.[1] To speak of righteousness apart from faith would have been to speak of light apart from the sun, of Himself apart from His Father. As He depended on His Father, so did the righteousness of men depend upon their faith in God. He lived in the perpetual vision of the Father, and knew that the sight

[1] It is true that St. Matthew occasionally exhibits Jesus as recommending "righteousness;" but the general tendency of the recommendations is, to hold up the righteousness to be sought as *the righteousness of God*, "seek ye first the Kingdom of God and *His righteousness*."

of the Eternal Righteousness implied the perpetual doing of righteousness. "The Son," said Jesus, "can do nothing of Himself but what He seeth the Father do." As it was with Himself, so would it be, He knew, with men. Could He but make them participators of His vision, they too would be rapt into communion with the Eternal Righteousness, and would be themselves made righteous. It was no more possible to trust in the Father and to remain unrighteous, than to feel the sunshine and yet to remain without the sense of warmth; faith implied righteousness.

"Thy faith hath saved thee," was a common saying with Jesus when He dismissed some diseased man cured of his disease. The nature of this faith He expresses on one occasion by saying, "Believest thou that I am able to do this." It may seem a very poor kind of faith, with little of the moral element in it—the mere belief in the *ability* of Jesus. Faith in the ability of a physician or remedy, has, as we know, great power in curing certain diseases: but it has sometimes furthered quackery and imposture, and might seem almost an unworthy condition to impose as essential to the performance of one of Jesus' mighty works. But it *was* a virtue, a righteous act, to believe that Jesus could do what He willed. Such faith differs as widely from faith in an impostor, as righteousness differs from imposture. The power of trusting, believing in, or—as Jesus sometimes expressed it—"receiving" a person, implies a power of being raised to some approximation to the level of that person. He that trusts in a prophet, so Jesus taught us, is imbued with the prophetic spirit; he that trusts in a just man is imbued with the spirit of justice; and in the same way he that trusts in the Son of God is imbued with the spirit of divine Sonship, which makes him one with the Son of God. In part, no doubt, the belief in Jesus was a virtue because it implied a promptness to believe also in His teaching, to believe in the kingdom of God, to believe in the Father in heaven, and, in a word, to believe in the ultimate fulfilment of all the good news of Jesus. But, after all, if anyone had asked, "Why am I to believe all this?" the answer would have been, not only "Because it commends itself to the conscience of every good man," but also, "Because it is Jesus of Nazareth who proclaims it." The personal presence of every good man makes a demand the same in kind (however different in degree) as that claim which Jesus made upon the faith of His companions. He did not proclaim Himself to be the Christ and call upon them consequently to believe in Him. Instead of this, He called upon them to believe in Him for what He was, and to draw their own inference as to His being the Christ. In other words He led them to believe that He was the Son of God by believing in Him as the perfect Son of Man. The faith that He demanded was of a very simple, undogmatic nature : it could not include belief in His Resurrection or Ascension ; we have no evidence to show that it included—and we have every reason to infer that it did not include—belief in the miraculous details of His Incarnation ; Jesus simply called on men not to drown the voice of their consciences, which proclaimed that His presence, His teaching, and His works were all those of one who could neither deceive nor be deceived, and who could not be separated from their conceptions of God. This faith, I repeat, was the same in kind as our faith in ordinary good men: but in degree it was infinitely greater. In phenomena and effects ordinary faith differed from faith in Jesus as much as ordinary man differed from the Man of men, as much as heated water differs from water heated to steam.

CHAPTER XV.

THE TRUE WORSHIP.

"BLESSED art thou, Simon, son of Jonah, for flesh and blood hath not revealed it unto thee, but my Father which is in heaven : and I say also unto thee that thou art Peter, and upon this rock I will build my Church, and the gates of hell shall not prevail against it :" these words may be said to celebrate not only the foundation of the Church, but also the birth of Faith. We cannot find a better illustration of Christ's success in creating Faith than will be afforded by a careful study of the circumstances of St. Peter's confession and Christ's blessing on it.

When Jesus pronounced this blessing on St. Peter, He was a fugitive. The days of His popularity had passed away, never to return, save for one brief outburst just before His death. There had been a time when it had seemed that Jesus might be accepted as the Messiah by all classes of His countrymen ; but that time had now passed away. When the new Teacher first appeared, recommended to the nation by the Prophet John, proclaiming the good news of the Redemption of Israel, attracting all hearts by His presence and by His cheering message, healing disease at a touch, and in particular banishing that most terrible disease of Possession which raged like an epidemic through Northern Palestine, Jesus of Nazareth had seemed at first, even to the Pharisees, a possible Redeemer. Other persons aspired to cure diseases and cast out devils with drugs and charms; but none of them could be compared for a moment with the great Wonder-worker of Nazareth. He proclaimed the Kingdom of God, which seemed tantamount to proclaiming revolt from the Romans. Surpassing all teachers and leaders of the time in popularity, Jesus of Nazareth seemed to the Pharisees at first a teacher who might be acknowledged and utilised. If only He could be induced to dispel a few misgivings on certain points of the law, if He could but satisfy them that He really did intend not only to fulfil the law—a doubtful phrase—but to obey the law, the Pharisees would probably have accepted Him: and while they were wavering, they did nothing to diminish His popularity with the poorer classes. But instead of satisfying the Pharisees He absolutely alienated them: the Sabbath, He said, was made for man, and not man for the Sabbath; not that which goeth into a man, but that which cometh out of a man defileth him. With a true instinct the Pharisees perceived that Jesus was no Saviour for them, and rather than that His influence should destroy theirs, as it assuredly would have done, they set themselves to destroy Him.

With the Sadducees and Herodians Jesus speedily became no less unpopular. If they had expected that the law would be relaxed by the new leader, and that a little more allowance would be made by Him for the luxuries and weaknesses and pleasant vices of mankind, they were soon undeceived by Jesus. The law, He said, was not to be destroyed, but to be fulfilled, or rather to be superseded by another law ten times more searching and exacting than the old one, extending to the heart as well as to the actions, and covering every department of thought, word, and deed. And in return for these intolerable restrictions He promised nothing but a "redemption," which when analysed resolved itself into an unsubstantial nothing. It was not long, therefore, before it became clear that for the Sadducees as well as for the Pharisees, Jesus was no Christ.

The last to desert Him were the peasants of Galilee, the hard-handed, true-hearted men whose fathers had fought for Judas the Galilean patriot, and who were ready to take up arms again at the bidding of Jesus of Nazareth, or any other leader who would promise the Redemption of Israel. Although He might be a little unsound on some points of the law, such as Sabbaths and washings, yet in spite of His heterodoxies they had followed Him faithfully at first. His mighty works showed that He had come from God: He proclaimed a Kingdom which seemed the exact copy of the Kingdom proclaimed by their former leader Judas the Galilean—a state in which all should be free, owning no master, and paying no service, save to God alone : if He seemed slow to give the signal for insurrection, they must remember He was a Prophet, and a Prophet's ways were not as the ways of common men : they must be patient and wait. But, as time wore on, and still Jesus taught and healed, and taught and healed, and nothing seemed to come of it, and He himself seemed patient, they grew

THE TRUE WORSHIP.

impatient. More than once had they attempted to force Him to place Himself at their head, but in vain. Little by little, doubts began to settle even on the trustful Galilean mind. Some of His followers began to fall away from Him as a dreamer and speaker of dark sayings, no Saviour of Israel. His great supporter, John the Prophet, whom Jesus Himself had called the greatest of the Prophets, seems to have expressed his own perplexity as well as the general distrust, when from the prison, which he was never destined to leave, he sent his disciples with one last appeal, if perchance Jesus might thus be moved to action: "Art thou He that should come, or are we to look for another?" But the only answer of Jesus to this prayer for rescue was a deliberate intimation that He intended to pursue His peaceful policy, accompanied by a rebuke for want of faith. Was it possible, asked the Galileans, that a Messiah, a Redeemer of Israel, could leave the last of the Prophets to pine in prison, or to die beneath the knife of the son of the Edomite? Meantime the Pharisees had been doing their best to rouse the jealousy of the Tetrarch of Galilee against this rebellious subject of his, who had dared to condemn divorce, and indirectly to stigmatize as adultery his connection with his brother's wife. Soon followed the execution of John in prison: and now at any moment the few remaining followers of Jesus might expect to see the mercenaries of Antipas entering Capernaum to arrest their Master for the purpose of hurrying Him to the same prison and the same death. Sullen and saddened by the death of the great Prophet, whose predictions seemed to have died with him, the Galileans now abandoned Jesus. Up to the last moment they had expected some miracle of release: but Jesus had neither worked a miracle nor accepted the offer of their services. Had He been the Messiah, He could have saved John by lifting His finger: but they had been mistaken; Jesus of Nazareth was not the Messiah. Thus it came to pass that Jesus, in danger of immediate arrest, unpopular with the lowest classes, persecuted and hated by the highest, was forced to flee from Galilee, the dangerous dominion of Antipas, and to take refuge in the dominion of Herod Philip. Here it was—near a town called Paneas or Cæsarea Philippi, close on the source of the Jordan—that St. Peter's confession was uttered and the blessing of Jesus was pronounced.

Try now to place yourself amid these circumstances and to realise the position of Jesus. For many months He had now been engaged in preaching the Kingdom of God, and not only preaching, but spreading it, healing diseases, casting out devils, forgiving sins. How soon that Kingdom would come He Himself had not known; nor, as He told His disciples, did He even afterwards know the precise hour and day of the arrival of that great consummation, that Day of the Lord, that day of Decision, to which every Prophet in Israel had borne witness. At first it had seemed as though the Good Tidings might have been speedily fulfilled. Now it was certain it would not be so. In what we should call "the drift of circumstances" Jesus clearly recognised the will of God. He had been rejected by the nation: yes, it was intended that He should be rejected. As John the Baptist had died, so also it was needful that the Christ Himself should die. Not only must He give His life, but He must also give His death for the Redemption of

Israel. His death could not and would not cut short the work of Redemption. He must triumph over death and the grave: but nevertheless He must die. All things that had been written in the Prophets concerning the sufferings of Israel the Redeemer of Nations, and the sufferings of the Messiah the Redeemer of Israel, must be accomplished in Him. But if He bowed willingly to the burden of sorrow, the Lord would give strength to bear; if He submitted to death, the Lord would give life out of death. From the Lord came sorrow and death, from the Lord came joy and life, as said the Prophet Hosea : " Come and let us return unto the Lord : for He hath torn, and He will heal us : He hath smitten, and He will bind us up. After two days will He revive us : *in the third day He will raise us up, and we shall live in His sight.*" This too must be fulfilled : the Messiah must die, but " in the third day He would rise again."

But though He should rise again, there must be a period of darkness and solitude for His faithful followers : how would they be able to endure it ? How far had He been able to prepare His disciples to carry on His work without Him ? For many months He had been sowing the good seed within their hearts : of all the seeds profusely scattered, was there one that had really found a place where it could spring up to life eternal ? Hitherto Jesus had been patiently working in the presence of His disciples, trusting to the silent influence of His nature upon them, making no proclamations about Himself, and applying no tests to ascertain His success or to prove their faith. But now the time admitted no longer delay. He felt that an hour was at hand for Him which would sever Him from them, and, as a father, before sending His children out into the temptations of the world, might subject them to preliminary trials as a test and means of discerning how far they are able to do battle with the world, so Jesus perceived that the time had now arrived when He must test the faith of His disciples, and, in that faith, His own success or failure. Sum up the results of all His thirty years of life, and what did they amount to? The great days of spiritual triumph when He had held multitudes entranced at the first utterances of the Good Tidings, the shouts of Hallelujah, acclamations to the Son of David, vacant wonder, obstreperous gratitude, professions of devoted allegiance, the faith of thousands, yes, the faith in Him as a great Teacher, a great Prophet, a great Wonder-worker—what did all that amount to? To nothing, absolutely nothing. He had known it all along; but if He had not, He must have known it in exile now. But beneath all this mere surface-feeling, had any substantial result been achieved? The time had now come to ascertain this. Before, when He was in the height of His popularity, it could not have been ascertained. Professions of faith in Him as the Messiah were rife among all the common people, and in repeating them the disciples would then but have been joining in the common cry: but now, if they still felt faith in Him, the unsuccessful, the outcast, the rejected, such faith as this would be not faith in the Teacher or the Wonder-worker, but in Himself, and this was what He wanted. What did His disciples think of Him? This was a question that He had never asked of them before; but He could not turn His face southward toward Jerusalem until He had asked it: for upon their answers would depend His success or failure. If the answers revealed in one single heart one single germ of living Faith, He had succeeded; if not, He had failed.

Both the kindness and the fairness of Jesus appear in the manner in which He tested His disciples. He does not confront them suddenly with the all-important question, but leads up to it with easier questions: in their dejected state a sudden test, without any preparation, might have surprised them into some mechanical expression of the prevalent gloom. On the other hand, He will not in any way bias their mind to any flattering answer by putting words into their mouths. On the contrary, He describes Himself, as usual, by that title of humility by which He habitually expressed His participation in the infirmities and weakness of men: "Whom say men that I, the Son of Man, am?" In contrast with the single confession of St. Peter which follows after the more difficult question that is shortly to be put, it is interesting to note the readiness with which this easier preliminary question was answered, not by one, but by all: "Some say that thou art John the Baptist: some, Elias: and others, Jeremiah, or one of the prophets." These then are the popular opinions about Him. Are the disciples satisfied with them, or what do they themselves think of Him? The crisis can no longer be delayed, and forth comes the question, upon the answer to which hangs the destiny of Christendom, "Whom say ye that I am?"

Pause here awhile before turning to St. Peter's answer, and, putting yourself now in the Apostle's place, ask yourself what you would have said, or not said, had that same sharp question been thus thrust home to your heart by one whom you felt that no flattery could conciliate, no hypocrisy deceive, no kindly evasion put off. Fugitives surrounding a fugitive who had utterly failed to bring about the Redemption He had promised—who were they that they should set themselves up against the apparent verdict of the Lord? Not thus had David, not thus had Barak or Gideon delivered Israel: if the Lord had been with Jesus of Nazareth, would their Master now be an exile? The upper classes of the people had rejected Him; the Scribes, the legitimate successors of Moses, had pronounced Him to be a heretic, an impostor; some had even declared that He was possessed by an evil spirit; the peasants of Galilee had fallen away from Him: who were they, then, that they should venture to dissent from the opinion of the whole nation and the deliberate judgment of the rulers and guides of Israel? The very place where their little group was sitting seemed adapted to engender depression and despair. Paneas the place was—so called from the heathen god; and high on the cliff before their eyes, polluting with its shadow the sources of the sacred Jordan, rose the marble temple of Pan, suggesting to the Galilean wanderers not only the abominations of its own special worship, but also the thought of the network of idolatrous polytheism which had overspread the civilised world—all but the little corner of despised Judæa. Moreover the place was known by another name no less ill-omened for the hopes of the followers of Christ—Cæsarea Philippi. As the name Paneas suggested spiritual abomination, so did Cæsarea speak of the all-pervading political abomination of the Roman yoke under which for now seventy years and more the chosen People of God had unavailingly groaned. The name Philip too was but a symbol of the policy with which the Romans disguised the fetters they imposed, utilising foreign princes as tools for subordinating its captive nations. Amid these surroundings, then, with Pan and Cæsar and Philip confronting them where they sat, or, if they looked eastward over to Galilee, with the axe of Herod Antipas ready to greet their Master on His return, and scowling Scribes and Pharisees ready to betray Him, and a sullen crowd ready to look on and acquiesce in His destruction, deserted seemingly by Jehovah and by the people of Jehovah, what chance had Jesus of success? And who were these twelve despised peasants of a despised district in a petty and despised nation that they should set themselves up against the whole world, east and west, Rome and Judæa, all for the Man who now sat before them patiently waiting for the answer to His as yet unanswered question? "Whom say ye that I am?" How were they to answer it? "Securus judicat orbis terrarum"—the invention of that bad proverb was reserved for the lazy superstition of after times, so that the actual words could not have been known to them: but the thought is innate in the vulgar side of every human heart. How easy to go with the world, how hard to go against it! How hard, and, as things looked, how very useless!

Against all this weight of opposition what positive proof had the disciples to justify their faith in Jesus? How very little did they then possess of that basis of historical knowledge which sometimes seems to us the essential condition of what we call a "saving faith"!

There is no evidence to shew that they were aware of the miraculous details of the Incarnation; they could not know, for they were yet to witness, the death of Christ upon the cross, and, indeed, they disbelieved in it when it was predicted to them; they could not know of the Resurrection or Ascension. But they had heard Jesus preach the Good Tidings of God, the Father of men, and His words had breathed conviction into their souls; certainly God must be the Father of men, and love the sinful as well as the just. But what did they know about this Father? Whenever they tried to realise the Father, they found the thought of Jesus indissolubly linked to the thought of the Father. They could not conceive of the Father apart from Him whom the Father had sent. Jesus Himself, meek and lowly though He was, had nevertheless spoken and acted as though He were one with His Father, and therefore entitled to their allegiance. He had forgiven sins in His Father's name, not to speak of countless cures and exorcisms of evil spirits. "Come unto *Me*," He had said, "and I will give you rest." No prophet had ever spoken like that; but with Jesus such language was habitual, and so far from interfering with, seemed to spring out of, His dependence upon the Father. It was because He was a Son, owing all things to the Father and being one with the Father, that He was able to do the works of the Father. His words, "*I* will give you rest," had been no idle promise. They had come unto Him, and they had found rest. Whatever Jesus might be to others, certainly He was the Christ to them; for besides the future redemption from the Romans, He had already redeemed them from their old sin-burdened state, and had made them free. A word from Him had changed the current of their lives and had brought to them light and life. He was the food of their souls, and in His presence they throve. Without Him, to live was death and darkness. If they deserted Him, to whom should they turn for their customary guidance and help, which was now as dear to them as life itself? No, they must trust in Him, He was their only hope. If God was not with Him, God must be evil, or there must be no God; but that could not be. No, there was a living God, and it could be no other than that Father whom they best knew as the Father of Jesus of Nazareth. Thus, in the strength of a divinely-implanted trust, it was given to Peter to pronounce in the name of the Apostles, and in the name of future Christendom, the first confession of faith— "Thou art the Christ, the Son of the living God."

To us in these days, when this narrative is read as the Second Lesson in our churches, St. Peter's confession appears a matter of course, and we are therefore naturally perplexed at the blessing pronounced upon it. But to Jesus, so far from being a matter of course, it was a solemn ratification of His work by the Father in heaven. For months He had worked on patiently, teaching in accordance with the eternal laws and processes by which God has revealed Himself to mankind since the Creation, not coercing, not obtruding, not pulling up faith by the roots to see how it was growing, but sowing it broad-cast as Nature sows, and waiting for the result. Now the result had come.

One at least of His disciples believed in Him with that kind of faith which lifts up mankind. It was God that had given this faith to the Apostle: God, and no one else, had taught him what sin and redemption meant, and what must be the nature of a Redeemer : it was God who had made Jesus necessary to the Apostles, so that they instinctively craved for His presence as the bread of their souls : it was God who, uplifting Peter above the level of his past life, in one of those divine impulses well known to the Prophets of Israel, had caused him to utter language his own, and yet not his own—not his own, because it betokened a higher level than he could have reached unassisted, and yet his own, because it sprang naturally from his past life and his impulsive, intuitional nature. For us who have not insight enough to distinguish between real and unreal faith, between professions of the lips and revolution of the heart, it is almost impossible to understand the importance attached by Jesus to what we call "mere words." But we may at least remember that where we surmise and imagine and think, Christ *saw*. This germ of trust, this mustard-seed of faith, transmitted from heart to heart, Christ saw springing up into a great tree wherein all the birds of the air might find refuge. Here at last was a definite solid basis of faith for centuries of spiritual life and action. Now, therefore, Jesus might prepare for His approaching death ; for His Church had been founded at last upon an everlasting foundation.

All this we *think* of and try to imagine, and for the sake of vividness we express it in metaphors : but what is to us a thought, was to Christ a vision. The future was to Him as the present, and all the involved consequences were discerned in the cause. Bystanders, who were not in the secret, would have seen nothing more than a group of Galileans earnestly conversing : but

Christ saw in this utterance a thousand other expressions of the self-same faith in word, and deed, and suffering—Confessors at the bar of emperors or princes, Martyrs amid the roar of amphitheatres, and then, in more distant times, generations after generations confessing Him always in the same spirit, though through other forms, through prayer, through labour, through long-protracted lives of patient expectation; all in the self-same spirit of faith, looking up through Him to the Father in heaven. Therefore, while others might see nothing but the rising fountains of the Jordan gushing from the red cliffs before them, Christ saw the streams of perpetual living waters struck open with the rod of faith to satisfy a thirsting world. Others might see nothing but Pan's temple of white marble on the brow of the hill above: but Christ saw silently uprising in that moment another Temple, a Temple not made with hands, which should remain when heaven and earth had passed away. This Temple was no other than the human race knit into one compact whole, and raised upon an everlasting foundation, to be the eternal habitation of the heavenly Father. That foundation was Himself: yet not Himself regarded apart from mankind, but Himself dwelling in the hearts of men through faith. This was the true Rock upon which the Church was to be built. It was not Christ looked at by Himself, it was not Peter, it was not faith: it was all these. It was Christ revealed by the Father to Peter through faith. It was Christ accepted by Peter through divine faith, in the name of the human race. Peter himself was but a Stone; but Peter thus accepting Christ, and through faith, identified with Christ, was a Rock not to be shaken for ever: "Verily, I say unto thee, Thou art Peter, and upon this Rock I will build my Church, and the gates of hell shall not prevail against it."

Verily, a wonderful and comfortable saying, true as long as humanity lasts! For what does it amount to? It amounts to this, that if men will but trust in righteousness, they shall share in the immutability of the supreme righteousness, and shall remain unshaken for ever. More than this, it implies a promise, without an *if*, that men shall trust in righteousness and shall be formed into one body, which shall ultimately triumph over all the weaknesses and sins that disorganize humanity. Who will assert that Christ's promise has not hitherto proved true, and is not now well on its way toward fulfilment? If any one is inclined to say that the present Church of Christ is but a poor result of so vast a promise, I answer, compare the morality of the present Church of Christ with the morality of the Roman religion of Imperialism, or even with the best times of ancient Paganism, and the vastness of the fulfilment even now will be apparent. Or if it be replied that this is only the result of the progress of eighteen centuries, then I answer, compare the Church of Christ with the Church of Mohammed or of Buddha, or with any other religion on the face of the earth, and the contrast will still more clearly reveal what Christ has wrought for us. If Christendom has not achieved all that it might have achieved, that is because it has too often believed, not in Christ, but in Christian systems and organizations; but so far as it has believed in righteousness, so far it has proved true Christ's promise that the gates of hell should not prevail against it.

THE TRUE WORSHIP.

Moreover we must remember that the spiritual Christendom is not to be measured by the number of persons at any given moment turning eastward and repeating the creed, but by the prevalence of the Spirit of Christ encouraging love and self-sacrifice among individuals and peace between nations, and by the subsidence of the old polytheistic spirit of aggressiveness. Wherever the human heart, aided by the indirect influence of Christ, has stood up in the might of God-given intuition and has declared its faith not in might but in right, there, we may be sure, has been something of that rock on which Christ's Church is founded. In our zeal for Jesus of Nazareth we must never deny that the work which He wrought on earth had been wrought before His birth on a smaller scale by the Word of God from the first, since the creation of mankind. Whosoever therefore from the beginning of the world has believed that righteousness is might, to him has been given something of the inspiration of St. Peter, and to that man shall be assigned a place in the divine temple which is founded on the eternal righteousness. But Christ by His life and death and resurrection and His mighty work in the Church for eighteen centuries has wonderfully strengthened our faith in the might of righteousness. He has so purified the hearts of men and changed their thoughts of God, that He has practically created heaven and earth anew for us: old things are passed away, all things are become new. The moral impulse which He gave to speed the human race on towards its ultimate goal is an accelerating force which will possibly soon begin to transport us into regions where we must expect new shapes of old truths, new circumstances of life whether social or individual. But St. Peter is likely long to stand in the presence of Christendom, as the living embodiment of that faculty of Faith or Spiritual Insight by which the sons of men have power on earth to forgive sins and to open the gates of heaven to one another. Where now is the Temple of Pan, or Cæsarea, or Antipas, or all the Herods, and even the Cæsars also? All vanished like so many mists and vapours of the night, rolling away at sunrise from the base of that great superstructure, wide as humanity, high as God's mercies, that Temple which can never perish because it is based upon those principles of human nature which must exist as long as there is a Father in heaven. Churches and sects and systems of philosophy may change and pass away; the Scriptures themselves might perish; the Apostles themselves might be forgotten; but, wheresoever there shall exist one human being believing from his heart that Right is Might, there will be found Christ's Church, founded on the imperishable Rock, and the gates of hell shall not prevail against it.

CHAPTER XVI.

THE TRUE FORGIVENESS AND THE TRUE SACRIFICE.

THE Sacrifice of Christ, as illustrated by the act of human forgiveness, is the subject of this Chapter. At first sight there may appear no comparison between the two. That great act which we regard as the central event of the history of the world may seem to stand by itself and to defy all illustrations by analogy. Faith, and not reason, may seem requisite here. For how can we ever hope to comprehend the nature of Christ, much less the nature of that mysterious sacrifice by which He reconciled man to God? That indeed can never be hoped. To comprehend any action of any human being is a most difficult, perhaps an impossible, task. Beyond the powers of comprehension and the limits of human logic stretch the "abysmal depths of personality." Yet in some degree to apprehend the nature of human thought, motive, and action, is not only possible, but essential, if we wish to form any conception of any human being. This is a truism about ordinary human beings: but it is also true about Christ. A Christ without motives is a Christ without the power of attracting our affection. To shrink from the attempt reverently to apprehend the meaning of His passion is to give up the hope of knowing Him and loving Him the better for His sufferings on our behalf. Surely that is not real reverence, but rather ends in nullifying the Cross of Christ.

I grant that many persons, simple and uneducated, have understood the mystery of the Cross by the intuition of affection. "I cannot understand, I love," often represents a most genuine understanding of the most divine mysteries; and to many believers of this kind I would sooner go to be instructed than to instruct. But unhappily to others the Cross of Christ is not a help, but a stumbling-block. "Yes," it may be replied, "and so it was to the Jews of old, and so it must always be." But the cases are different: the Jews stumbled at the Cross because they could not endure the thought of a Messiah dying the death of a slave; some sceptics of modern times, on the other hand, reject the Cross because it comes to them associated with doctrines that seem to them absolutely immoral. If without shaking the faith of believers we can remove any of the difficulties in the way of those who doubt or disbelieve, reason will be employed in its right position, not to replace, but to prepare the way for, faith.

Here, as elsewhere, we must pursue the path of analogy. We shall reason in the faith that man at his best is the best image of God, and that the spiritual processes of man are the best guides to the spiritual processes of God. "The rainbow is made in the sky out of a dripping cloud; it is also made here below with a jet of water. Still therefore it is Nature which governs everything." This doctrine we shall apply from material to spiritual nature, believing—to transfer the words of Bacon a second time—that "the supposed divorces between ethereal and sublunary things are but figments, superstitions mixed with rashness, seeing that it is most certain that very many effects have place not only here with us, but also in the heights of heaven." As, therefore, when we speak of Christ's love and of God's Fatherhood we are obliged to think of some standard of human love and human fatherhood, so we shall endeavour to rise to the conception of Christ's forgiveness and Christ's sacrifice by starting from human forgiveness and human acts of sacrifice.

Human forgiveness we found to be, not an easy task, but the most difficult imposed on mankind, requiring for its perfect performance, first, some kind of sacrifice or giving up of self; secondly, faith in God as the Father of man, and in man as the child of God; thirdly, love of man and sympathy with him; fourthly, hatred of sin. A fifth condition was rejected, as being not essential, though generally requisite: this was, some outward sign of the inward spiritual act. No man, as we said above, had all these qualifications in perfection. But only in proportion as he had them could any man approximate to an act of perfect forgiveness.

Of all but the last of these four qualifications little need be said to prove that Christ must needs have had them in perfection. As for the giving up of self, surely the most sceptical cannot deny that Christ's whole life was a sacrifice. His actions, His precepts, and His influence, after death, in His disciples, all prove this. The Son of Man came, not to be ministered unto, but to minister; He came not to do His own will, but the will of the Father; He was among men as one that served. His life was an expression, in act, of the words, "Thy will be done." As to Faith in God, or rather sight of God, it appears in the very name to which He instructed His disciples to offer up their prayers—the Father in heaven. He speaks of the Father as of One for whom no mercy is too great, no care too petty, without whose will not a sparrow falls to the ground, who does not scorn to provide for the adornment of the lilies of the field, and who therefore may be trusted to care for the welfare of men, who are His children. The Father can will nothing but what is right and good, and therefore the Father's will must be that the lost children of Israel shall be redeemed and the sick made whole, the prisoners in the bondage of sin shall be delivered, the ears of the deaf shall be unstopped to receive the good tidings of salvation, the eyes of the blind shall be opened to the light of truth, the tongue of the dumb shall be loosened to proclaim the praise of God, the lame shall leap like a hart upon the paths of righteousness, the starving shall receive the bread of everlasting life. Let the Rabbis cast out sinners from the synagogues; God is able and willing to restore them. With God all things are possible, even to the saving of those who are rich and prosperous.

Closely allied to this faith in God the Father of men, is faith in men the children of God. Harlots, traitors— for publicans were traitors to their country—seemed to Jesus to be made (originally, at all events), no less than Rabbis, in God's image: and none were so far fallen that they could not be lifted up again by faith in the heavenly Father. Of all God's creatures, man was, in the eyes of Jesus, infinitely the greatest and noblest, owing his dignity not to any adventitious ornaments, but simply to his God-given nature. Rank and pomp went for nothing with Him. What was highly esteemed by men was an abomination in the eyes of God, and the borrowed glory of Solomon was infinitely inferior to the clothing of a lily of the field. To be rich and noble was nothing; but to be a man, to be in God's image, a child-elect of God, that was to be something great indeed, of more value than many flowers of the field and many sparrows. In indignant rebuke Jesus reprobates the formal president of the synagogue who would have shewn less consideration for a child of Abraham than Moses shewed for an ox or an ass. Great by nature, man, He predicted, should be greater still when admitted into the new kingdom, or family, of God. Then every aspiration of humanity would be satisfied, and all the present fogs and mists of miseries which enwrapped mankind, tinged by the light of God, would change into haloes of glory round the heads of the saints. There would be new ranks and new gradations of nobility about the throne of the King of heaven. The new dependent type of warrior should struggle with the old aggressive type and be victorious. The self-sufficient, complacent, exultant character should perish from the earth and make way for the meek and lowly. About the steps of the Royal throne and in the palace-courts of the Father should stand in their several places the mourners, the meek, and the merciful. In His presence-chamber there would be the pure in heart, and He would hail peacemakers as His children. Once admitted into this new kingdom or family of God, the humblest of men became forthwith the greatest of created beings, greater far than any priest or prophet of the past, greater than the last and greatest of the prophets—John the Baptist himself. For such exalted beings as this new race of heaven-born men, the Sabbath was but an instrument, the winds and waves, and all the elements of nature, were but subservient ministers: food and raiment would come to them naturally if they but followed the will of the Father; they might be persecuted, yea, put to death, yet—strangest of paradoxes—not a hair of their head should be injured. The disciples of Christ should not be inferior to their Master Himself in the power of doing mighty works; even greater works than He had done should they do, and the greatest power of all was expressly communicated to them. They, as well as He, were to have the power of "forgiving sins on earth."

But with faith in man as he ought to be, and might be, there went also love of man as he *was*. Christ did not, as some men do, reserve His love for the ideal man that never appears in practice; nor did He, as some religious people do, shew kindness to a man, not for the man's own sake, but for the sake of a principle, or for the sake of an eternal reward. He loved men for themselves, for what was in them of their own. Deep down beneath the accumulations of evil thoughts and vicious habits, He could discern the buried image of His Father, and knew that it belonged of right to the sinner, and in virtue of that, Jesus of Nazareth could love even a sinful man for the sinful man's sake. But on this we need not dwell. The love of Christ for sinners, how naturally He lived and moved among them, how expressly He declared them to be His peculiar care, and how richly His love was rewarded and justified by their gratitude and penitence—all this is the common-place of the Gospel narrative.

Far less prominence, and as it seems to me, far too little prominence, is given in our thoughts to the next and last requisite for forgiveness, I mean hatred of sin. We do not sufficiently understand the feeling—nurtured in Israel and pervading all the national literature—of antagonism and internecine hostility to sin, as being itself hostile to Jehovah. In our modern desire to avoid brutality and vindictiveness, we sometimes ignore even that righteous recoil from injustice or oppression, or sins against society, which has received the name of "resentment:" still more do we ignore the higher and nobler recoil from sins, considered as sins against God. "Do not I hate them, O Lord, that hate Thee? Yea, I hate them as though they were mine own enemies" —to us this sounds almost blasphemous; yet it conveys a truth which we are in danger of forgetting, that though we are not to hate sinners, we are to hate sin.

Does it seem strange to us that the Healer of sins should also be the Hater of sins? Is it not rather consonant with our every-day experience? How often is it found that a man who has himself known what it is to sin, and who hates sin because he has suffered from it, knows best how to forgive sin! The men of cold philosophic temperament, the men of weak passions and strong sense, who have an amateur acquaintance with vice, and have formed paper theories about temptations—are they the world's great forgivers? They have sinned little, and too often they have also loved little and forgiven little.

The Forgiver of the world must be touched with the sense of our spiritual as well as physical infirmities. He must have known what it is to be hungry, and homeless, and weary ; what it is to hope and to be disappointed, to find friends and to lose them, to love and to be not loved or not understood, to trust and be betrayed : but all this would have been as nothing unless He had also known what it was to sin. How Christ could have been Himself sinless and yet could know sin, and bear sin, and so closely identify Himself with sin that He was said by the Apostle to have been made sin for us—this must always remain for us a mystery incomprehensible. Yet we may partially apprehend it if we strive to bear in mind, in the first place, the horror with which He who was in the bosom of the Father must have regarded that principle of evil which divides men from the Father, and, in the next place, the infinite force of the love and sympathy with which He linked Himself to sinners. If we wish in some faint way to realize Christ's sense of sin we must try to understand the Psalmist's loathing of it as a foul disease, like some internal leprosy eating to the very bones and marrow of the sinner. Let us try to imagine ourselves in the possession of perfect health, and preternaturally gifted with insight into the laws of health, and with a knowledge of the highest possibilities of physical welfare, so that every time we look upon a sick man, or even on a man a little below the average in health and vigour, we are struck not only with the feeling of pity for the pain and feebleness, but also with the thought, "All this misery might have been spared, and might have been exchanged for a state in which mere existence would have been a delight." With all these adaptations for an environment of health let us imagine ourselves placed amid a world of diseased humanity, where disease is not the exception but the rule; suppose corruption substituted for health, perpetual pain for the unconsciousness or pleasure of existing, every organ deprived of its faculty, and remaining only to be a witness of wants not satisfied and of gifts not given; distorted limbs, dumb or inarticulate tongues, feet halting, sightless eye-balls, the dull stare betokening deafness, or the vacant look of idiocy, and in a word, the world one great receptacle of physical woes such as Adam saw in his vision of the uture, a place—

>"—sad, noisome, dark,
> A lazar-house it seemed, wherein were laid
> Numbers of all diseas'd; all maladies
> Of ghastly spasm, or racking torture, qualms
> Of heart-sick agony, all feverous kinds,
> Convulsions, epilepsies, fierce catarrhs,
> Intestine stone and ulcer, moping melancholy
> And moon-struck madness, pining atrophy,
> Marasmus, and wide-wasting pestilence,
> Dropsies and asthmas, and joint-racking rheums.
> Dire was the tossing, deep the groans; Despair
> Tended the sick, busiest from couch to couch;
> And over them, triumphant, Death his dart
> Shook, but delay'd to strike, though oft invoked
> With vows as their chief good and final hope."

Yet all this does not come near a hundredth part of what Jesus saw when He cast His eyes round the spiritual lazar-house of this most sinful world. Adam saw none but transient maladies, lasting for no more than a single human life: Jesus discerned diseases infinitely more wretched in their effects, more fatal, and more durable. The triumph of Death that saddened the eyes of Adam was but a brief triumph over frail flesh and blood: but to the eyes of Jesus, while eternal Life was at hand within the reach of every sin-stricken wretch, yet there appeared, mocking at rejected life, eternal Death enthroned in the soul of every formal Pharisee, triumphant with a triumph that enslaved spirit as well as body, wresting the souls of men out of the extended arms of God their Father, and hurrying them to the chains of darkness and death. If, as Milton tells us, the vision of disease had such power to touch the heart of Adam that he could not but weep, "though not of woman born," what tears might we not expect to fall from Him who chose as His special title, "the Son of Man," and who embraced all humanity, past, present, and to come, in the bonds of spiritual brotherhood?

That word "brotherhood" suggests yet one more thought that may help us to understand the power of Jesus in forgiving. One reason why we do not comprehend Jesus and His motives is, that we have little power of sympathy ourselves, and cannot comprehend how powerful a motive sympathy was in Him. The notion that His power of bearing the sins of the world is in any way to be illustrated by that poor, weak, stunted feeling which, so far as it extends towards all mankind, is so inert in our hearts, seems to us vague and unsatisfactory. Yet at least we know, or may, what it is to sympathize with a narrow circle, brothers and sisters, parents or children, or very intimate friends. Now suppose some of those who are closest to our hearts to commit some grievous, shameful sin: do we not feel it? By "it," I do not mean the discredit that may attach to us from our relationship or connection with the offender; I mean the *sin* itself. Do we not, in proportion to the genuineness of our affection for the offender, put ourselves in his place and feel his sin, and bear his burden as though it were our own? But to Jesus the whole world was a circle of brothers, loved by Him with an affection surpassing far the love of human brotherhood [1]

With all these qualifications for the divine task of forgiving, that Jesus should have forgiven, and should have imparted His own righteousness to those whom He forgave, will surprise no one who understands what forgiveness means. But Jesus also forgave in the name of His Father. He set no limitations or qualifications to the scope of His forgiveness, He did not say, " I forgive you so far as man can forgive, leaving the rest to God." On the contrary, He declared that He had authority to forgive sins here on earth, without waiting for any future state. This, too, is readily intelligible, and may be illustrated by the forgiveness of little children by their human parents. We saw above that for very young children the father is the only possible representative of God and humanity or society: the father forgives wholly in such cases, and the child feels wholly forgiven. Much more would the Son of God forgive sins wholly in the right which He possessed in virtue of His oneness with the Father. As the Psalmist identifies himself with Jehovah in thought, for the purpose of expressing his hatred of God's enemies, "Do not I hate them that hate Thee, O

---

[1] May not some illustration of the sympathy of Jesus with sins, not actually committed by Him, be derived from the authenticated instances in which the spectators of *physical* injuries inflicted on others have been themselves *physically* affected with corresponding injuries? See Dr. Carpenter's *Mental Physiology*, p. 680, for instances of this phenomenon, supported by what Dr. Carpenter pronounces to be "excellent authority."

God ? Yea, I hate them as though they were mine own enemies," so Jesus uses His identification with the Father for the purpose of forgiving those who have sinned against the Father. There is nothing unnatural in this, nothing that implies that Christ forgave in virtue of His divine nature and not in virtue of His human nature. On the contrary, He expressly tells us, not that the Son of God, but that "*the Son of Man* hath power on earth to forgive sins," and these, too, sins committed not against Himself, but against God.

It is of course but a form of words, yet it is somewhat more than a metaphor to say that Jesus *saw* the process of forgiveness. One or two phrases in the Gospels remain to indicate the nature of these visions of Jesus, but nothing indicates, or can indicate, the clearness with which He saw in each sinner the bandage of darkness round the eye of the captive and torpid soul, laden with the fetters of sin ; then the awakening at the sense of His presence, the increased oppression of the oppressor, the struggles against the bonds, and the effort to open the long-closed eyes to the light ; above, in heaven, the choirs of expectant angels hushing their harps in preparation for new songs of joy over "one sinner that repenteth ;" then the intense strain and sudden shock of conflict, and the shattering of bonds and the opening of the blind eyes, while the guardian angel of the repentant sinner, roused from its long torpor, turns its averted face once more to the Throne, henceforth always to behold the Father which is in heaven. Every act of forgiveness was a work "prepared" for Jesus by the Father : the real act was performed not on earth, but in heaven, up near the throne of God. As for the stir and bustle of it on earth, all that was nothing but the faint echo of the sound of the act performed in heaven.

The wonder to me is, not that Jesus forgave, but that in some cases He did not forgive. I can understand how the publicans and sinners were lifted up by His very presence into a new atmosphere of hope and life, self-reproach and self-respect, joy and sorrow, love of God and hate of self, and were carried by Him irresistibly into the presence-chamber of the forgiving Father. This is natural and intelligible; but that so many should have had the power to resist Him, and to keep out the forgiving influence—that is the great mystery of mysteries. Doubtless in some future state this problem will be solved. Not one word or look of Jesus will have been wasted even on the Pharisees or the Son of Perdition. The inevitable hardness caused by their resistance to Him cannot remain for all ages the sole result of Christ's influence even on those whom He condemned as hypocrites and vipers. "I have not come to send peace on earth, but a sword:" true, yet that sword cannot eventually destroy anything but what is entirely evil. Even when bearing the sword Christ can never cease to be the Prince of Peace.

But this power of forgiving, from its very nature, must have been singularly painful. The stress and strain of identifying Himself with sinners at all times, and more especially in the crisis when the emotional shock was being conveyed, must have been something more than a work of unmixed pleasure. "A man of sorrows and acquainted with griefs" is indeed the true description of at least one side of the life of Jesus. Indisputably the sorrows of Jesus were not the mere sorrows and griefs of homelessness, poverty, and hunger, or even the desertion of friends; all these were overshadowed by a far deeper sorrow, such as has been hinted above, the sorrow for the sins of humanity. Jesus did not wear the aspect of sorrow, at all events during the earlier part of His teaching. Yet even when He sat at feasts, it is not to be supposed that it was entirely pleasurable to Him to be the witness of the hardened coarseness of some, the unintelligent wonder, or slavish formality, or half-formed penitence of others, the misappreciation of all. At other times the sadness of Jesus appears plainly. The tears and groans of Jesus near the grave of Lazarus seem to have arisen not for the sake of Lazarus, but for the faithless mourning of the survivors. He sighed when He looked up to heaven and loosed the tongue of the dumb man. A fuller expression of this feeling is found in the words uttered immediately before the healing of the lunatic child, "O, crooked and faithless generation! How long shall I be with you, how long shall I suffer you?" But the keenest of all His expressions of anguish was in the garden of Gethsemane, where He said, "My soul is exceeding sorrowful even unto death," and besought the Father that, if it were possible, this cup might pass from Him.

Thus we are led from Christ's forgiveness of sins to Christ's sorrows, and from His sorrows to His Passion and Sacrifice on the Cross. In the truest sense of the word, the whole of Christ's life was a sacrifice, a giving up of self to God: but in what sense was His death a sacrifice? A thousand hymns and psalms in the language of every Christian nation reply, or seem to reply, that it is the physical and bodily sufferings of Christ upon the cross that constitute the great sacrifice. "Raise your eyes," they cry, "to the cross upon which He hangs with pierced hands and feet, and with the crown of thorns on His brow, tormented with raging thirst, and surrounded by the execrations of His countrymen: all this Christ bore for you." Thus has the appeal of the Cross gone forth to men, and to many of the poorer and the simpler sort it has spoken with a plain and helpful meaning. They have unconsciously felt that all these sorrows borne for men denote a readiness to bear other deeper sorrows of which they could take no cognizance, or which they could not express in words. But for some, who are not carried away by sympathy into an intuitional apprehension of the mystery of the Cross, the excessive emphasis laid by many theologians upon the physical pain of the crucifixion has created a stumbling-block: "To common men," they urge, "the thought of death is terrible, but not to all, not to the highest: and as for the mere physical pains of a lingering death, many a disciple of Christ has endured sufferings far more acute and protracted than the recorded sufferings of the Master Himself. Surely there must have been something beside these things that could cause the soul of Jesus to be exceeding sorrowful even unto death, or to cry, 'My God, My God, why hast Thou deserted Me?'" Undoubtedly there was something more. Physical pain must have been a very small part indeed of the sufferings of the cross. In order to bring this home to our imaginations let us make a supposition quite conceivable and natural, though to us, soldiers of Christ's cross, the very mention of it seems shocking, and almost profane. To some of us it may seem that the Sacrifice fore-ordained before the foundation of the world must have been from the first connected by Providence with that emblem which once suggested all that is vile and repulsive, and is now sacred to all Christendom. But suppose that Christ, instead of having been put to death by the Romans, after their national custom, on the cross, had been slain by the Jewish punishment of stoning, or that, like John the Baptist, He had been beheaded. Will any one venture to contend that His life and death would have been less of a sacrifice for us? But suppose again that instead of being killed at once, He had endured a lingering death in prison, dying at last what we call a natural death: thus dying, would He not still have been our sacrifice? Surely there can be but one opinion here. All of us will feel that the death upon the cross was pre-eminently the fittest, a death of humiliation, a death fit for Him who came not to be served, but to be the Servant of mankind, a death which has exhibited Him as no other death could have done, erect and clear to the adoration of a wondering world: but we shall none the less unhesitatingly admit that the sacrifice of the Eternal Son of God does not depend for its genuineness and saving power upon the shape of the instrument in which or by which He may have suffered. In whatever circumstances Jesus might have lived, and in whatever manner He might have died, being what He was, He could not fail to make His life and death the supreme Sacrifice of the world. The cross and the physical sufferings on the cross are therefore but the outward and visible expression of the inward and invisible Sacrifice which Christ was offering up for man to God every hour, every moment, of His life.

What that sacrifice was, as I have said repeatedly, we never shall in this life comprehend: but thus much we do perceive, that it was something in Jesus corresponding to our faculty of sympathy with sinners. It was the will of the Father that Jesus, who hated and loathed sin with an intensity inconceivable to us, should not only live among sinners, but also share their thoughts and even the burden of their sins, " bearing," as Isaiah says, " our sins and carrying our iniquities."[1] Only in this way could the Son of God make any sacrifice to the Father. To bear hunger and poverty and persecution was for Him easy: but for the Sinless to bear sin—that indeed was a giving up of the will, a sacrifice even for the Son of God. At all times it was a weariness, an effort, a strain. To recover from it He would go apart at times to be alone. But on the eve of His crucifixion He had to prepare for a greater strain than had ever before befallen Him. The sins of His countrymen, culminating in their supreme expression of malignity, were to compass Him round, and He must bear them all in the hour of ebbing strength and weakening human will, with no power now of going apart into the wilderness to " rest awhile." If anything could shake a divine faith in God as the Maker of men, and in men as the children of God, it must have been the quickened spiritual perception of the exceeding sinfulness of sin just at the moment when the human will was failing. It was no mere crowd of Pharisees and priests that Jesus saw and heard taunting Him in His dying moments: He saw, triumphant, Satan bestriding a fallen world, and heard the challenge of the Evil One claiming mankind as his lawful prey. As

[1] For the meaning of this phrase, see Chapter XIII.

truly as ever champion of flesh and blood fought against and overcame with substantial weapons a visible human foe, so truly did Jesus of Nazareth for Himself and for each of us wrestle with and overcome that horrible spirit of doubt and calumny which is the author of all evil. The invisible victory of Jesus, indeed, is the real contest of which all visible contests are but the poor metaphors and paintings in this unreal world of sight. If He had failed us in that moment—though He could not have failed—then it would have been better for the world that it had not been created.

Before the cross of Christ we all stand, from our childhood upwards, as before some mysterious altar; all of us striving to offer up our several sacrifices. We wish to offer up ourselves wholly to God, our better nature to be purified by Him, our worse nature to be utterly destroyed. But we cannot accomplish our wish. Dread of God, distrust of ourselves and of the destinies of humanity, suspicion and dislike of our fellow-men, a thousand shapes of selfishness come in between us and our purpose. For years perhaps we stand idly spinning our flimsy schemes of salvation out of the theological cobwebs of the past; and meantime Christ helps us not. He is too far above us, His motives too inexplicable, the merit of His death and passion so obscure, so seemingly arbitrary. We cannot understand, we cannot love Him. But suddenly, or perhaps, more often gradually, it is borne in upon us that Christ really was a man; had motives; had something more than flesh and blood and the outside semblance of a man; had joys, sorrows, fears, hopes. Then we leap to the thought of what He must have been, if He was indeed a man, what His love, what His pity, what His forgiveness must have been worth; what must have been the nature of His deepest sufferings and sorrows. Love so divine, we feel, must transcend all limitations of time and space. We feel that He who loved once thus, must love thus still, and must love for ever, must love all the world. Jesus in power still loves and sympathizes and helps no less than Jesus on earth. Straightway our thoughts go up to Him as our Help and Saviour, our Source of all good. He is no mere pattern or copy outside us for us to imitate. God forbid, and woe to us if it were so! He is our life, the breath of our being. Copying and imitation imply separation, judgment, criticism. We cannot judge, we cannot criticize; His sacrifice and nothing less can express for us the true meaning of our lives and the offering we owe to God. "Christ is our only sacrifice," we cry to the Father, "we cannot offer Thee any sacrifice of our own; take His as ours." And God does take it. Not by forensic transactions, or by any theological make-believes, but by the simple processes, divine but human, of trust and love, He raises us up to the height of that great sacrifice, and making us one with Christ, accepts us in Christ as His dear children. Thus is the sin-offering offered for us, our lower, sinful nature taken away, cast out, and consumed, and all the sorrow and burden of our sins lifted from off us and buried in the tomb of Christ our Saviour: and so is realized for each of us that ever true Dream which tells us how Christian "ran till he came at a place somewhat ascending, and upon that place stood a cross, and a little below, in the bottom, a sepulchre. So I saw in my dream that, just as Christian came up unto the cross, his burden loosed from off his shoulders, and fell from off his back, and began to tumble, and so continued to do, till it came to the mouth of the sepulchre, where it fell in, and I saw it no more."

CHAPTER XVII.

THE TRUE SOCIETY.

How Jesus, accomplishing for us the revelation of the Family, inspired mankind with trust and affection, we have attempted to show: we now proceed to ask how far He accomplished for us the revelation of Society. We found that the influence of society on Rome and Israel was powerful and beneficial, but defective. In both countries it was an exclusive influence. In Rome, as soon as it ceased to be exclusive, it ceased to be ennobling; in Israel it remained exclusive to the last. In Rome it was also aggressive, patriotism presupposing the desire to lower other countries in order to raise one's own. From these defects patriotism came to ignoble ends, taking refuge in a despotic theocracy both in the East and in the West. In the rest of the Empire they apotheosized Cæsars; in Israel, law.

It might have seemed natural that Jesus should set aside the influence of society and work without it. Wrapped up in the perpetual vision of the Father, He might have conceived as His ideal of the new kingdom a great Essene community, in which each child of God should stand by himself contemplating singly the perfection of the divine Fatherhood; a society in which members might meet for joint worship and work, but, for the rest, apart; a brotherhood of contemplative hermits. But this was not the ideal of Jesus. Little as He says about the nature of the society which He intended to found, He gives us plainly to understand that it was a working society, implying constant and close intercourse between its members. The Church was to hear and decide disputes: the members were to have and practise the power of forgiving sins; the sign by which they were to be known was their love toward one another: the duty of loving one another as each loved himself was the only law imposed on the society, and in the fulfilment of this duty, and its necessary accompaniment, the love of God, consisted perfection. Again, the society was to be aggressive: the members of it were to go forth to seek and save that which was lost, making perpetual war against Satan; he was to be foremost and chief in the society who was, not the most profound in contemplation, but the most active in serving his fellow-men. All this implies, not a community of hermits, but a phalanx of warriors.

In His society there were to be no distinctions of rank except such as arose from distinctions of service. The least would represent the Master: the greatest could represent no more. The object of the whole society was the same, war against sin. The weapon with which they were specially armed by their Master was that new sword of the Spirit which He had Himself introduced into the world, the power of forgiving sins. The Church of Christ was a spiritual Sparta, a society of combat. Yet they had no detailed code of laws and regulations, such as Lycurgus bequeathed to his martial fellow-countrymen, laying down principles of government, and entering into the minutest details of the life of the home, which was to prepare them for the combat abroad. The difference here between the two lawgivers, is striking. The Spartan, after mapping out the life political, military, and domestic of each member of his state for all time, is said to have bound his countrymen to obedience to his legislature by exacting from them an oath that they would obey it at least till he returned home from an intended journey: upon which the lawgiver exiled himself for ever. True or false, the story exactly illustrates what Christ's commonwealth was not. Lycurgus left laws behind him and secured obedience by his eternal absence. Christ left no laws behind Him, and by His last Will and Testament bequeathed to His society no code, no precepts, no secret charm of policy, nothing but His eternal presence in the hearts of all His followers. This was His only legacy, Himself to be their life and the food of their souls.

Yet it must not be thought that, because Jesus laid down no code, therefore He attached no importance to the influence of His society as a whole upon its individual members. On the contrary, He taught His disciples to regard themselves as inseparable from the collective body. In their prayers they were to call upon God not as "my Father," but as "our Father:" wherever two or three were gathered together in His name, there He promised His special presence. If two or three agreed in prayer, that prayer should have a special force. The whole world was to be henceforth a family, a brotherhood looking up to the common Father. His disciples were not to be able to look upon a human being without recognizing in him a brotherhood or possibilities of brotherhood that pointed up to the Father in heaven. No legislation of a Lycurgus could be more exacting than the demands of Jesus upon every department of the life of His followers. Wherever they went, whatever they did, they carried with them a law, not localised or limited like the law of Moses, but ubiquitous, regulating conduct to Gentiles as well as to Jews, and extending to thought and word as well as deed. This law was His Presence, or His Spirit, and it was pre-eminently a spirit of brotherhood, of love, of fellowship. By His disciples this Spirit was so familiarly associated with the feeling of fellowship that, when they prayed for its presence, they habitually spoke of the "fellowship of the Holy Spirit."

Obviously the society thus introduced by Christ is free from the grave defects inherent in the Roman and Jewish nations at the time of His birth. It is aggressive, as was Roman society at its best; but it is beneficently aggressive, and it will never cease to find scope for legitimate aggression. The Roman patriotism called forth unselfishness in its citizens in their mutual relations, but it was exclusive always, and at last oppressive; and, when Rome was empress of the world, Roman patriotism ceased to have reason for existing. But the patriotism of the New Jerusalem, while calling forth self-sacrifice in its citizens, benefits also those whom it attacks, and, to the world's end, as long as there is a trace of evil and sin among mankind, will always find scope for its energies. Again, the Christian patriotism has no less of the spirit of holiness and allegiance to God than had the patriotism of Israel. It hates sin as much and loves righteousness as much: but it makes war against sin more actively, and both in hate and love it is less exclusive and formal. It combines the holiness of the Jew with the inclusiveness of the later Roman empire, absorbing into its circle each province as soon as conquered, and admitting each newly-subjected enemy at once and without condition into the full cosmopolitan franchise of the children of God. In a word, the principle of Christ's society was that the relationship of the family should pervade the world, the state, the city, the district, the family, and not only this, but also every chance collection, every fortuitous "two or three" of human beings. There is no truer realization of the saying that "the great multiplication of virtues resteth upon societies well ordained and disciplined," than is to be found in the policy of Christ.

The very simplicity of the basis which Christ laid as the foundation for His future society, has blinded some persons to the obvious fact that He was the greatest social reformer that ever lived. So far from contemplating an isolated life of contemplation for His followers, He made it part of their religion to be sociable. There is not one of His precepts that does not directly or indirectly point to a future organization of society, and that does not make war against the principles that would disorganize society. All this He so takes for granted that He does not think it worth while to say in so many words, "I intend to reform social life;" but the constant mention of the Kingdom of God and of the Father in Heaven, bears witness to the social aspect in which He always regarded mankind. In every point it might be shown that the life and teaching of Jesus was intended to supply the links necessary, just at that crisis in the history of the world, to reunite and reorganize a society that was on the point of falling to pieces.

When Christ came into the world, He found the pagan nations worshipping power. They had worshipped power under the form of Polytheism; they were now drifting into another worship of it under the form of Imperialism. Now the worship of might is a sure forerunner and cause of the decay and disorganization of society; it is a religion of conquerors, not the religion of a peaceful society. Against the worship of might therefore Jesus set up the worship of a Righteous Father of all men. Have we ever sufficiently considered how much social reform was implied in this novel worship? It is true that we, even in these days, have not yet followed out our worship to its legitimate conclusions; but it has already had most weighty consequences. When Christ bade His disciples pray to "Our Father which is in Heaven," He virtually enacted for His followers the abolition of slavery; just as, when Mohammed declared that "there is none in the heavens and in the earth but shall approach the God of Mercy as a *slave*," he virtually enacted for his followers the continuance of slavery. Again, Christ found the nations of the world disunited by their old polytheistic religions, so far as they still adhered to them, and Israel itself indulging in the same exclusive spirit. In opposition to this spirit He expressly declared that there would be a blending of nations in the Kingdom of God; many would come from the east and the west and would

THE TRUE SOCIETY. 275

sit down with Abraham and Isaac in the Kingdom of God. More especially in Christ's treatment of the Law of Moses does He appear in the light of a reformer of society. Had He been bent upon founding a sect of hermits, He might have been expected to encourage the rigid observance of Sabbaths, fastings, purifications, and the like, all of which, by fixing the thoughts on the divine Author of these institutions, might be supposed to foster contemplation and solitary worship. But Jesus rejected them because they were unsociable, and because they hampered the free and healthy intercourse between man and man. In the same spirit He condemned the selfish moroseness of rich men who suppose that they have no responsibilities to society; He condemns violence; He inculcates respect for the weak and lowly, and, appealing to the down-trodden classes of society, He calls upon them to enter the Kingdom of God on the strength of that new power of forgiveness which He had introduced into the world.

If it be said that all this is rather destructive than constructive, and that it is necessary to show on what definite principle Christ intended to construct society, I reply that all paper schemes of government, if they do not fail at once, are sure to be narrow, transient, and liable to perversion. The absence of a code for His Church was not only a protest on the part of Christ against the literalism of the Jews, but was also necessary for the transmission of His organizing influence to the future society. It was the beauty of Christ's policy that He left no code to be idolized, distorted, and disputed about. His constructiveness consisted in being what He was, and in bequeathing Himself to His disciples as a moral force for all posterity. One law alone He left to the citizens of His kingdom, that they were to love one another as they loved themselves; and, having inspired them with moral power to carry this rule into effect, He left all details of execution to be stated by the countless varieties of the circumstances of the future. But what can be more fundamentally social than Christ's Kingdom of God? The King was to be a Father of all men: the only sign of citizenship, and the only law of the kingdom, was love. Why then should it be asserted that Christ did not organize society, simply because He organized it, not after the rough manner of statesmen by nations or provinces or towns at a time, but after the manner of Nature proceeding outward to the race from the individual, and yet at the same time proceeding inward to the individual from the whole human race? St. Paul exactly expressed Christ's system of society when he described Christ's followers as inseparable limbs of one body, and he exactly expressed the nature of Christ's constructiveness when he described the society not so much as being organized by Christ, but rather as being a living body of which Christ was the head, or, still better, as *being* Christ Himself.

The great obstacle to reform in all nations has been that servile spirit of conservatism (I do not deny that there is a righteous spirit of conservatism) which is bred by bestial contentedness, by disregard of the troubles of others, by the fear of arousing in the masses desires that can never be satisfied, by the want of faith in the guidance of a Supreme Reforming Spirit who is bent on conforming mankind to Himself throughout the ages, and by a consequent idolatry of rigid traditions or codes of the past. The Spirit of Christ, on the other hand, is, from every point of view, a reforming spirit. It engenders in us aspirations which necessitate perpetual effort and improvement; it haunts us and harasses us with an uneasy feeling that something remains to be done as long as we see a single human being in a position which we ourselves should not desire to occupy; it relieves us from the fears that retard reform by teaching us to place confidence in the destinies and tendencies of the masses of mankind; it leads us to avoid force and violence and dislocating revolutions, and to imitate what Bacon calls the great innovator Time, but what we should rather call God, who "innovateth greatly but quietly, and by degrees scarcely to be perceived;" lastly, while it protests against the idolatry of the outworn past, it warns us that every jot and tittle of God's teaching in the past must be revered and fulfilled, and, instead of prescribing to us an unchangeable standard of conduct, it leaves us free to ask counsel of circumstances as to what is fittest, while promising us the continual promptings of God's Spirit to teach us what is best.

It is because true Christianity is so very reforming a religion that it must always seem to be visionary and unpractical: so much will always appear remaining to be done by the true Christian Reformer. After eighteen centuries of Christianity we are only just entering upon the new phase of society contemplated by Christ when the distinctions of rich and poor, powerful and weak, shall be, not perhaps obliterated, but at least consecrated to the good of the community. Slavery has been abolished; duelling, through the indirect influence of

Christ, has been greatly diminished; but war still thrives, unchristian distinctions are still kept up between rich and poor, and no one can say that the masses of mankind are as yet placed in the position that Christ would claim for them. Wherever we look we find Christ's measures of reform as yet only imperfectly carried into effect.

"Then, by your own confession, Christ's Society is a dream, and has never yet been realized." Certainly it has not yet been realized, and probably will not be even approximately realized for some century or more, perhaps for many centuries to come : but it has already saved mankind from ruin, and raised it steadily up to its present position. Had it not been for Christ's society, the framework of the civilized world would have fallen completely to pieces after the fall of the Roman empire. It is not sufficiently recognized that ancient society was absolutely dependent on a basis of wretchedness and servitude. For every free citizen of Athens there were some half dozen or more of slaves; a Roman noble in the times of Christ presupposed a whole regiment of slaves. If any Roman had predicted in the times of Christ that a time would come when this foundation of misery would be withdrawn, and society would still remain intact and progressive, he would have been scoffed at by his countrymen as a being more fatuous and contemptible than even a professional augur. But Christ has effected for mankind this seeming impossibility, and has effected it quietly, without " servile wars," without bloody revolutions. Who then can deny to Christ the name of a great practical Reformer?

It may be said indeed that even in modern Christian

States this inequality of happiness still remains. Even now in England, as once in Greece and Rome, " good society, floated on gossamer wings of light irony, is of very expensive production: requiring nothing less than a wide and arduous national life condensed in unfragrant deafening factories, cramping itself in mines, sweating at furnaces, grinding, hammering, weaving, under more or less oppression of carbonic acid—or else, spread over sheep-walks, and scattered in lonely houses and huts on the clayey or chalky corn-lands, where the rainy days look dreary." True: but it is the merit of Christ's re-organization of mankind that He goes down to this very lowest stratum of society and exalts it in two ways. On the one hand He appeals to it directly, by consecrating all labour and every condition of life as equally holy, and by holding out hopes of equal future blessedness to peasant and to king; and on the other hand He ameliorates it indirectly by making the other classes of society uneasy at the spectacle of their brethren toiling below them. Old Cato recommended his countrymen to work their decrepit slaves to death; but the Christian spirit of humanity devotes itself unweariedly to the discovery of inventions for minimising the hardships of toil, and of late years the Christian spirit of fairness and justice is at last beginning to recognize the rights of manual labour to a far greater share in the comforts, and pleasures, and culture of life. Very much more will be done in this direction before this century has passed away; but even as things are we may say that wherever the spirit of Christian fellowship is present, there we find life and progress; wherever it is absent, there we find decay.

Many of those who might be disposed to blame the tardy realization of Christ's policy, would probably be found among those who believe that the human race has existed, not for six thousand years, but for a much longer period. Those who believe in the fascinating theory of evolution can better afford to wait than those who do not. If it took so many thousand years first to create man, and then to develop him to a state fitting him even to receive the seed of the spirit of brotherhood, surely we may naturally expect that a few thousands of years will be required to foster and rear that seed into a vigorous life. Evolutionists ought to be among the most ardent believers in the future of humanity and the most patient waiters for the development of Christ's grand scheme. That it should not succeed, and not be realized in some shape at some future time, must seem surely impossible even to those who reject the worship of Christ, and reserve their worship for humanity: and even those who are not Christians ought to acknowledge that Christ's partial success hitherto implies a very great personality influencing mankind by taking advantage of the natural laws of humanity, a personality not to be blinked by philosophers, nor to be despatched in a sentence as "the real or ideal founder" of Christianity.

CHAPTER XVIII.

THE TRUE ATTITUDE TO NON-HUMAN NATURE.

WE agreed above that the peculiar lesson learned by men from the vaster phenomena of Nature is awe. No human virtue or passions impress us with quite the same awe as we feel at a thunderstorm, or at the sight of a snow-topped mountain or a vast sea, or even at the common sight of the sky and the stars. But by awe we did not mean such servile fear as that which made the Moabite crouch before Moloch, nor the blank alarm with which men regard an epidemic: awe always implies some degree of reverence, some looking up to a Being greater than ourselves, whose ways are not our ways, but much greater and grander than ours. We may not go to the length of actually believing in a Person behind the phenomena, but in any case there must be some feeling of trust or faith such as could not be produced by a mere machine known to be a machine, however vast and complicated.

In two ways Christ has increased and purified for us this feeling of awe—first, directly by giving Himself to us as an object of awe: secondly, and indirectly, by making Himself the Mediator between us and Nature, and by introducing us to a new and purer awe of the material world, its laws and processes. Of the first of these two lessons little need be said. He that knows Christ at all knows what it is to feel awe. Not only His manifestations to His disciples after His death, not only the wonderful acts of healing performed by Him before His death, but His superhuman goodness, His unbounded trust in God, or rather insight into the working of God's will, His sense of sin and power of bearing sin, all impress us with the conviction that we worship in Christ one who is a man, yet "not our selves;" one who may be loved and trusted without limits, but with that kind of love and trust which, instead of being cramped, is developed by simultaneous awe.

This we must all feel. Non-Christians as well as Christians would recognize that Christ has supplied the world with a new and great object of reverence. But the next point requires more consideration. It is this—that Christ, taking us into Himself, has placed us in a new attitude, His own attitude, towards Nature, which increases and purifies our awe of Nature. The attitude of Christ towards Nature may be illustrated by many of His words and works; but one of the best illustrations is to be found in the Temptation. Whether it narrates a dream or a trance, or any other kind of vision—equally real in any case—we shall learn much from the narrative which describes how Jesus resisted the three inducements to turn stones into bread, to cast Himself down from a pinnacle of the Temple, and to secure the empire of the world by doing homage for it to Satan.

I pass to the consideration of the Temptation as a

natural phenomenon. But when I say natural, I mean natural for such a one as Jesus of Nazareth, and not by any means natural for an ordinary Prophet, still less for an ordinary Israelite, least of all for an ordinary Englishman in the nineteenth century. But if anyone rejects the explanation I shall give of the narrative, and says, " The whole story seems to me a myth," then I reply, " Well, if it is a myth, is it not an admirably invented myth, containing a great deal of spiritual truth consciously or unconsciously imbedded in the narrative by the inventors of it? And if we take the trouble to search to the bottom of this myth, may we not hope to find some light shed upon the actual life and character of Christ by those early narrators or inventors?"

Let it not be thought irreverent if we endeavour to understand something of the details of Jesus' temptation, and to give a human meaning to them. We know indeed that we cannot fully sympathize with Him, we cannot feel as He felt. Not all the biographies of all the St. Pauls, the St. Augustines, the St. Francis', the Luthers in the world could ever enable us to do that fully. But we must try to do it; for, only so far as we can feel as He felt can we love or trust in Him, or be worthy of the name of Christians. Since He was a man, we are to assume that His temptations were human, or even, in the strong language of the New Testament, that " He was tempted in all points as we are." Now it is in the transitional stages of men's life, notoriously in early manhood, and perhaps quite as much, though less notoriously, in the passage from the enthusiasm of early manhood into the sober prudence of middle age that the strongest temptations naturally befall us. New feelings, new passions, powers, and wishes (new, or if old, latent) make themselves felt and crave expression and satisfaction : and the question arises, In what kind of action ought they to be expressed and satisfied? These new powers cannot be stifled without peril : a man cannot make himself a boy again : they must be directed; and if rightly directed they lead to the fulfilment of one's highest nature—if wrongly, they end in wreck. To all men, and not merely to statesmen and politicians, there comes more than once in the course of nature such a crisis. The temptations of Jesus, being human, cannot have been exempt from the general law of human temptations. As high as His faculties are above ours, so high are His temptations above ours. But He too must have been tempted, as we are, to use His faculties for inappropriate ends. Keeping therefore the law of human temptation steadily in our minds, let us pass to the consideration of the Temptation to turn the stones into bread.

It is certainly possible that, as Satan subsequently tempted Christ through the medium of the Apostle Peter, so now he may have offered this suggestion in the person of some casual passer-by, or some curious visitor who came to spy out the secrecy of the retiring prophet. This supposition somewhat resembles the account of the incident as it is given by Milton. It is more likely, however, more in accordance with the solitude and loneliness of the picture, that the voice of temptation, though it strove to blend itself with the consciousness of Jesus, so jarred upon His sinless nature as to present the effect of an external voice. But be the form what it may, the essence of the temptation lay in the suggestion, " Turn these stones into bread." Why should He not? Moses was said to have done something of the kind; so also Elijah and Elisha. They were merely prophets: what might not be expected from the Son of God, in whom God was well pleased?

The very modesty and humility of Jesus contributed to the force of the suggestion. Up till now He had been in the seventh heaven, in communion with the Father, hearing words unspeakable, rapt into paradise, indifferent to earth and earthly things, to sense and the things of sense, and now the Son of God was reminded that He was hungry by the pangs of appetite—what a humiliation and unseemly contrast, *if* He really was the Son of God? Could the Son of God feel a desire, and that desire remain for a moment ungratified? Body and mind were faint and weak with hunger. Was the want of a meal to retard or cramp the work of the Saviour of the world? Could a being so limited, so dependent, really be the Son of God?

It has been said above that the temptations of humanity generally press heaviest at those critical periods when one age is supplanting another, and is bringing with it new faculties and new duties. It is difficult for the man who was yesterday a youth, at once to shake off youthful thoughts and actions, and to see the ideal of manhood. And to Christ, recently perhaps made for the first time fully conscious by the Voice from heaven of His superiority to all the judges and kings and prophets to whom He had looked up in childish days, must there not now have come a period of transition when it became necessary to mark out the new course of action appropriate for the Son of God? He felt within Him certain powers not vouchsafed to ordinary men. He, the Son of Man, was omnipotent, not because He could do as He pleased nor because He could induce the Heavenly Father to grant His will, but because His will was identical with the will of the Father. Whatever the Father willed the Son willed, and in that obedience He found perfect power. The question therefore arose, What use was He to make of the great faculties which had hitherto lain unexercised, but now called for action? These faculties had in greater or less degree, so it was recorded in the Old Testament, been bestowed on many of the ancient prophets, and they had with their aid done many mighty and startling works. What should be the new works, excelling in might and marvel, that should indicate the operation, not of a prophet, but of the Son of God? This was an intellectual rather than a moral doubt. The first part of the temptation, "If thou be the Son of God," was a moral trial; the second part assumed His sonship, but suggested actions unworthy of a Son of God. But both intellectual and moral doubts blended together and found expression in the suggestion, "If Thou be the Son of God, turn these stones into bread."

The answer to this suggestion was not what we might have expected. It was not, "I will give no sign to satisfy incredulity: I will not experimentalize with faith," but—"It is written, man shall not live by bread alone, but by every word that cometh out of the mouth of God." The deliverer of Israel identified Himself with Israel, and in His trials recurred to the trials of

His nation. If they had hungered, why should not He? if they had been chastened, why might not He expect, not indeed chastisement, but the kind pain that comes with chastisement, and welcome it as a mark of fatherly love, and not of anger? "And thou shalt remember all the way which the Lord thy God led thee those forty years in the wilderness, to humble thee and to prove thee, to know what was in thine heart, whether thou wouldest keep His commandments or no. And He humbled thee, and suffered thee to hunger, and fed thee with manna which thou knewest not, neither did thy fathers know, that He might make thee know that man doth not live by bread alone, but by every word that proceedeth out of the mouth of God doth man live. Thou shalt also consider in thine heart that as a man chasteneth his son so the Lord thy God chastened thee."

Jesus deliberately accepted the inconveniences of the desert and the pangs of hunger as the loving schooling of a heavenly Father, and as a proof, not a disproof, of his sonship. The divine system of nature contains many ordinances tending to the education and the spiritual rearing of mankind—prosperity and adversity, labour and rest, famine and fulness. It was not for Jesus, out of respect to His own comfort, to interfere with that orderly providence. It was the mark of a weak and selfish king to find the ideal of power and royalty incompatible with subjection to the wants and weaknesses and sorrows of common men—

"I live with bread like you, feel want,
Taste grief, need friends; subjected thus,
How can you say to me—I am a king?"

Very different was the royal idea of Jesus. For the sake of His subjects it might be hereafter His duty to use mysterious powers, but not for Himself—He could help others, Himself He could not help. A superiority in suffering and in sympathizing, in loving and forgiving —that was the claim asserted by the Son of God: He claimed no other precedence. Had it been otherwise, had Jesus, on every occasion of need, had recourse to His divine powers to lighten His own burdens—then indeed systematic theology might have striven to extract some moral from His life; but, raised above the level of men, He would have been a non-human idol, a "mysterious amalgam" of humanity and divinity, and for all the purposes of love, trust, and awe He might as well never have existed.

As this temptation vanished, another appeared in its place, which, though put third by St. Luke (who aimed at chronological arrangement), may better be considered in the place which St. Matthew gives it. Jesus had rejected the suggestion that the Son of God must exempt Himself from the inconveniences and dependences of a son of man. To suffer was to be strong; to obey was to be a king: in perfect dependence on the Father's will He found perfect independence of material things. What mattered the laws of nature and limitations of humanity to Him? What could separate Him from the love of God? Could hunger? He had proved that it could not. Could peril of death? That was the question which now arose.

As He mused on the dependent independence, the ineffable happiness and security of a Son of God, He recalled the words in which the Psalmist describes the safety of God's chosen child: "He that dwelleth in the secret place of the Most High shall abide under the shadow of the Almighty." Then followed the lofty strain in which the child of God is addressed: "He shall cover thee with His feathers, and under His wings shalt thou trust: His truth shall be thy shield and buckler. Thou shalt not be afraid for the terror by night; nor for the arrow that flieth by day; nor for the pestilence that walketh in darkness; nor for the destruction that wasteth at noonday.... There shall no evil befall thee, neither shall any plague come nigh thy dwelling. For he shall give his angels charge over thee, to keep thee in all thy ways. They shall bear thee up in their hands, lest thou dash thy foot against a stone. Thou shalt tread upon the lion and adder: the young lion and the dragon shalt thou trample under feet." And last came the responsive blessing of Jehovah upon His obedient child: "Because he hath set his love upon Me, therefore will I deliver him. I will set him on high, because he hath known My Name." Immediately, with these words in His mind, or perhaps upon His lips, Jesus found Himself upon the pinnacle of the temple in Jerusalem.

It may have happened to the reader, while walking along the cliffs of some rock-bound coast, and looking dizzily over the edge at the waves that break far down out of sight beneath the hollowed rock, to reflect sometimes in the midst of mirth and health and sunny holidays, that, spite of his present thankful happiness, his harmony with nature and glad aspirations, one leap or one false step would place him where not all the prayers and praises and aspirations of the universe could save him. Such thoughts bring with them a kind of sickening lower kind of awe for what are called the laws of nature, and a certain contempt for the humanity which only exists in happiness as long as it is content to be the subject of Nature, not without a shade of distrust in the personal existence of a Ruler of the world and in His care for each individual human being, since He has attached such terrible penalties to carelessness, and since, though He may forgive in another world the want of present piety, He often refuses to forgive in this world the want of thought. Months or years afterwards, when walking through crowded streets, or perhaps seated alone in one's study, a man recalls unconsciously that transitory thought; and, in a moment, study or streets disappear, and he is on that rock-bound coast again, with the roaring sea once more beneath him, listening to the voices of the breakers as they cry, "Thou art not a child of God, but only dust. If thou deniest, come down to us, and try whether we shall not scatter thee into thine original atoms."

As a child Jesus must have seen the magnificent, though unfinished structure of Herod's temple, the pride of every citizen of Jerusalem, the admiration of every pilgrim from the provinces, and upon any Jewish child the sight must have left no slight impression. The "pinnacle," or battlement, of the temple was exceedingly high, and may perhaps have been proverbial for its height. A leap from the "pinnacle" of the temple may perhaps have been a common phrase to represent a fatal fall, like a leap from the Tarpeian rock at Rome, or a leap from the Monument in London. We learn from Josephus that it caused dizziness to look down from the southward side of the temple into the valley below. But a still more important fact is that from this "pinnacle" or battlement James, the brother of Jesus, is said to have been cast down by the Jews. We need not assert that the account of James' martyrdom as it is quoted by Eusebius is in all points trustworthy; yet at least it renders probable the supposition that the "pinnacle" was notorious for its conspicuous position and for its height.

Now, therefore, in a moment, while wrapped in meditation on the divine promises, and appropriating to Himself the words of the Psalmist, "He shall give His angels charge over me to keep me in all my ways. They shall bear me up in their hands, lest I dash my foot against a stone"—the stones and the desert faded from His eyes, and He was high in air, dizzily clinging to that well-known summit, and hearing the voice, "If Thou be the Son of God, cast Thyself down."

Such a temptation as this would have slight power against us. The tenacity with which we cling to life, and the dulness of our faith in a heavenly Father, arm us with thick panoply against it. But we must not thence infer that it was no trial for Jesus. He had a boundless faith, an infinite love, a trust illimitable; He cared not for self or life: He longed to bear the pains and troubles of His fellow-men: He knew no law but universal love; why then should He not cast Himself down? He had been tempted before to break the orderly Providence of God for His own comfort; now He was tempted to submit to it, to throw Himself in blind trust upon it, to His own peril, and to see whether God would not break it for Him. He had submitted to hunger in reliance upon God, let Him now submit to the peril of death in the same reliance. Why stand there, timidly clinging to the pinnacle, when choirs of angels were ready to bear up His feet?

In all ages, long before the Epicureans and Stoics had ever defined their dogmas, and long after their definitions had been forgotten, two extreme courses have suggested themselves to men in trouble—to suffer all circumstances or to control all circumstances: and men have debated within themselves which was the nobler. In the former temptation Jesus had been solicited to join the school of Epicurus; now the Stoical temptation was before Him. The intuition of Jesus had taught Him what we have learned by the long and tedious process of centuries, that the laws of nature are not to be overridden. The same intuition now taught Him what perhaps some of us have yet to learn, that the law of human will is as natural as the other laws of nature, and that the ideal human life is a mixture of obedience and control: that God's will is being fulfilled in all things, and to His will our wills are subservient, but that, however inexplicable it may be, "our wills are ours," and are not to be lightly cast away. Thus in the temptation to suffer, as well as in the temptation to act, Jesus recognized that suffering as well as action must be regulated by obedience to the divine will. The lesson of the temptation was the same as the lesson of the passion. "Though He was a Son, yet learned He obedience." His temptation was to give up life, His duty to cling to it. To try experiments with suffering was to tempt God, and it had been written, "Thou shalt not tempt the Lord thy God."

The second temptation having been resisted like the

first, the tempter fled, but only to return a third time with a different suggestion. The divine Sonhood of Jesus was no longer disputed, His claim to kingdom not controverted; but the manner in which His kingdom was to be attained now came into question. The Son of God was to be a Son of Man, subject to human wants, liable to human dangers, and under an obligation to act as well as to suffer in human methods. His humanity was not to be a mere honorary title, as when a prince of the blood receives the commission of a subaltern in the army, and is lieutenant one moment and prince the next, at his own pleasure. There was to be no favouritism nor exemption for Jesus. If He was to conquer and to achieve kingdom, He must achieve it by the actions and virtues of humanity. But since He was to achieve a kingdom by human actions, must He not employ human methods, and study the history of human successes?

In a moment He was on a lofty mountain, His own Galilee beneath Him, Judæa and Syria near at hand, Parthia and Asia farther off, and farthest of all, beyond the great sea, a dimmer vision of the power of Rome. As Jesus included in one rapid glance the kingdoms of the earth, the thought came, What was the secret of kingcraft, by which these kings had climbed to their thrones? Violence and deceit, oppression and servility were the steps that led downwards to a Herodian throne, and the same arts that gained, were doubled to preserve power. Even if Jesus turned His thoughts to the distant centre of power, beyond the sea; what was the secret of Roman rule? What was their motto but " Divide and conquer"? Look where He might, force and cunning were the secrets of empire. This sweeping condemnation could not have been passed upon the world in the days of Aristides or the Decii. But now patriotism had passed away, and patriots were out of date. In His own country Judas of Galilee had met with failure and death; and, if the fame of Cato or Cicero had reached His ears, their miserable ends would but conspire to prove that patriotism must henceforth be a failure.

What, therefore, in this corrupt condition of affairs should be the policy of the would-be king of men? Ought He not to recognize it, as a physician recognizes, in order to cure, the disease of his patient? Other kings came, like thieves, to despoil the sheep whose shepherds they were bound to be; Christ's kingdom, when once established, would bring with it universal peace and happiness. To bring about so vast and desirable a result, was it not worth while to make some temporary truce as it were with unrighteous Mammon against itself, to "divide" Mammon in order to "conquer" it, to contest arms with arms, cunning with cunning, compromise with compromise? If it really was the object of Jesus to benefit mankind, was it too great a sacrifice to expect of Him that He should stoop to their level and condescend for a time to their weaknesses in order to raise and strengthen them permanently? Did not the order of things seem to show that men could only be ruled by cunning and violence? Was it not really true that mankind seemed to have been surrendered to a "spirit of this world," who claimed the kingdoms of the earth, and bestowed them on whom he willed? Did not a spirit so powerful deserve some recognition, some respect, it might almost be said, some homage? Thus for an instant there arose before Jesus that terrible phantom which has darkened many doubting hearts, the suggestion that God is not the supreme ruler of the world, that men are not the children of God but the servants of Satan, that kings and courts, councils and armies of men, nations and national policy, are reserved to be the prey of the Devourer of human souls, while God the Father dwells only in the cottage, the desert, and the church. To a pure saint who was intent on his own personal safety and righteousness, the natural consequence of such a thought would take the form of a temptation to give up active philanthropy and to leave men to their fatal slavery. To Jesus, whose object was the welfare of the world, the temptation took a very different shape. He was tempted to share men's slavery in order to make them free. Conscious of His powers and purposes, Jesus might well feel that there was need of only a moderately fortunate combination of circumstances to ensure Him universal empire, and fulfil in Him the current prophecy of "the conqueror from the East,"—if only He could steer safely through the slighter dangers that beset the candidate for a throne. For all the greater emergencies of the struggle, for all the crises that call for the foresight of a prophet, the intuition of a seer, and the rapid execution of a king, He was prepared. But for the minor details necessary to secure respect and obedience and the enthusiasm of the vulgar, for the tact, the *finesse*, the compromising faculty, the judicious ostentation of successful politicians—for these arts He was not prepared. As little was He prepared for the arts of a successful general. If Jesus was averse to deceit, He was equally averse to violence. He would recognize no law, He would appeal to no motive, but that of love. His only policy was the policy of the Word of God, which, since the creation, had recognized love as its highest law, and the family as the ideal State. But His temptation was to recognize selfishness as a power in the world, to work through the fear of violence and the hope of gain, and to save men from selfishness by Himself appealing to it and utilising it.

This was the last and hardest trial of all—the last and hardest, as poets have told us, for all really great men who sympathize keenly with their fellow-creatures. To beings of limited capacity, unable to do much good or evil, such a temptation, like all the temptations of noble natures, may seem unreal. But a king, a healer, a shepherd of the human race has never been able to hear unmoved the cry rising up from the toiling, struggling masses of his fellow-creatures—

"To do a great good, do a little wrong."

We know enough of the history of the times of Jesus, the break-up of patriotic feeling and national religious thought throughout the world, the lifelessness that pervaded the perfect machinery of the Roman empire, the spread of superstition and scepticism, the failure and unpopularity of philosophy, contrasted with the life and vigour and self-sacrifice of the Galileans, to see that, had Jesus succumbed to the tempter's solicitation, the tempter might have kept his word. By temporary homage to the spirit of selfishness Jesus might have achieved an empire coequal with the then known world, exceeding in the durability and perfection of its government, in the wisdom of the governor, and the enthusiastic obedience of the governed, that empire which was founded six hundred years afterwards by the Arabian who—combining the sword with the Koran—confessed the supremacy of the spirit of this world, and verily received his reward.

To put away so bright a prospect was no slight trial, and called for a special resistance. Jesus did not argue or debate the question of supremacy, or of the lawfulness of war and diplomacy. That men are selfish and can best be ruled, at least under ordinary rulers, by a partial appeal to their selfishness, that complete honesty is not, at all events in its immediate results, the best policy—these are truths that admit of no denial. Jesus does not deny them. Nor does He enter into the mysterious question, why men were given over to sinful and weak rulers?—why sin and weakness are tolerated in the world by God? He holds fast to the one great truth which can be demonstrated to none of us, but can be felt by all, that spite of the appearances of discordant powers in the world, we are none the less governed by one God, to whom alone our allegiance is due. But so keen a temptation required something more than mere passive resistance. As in later days, when the tempter spoke through the mouth of His most ardent disciple, the violent attack called forth an active repulse, so now the dialogue with the evil spirit was finally broken off: "Get thee behind me, Satan : for it is written, thou shalt worship the Lord thy God, and Him only shalt thou serve."

In rejecting this last suggestion of the spirit of this world Jesus sealed His fate as far as this world is concerned, and deliberately preferred present failure to present success. It has been said of the typical reformer that "he is apt to treat adverse circumstances as if they were accidents or anomalies in nature having no right to existence, and thus, more or less wilfully, shuts his eyes to the force of events on which he purposes to operate, and which will, in any case, operate upon his principle. He hurls a favourite principle, which may be a very just one, into the world not sufficiently prepared for it, which has not reached the due level of its evolution, and which therefore is necessarily hostile to it. . . . . Adverse circumstances, which they in their passion would not recognize, but which, as rational beings, it behoved them to have recognized, have swept them away: and the truth which they have been upholding has been for a while the victim of their indiscretion." Put the first for the nineteenth century, and make the corresponding changes of phraseology, and we have here the very suggestion to which Jesus would not listen. He persisted in regarding sin and vice as if they were "accidents or anomalies in nature, having no right to existence." He would not, indeed seeing so clearly into human nature as He saw he could not, recognize as realities these "adverse circumstances." Rather than float down in triumph on such a stream, He preferred to be "swept away." Like many other martyrs and reformers, He was "swept away." But it seems probable that martyrs and reformers have understood their business better than critics.

CHAPTER XIX.

THE TRUE SPIRIT OF SCIENCE.

IT is often urged, as an objection against faith in Christ, that although His life is in many respects pure and admirable, yet it is one-sided and deficient. A man ought to live, we are told, not only in the Good (that is, morally), but also in the Whole (that is, scientifically), and in the Beautiful (that is, artistically). Now it is commonly supposed that there is an antagonism between the Spirit of Christ and the Spirit of Science. Christ is said to "have had no attitude at all to science ; never to have so much as dreamed of it." Many go even further than this in their thoughts, and entertain a suppressed belief that Jesus of Nazareth intended actually to discourage science, and that, were He now living on earth, He would set His face against the wonderful scientific discoveries of this century as being snares and temptations to mankind, or, at all events, as insignificant in comparison to the one grand object of life, the salvation of the soul. Many religions are undoubtedly unfavourable to science. Some commit themselves to definite theories about the creation of the world, or about the history of certain epochs, stifling science with an orthodox cosmogony or with orthodox versions of history ;

others engender a fear and terror that paralyses research; others inculcate lifeless and servile rites, which formalities directly or indirectly check the natural flow of reason. I shall endeavour to show that the Spirit of Christ does none of these things, and does everything that is contrary to these things.

But we must first explain in what sense we shall use the word Science. The word might have been used to mean all knowledge, including knowledge of God and of morality, of social and political order, as well as knowledge of the scientific subjects commonly so called. Indeed we do sometimes speak of social science and of moral science. But the word has of late (perhaps perniciously) come to mean not all knowledge, but the knowledge of those subjects in which human will does not disturb the sequence of natural phenomena. In this narrow sense we shall employ the word. Be it remembered, however, that it is a narrow, a very narrow sense, and that a Redeemer of mankind might be well worthy of the name, even though he put this narrow department of human life entirely on one side and said, " I come to make men hope and trust, that they may know God to be their Father, and themselves to be His children, and that, through this knowledge, they may know their duty. If I can give them this knowledge, which is only to be attained by combining trust with reason, I shall have bestowed on mankind the best of all sciences, and may fairly claim to be ' the first of those that *know.*'"

But I maintain that what Christ did for mankind extended far beyond the mere province of spiritual or moral science, and pervaded natural science itself, or science in its narrow signification. This being the case, we will give up the advantage that we might derive from using the word science in its ample and scientific sense, and we will use it throughout this chapter in its narrow meaning, as applied to nothing but what is called Natural Science. Now there are two ways in which a great Reformer may encourage science. In the first place, he may create favourable circumstances for study and research; in the second place, he may, by his life and influence, engender in mankind the scientific habit of mind. I shall endeavour to prove that in both these ways Jesus of Nazareth prepared the way for the discovery of scientific truth.

It will scarcely be disputed, I imagine, that an environment of social, and political, and moral order is favourable to the discovery of the order of Nature. Independently of the indirect advantages of peace and leisure, it can hardly be denied that order in the State and in the mind suggests an orderly sequence in Nature. The prophets of Israel, for example, when they protested in the name of moral order, against the apparent subversions of it by temporary disorder, indirectly contributed to the recognition of Law in the visible as well as in the spiritual world. That Babylon must fall, or that Assyria or Egypt must fall, not because the prophet wished them to fall, but because these overgrown empires were trampling down the Truth, and violating the laws of Righteousness, Justice, and Mercy—the recognition of this inevitable sequence of cause and effect in the spiritual world was not without a scientific as well as a moral consequence on human nature. Taking up this doctrine of the prophets, Christ delivered it from its unscientific national exclusiveness, and applied it at once to the human race, and to each individual in the race. " There is a law in spiritual things," He practically said to mankind," you are not good by accident, or bad by accident, you are not punished by chance or rewarded by chance, there is no such thing as casualty and caprice, you are surrounded by invisible causes inevitably producing sensible effects." This message He accompanied by the proclamation that this inevitable order must be obeyed and trusted in, as being the will of an all-loving Father. Such was the general tendency of Christ's teaching : but we now proceed to consider it somewhat more in detail with special reference to its influence on the scientific spirit.

The scientific spirit may be regarded in two aspects, the moral and the intellectual. Morally the scientific man must love truth and hate falsehood : he must regard facts as things sacred, not to be tampered with, but to be revered as the expressions of Nature's meaning. He must not merely accept truth with an otiose assent, not merely welcome it, but be enamoured of it, woo it, forget himself and his own petty interests in the absorbing enthusiasm for it. After a manner, he may be almost said to worship it and to feel that it is his mission to seek after it. Now he cannot easily feel this passion for truth and this sense of mission in the search after truth, unless he also feels that it is good for him and for mankind to find out as much as possible about the truth. The man who approaches Nature servilely crouching before it in terror, or aggressively despising it as though it were an impostor, is, in either case, disqualified for dispassionate scientific observation. He is the slave of prejudice, and prejudice is the parent of mal-observation and error. It may be urged indeed that for a man to "feel that it is good for him and for mankind to find out as much as possible about the truth" is a prejudice. But the difference is obvious. This last is a prejudice in favour of truth as against falsehood, and this can lead no man wrong: the former are prejudices in favour of one conclusion against another conclusion, and these can in the long run lead no man right. We are therefore justified in maintaining that a moral prejudice in favour of the ultimate utility of the discovery of all truth is a useful stimulus in scientific investigation.

Closely akin to the belief in the ultimate kindness of truth, so to speak, is the belief in the ultimate discoverableness of truth. Clearly theology may be in this respect a useful friend to science, or a formidable foe. If men believe in a religion which asserts that God fashioned man as an artificer fashions an image out of clay, and did *not* breathe any particle of the Divine essence into him ; which exhibits God as an inscrutable Sultan, whom to hear is to obey ; which calls God the Merciful and Compassionate, not because love is of the essence of His nature, but because, though all-powerful, He forbears to use His might for man's destruction ; and which asseverates that "verily, there is none in the heavens and the earth but shall approach the God of mercy *as a slave*"[1]—then it is obvious that so servile a theology cannot but discourage or annihilate the pursuit of truth. Accordingly, among Mohammedans, "it is the will of God" has proved an effective barrier to scientific speculation. What reason has the believer in an inscrutable

[1] See Osborn's *Islam under the Arabs*, Longmans and Co., p. 25.

Sultan for supposing that the laws of the universe are discoverable by the slaves of God? How much more will the seeker after truth be encouraged in his search if he can believe that "God hath set the world in the heart of men," or, in the words of Bacon, that "God hath framed the mind of man as a glass capable of the universal world (joying to receive the signature thereof) as the eye is of light!" Such a hopeful prejudice in favour of the ultimate discoverableness of all truth will be engendered by all theologies that teach us to worship a good God, but by none more than by that theology which teaches us, while we adore God as a Father, to respect men, not as His slaves but as His children, whose duty it is not only to hear and to obey, but also to hear with intelligence, and to obey with love.

The intellectual characteristic of the scientific spirit being generally understood, requires little to be said about it. It consists in the recognition of the sequence of phenomena in Nature as being necessary and not subject to interference. Whatever he may desire or hope, the man of science will not allow desire in the slightest degree to bias his scientific investigations. On the contrary, he will be carefully on his guard against allowing the "dry light of reason" to be drenched with the passions of flesh and blood. In a word, the leading characteristic of the scientific spirit, intellectually considered, is to recognize the inevitable. Poets and dreamers deal with the *might be*, but men of science deal with *must*.

I shall now attempt to show that Christ by His actions, His utterances, and His whole theory of Nature and of human life, tended to encourage the scientific spirit, whether morally or intellectually considered. In passing first to the actions of Christ, I shall not be blamed by the sceptic for putting aside, at least for the moment, those miracles of Christ, which, if historically accurate, must necessarily be accepted as violations of all known laws of nature. According to our principle, these must be regarded as accretions round the original narrative, and must, therefore, for the present, be disregarded. But, in passing, I must deprecate the charge of arbitrarily putting aside everything that militates against my views of Christ's life. Sceptics at all events (and it is to them that I am addressing myself) have no right to bring this charge. They ought to admit at once that there is nothing arbitrary in putting aside all that is, on the face of it, unnatural and legendary, and yet retaining all that is natural and intrinsically credible. The only objection that should suggest itself to them is this, "How can you feel sure that the same causes which led the early historians of the Church to introduce legendary narratives, did not also lead them to invent other narratives of possible events, and accounts of possible utterances, all which may rest upon the same unsound basis as those very legends which you are putting aside?" My answer is that the Gospels contain a thread of narrative which is far beyond the invention of any human being, or collection of human beings; that they exhibit a Life and Character, the portraiture of which—if no such Being had ever existed—would entitle the painters of it to a place far, very far, above our own Shakespeare, and that the hypothesis of a collaborative production of a Christ by a little knot of

Christian philosophers will always stand condemned as an absurdity by the common sense of mankind. Moreover, it would be easy to show how all the miraculous part of the narrative may have arisen without the slightest falsification, or intention to deceive, and in many cases the result of mere misunderstanding. How this may have been I shall try briefly to indicate hereafter.[1] For the present let us return to our immediate subject, which is the non-miraculous actions of Christ, His utterances, and His theory of life, considered with relation to their influence on science.

First, then, the actions of Christ plainly recognize the inevitable *must be*, and the sequence of cause and effect. It is true that He worked sudden and remarkable cures, which, though not supernatural in the sense of violating the laws of nature, are yet supernatural in the degree in which they exhibited the power of His personal influence upon those who surrounded Him : but He recognized the necessity of faith for the performance even of these cures, and, where faith was absent, it is expressly recorded that He was not able to do any mighty work. Moreover, there is no trace (as far as I know even in the suggestions of enemies) that His faith in His own Divine powers ever led Him to attempt any action in which He failed. There is nothing in the life of Jesus like the conduct of the Egyptian false prophet, who led thirty thousand Jews from the wilderness into the neighbourhood of the Roman garrison in Jerusalem, to see the walls fall, as the walls of Jericho had fallen in the days

---

[1] I have relegated the sketch of this theory to an Appendix, partly that it may not break the argument here, and partly that it may not obtrude itself upon those to whom the miracles, literally taken, present no difficulty, whom I should advise not to trouble themselves about the Appendix.

of old. The Egyptian's promise of a definite sign at a definite time was just the kind of pledge that Jesus persistently refused to the importunate Pharisees. His signs and mighty works of healing flowed naturally from Him, as words of pity from us : they were the natural expressions of what He felt, or rather saw. They were the results of insight into law, not violations of law, and they proved themselves, by success, to be in accordance with the deepest laws of Nature.

In modern times Christ's acts of healing, so far from being regarded as the basis of faith in Him, have come to be looked on as stumbling-blocks. I have said elsewhere that most of those miracles which are not acts of healing appear to me to be later accretions round the original narrative, and often the results of a mistaken interpretation of metaphorical language ; but the miracles of healing, however the narrative may be here and there brightened by later picturesque detail, rest on a different footing, and must be accepted as having a basis of actual fact. It is not possible to study physiology in however rudimentary a manner without recognizing that certain diseases, in particular paralysis, are susceptible to cure by a sudden emotional shock. How far Christ's miracles of healing may be explained in this way, as being natural in kind and supernatural only in degree, or how far the narratives may have been subjected to non-historical picturesque development and exaggeration, I am not prepared to say.[1] But I do not think it is possible to study the Epistles of St. Paul and the history of the

---

[1] Dr. Carpenter's *Mental Physiology*, p. 680, contains instances of physiological phenomena authenticated by "excellent authority," quite as wonderful as some of the most startling of Christ's miracles.

early Church, without recognizing that the early followers of Christ, and *à fortiori* Christ Himself, had a remarkable power of healing disease.

But it is objected that though Christ probably did work acts of healing, yet He *ought not* to have worked them. "If He had power over men's bodies (which we will grant for argument's sake), then that power was a disturbing element, obscuring His real greatness, not helping it." This objection is to me quite unintelligible. If it be once admitted that Christ had the power to work cures in a natural way, sometimes without His volition, through the mere force of the faith of the diseased, but more often by some exercise of will on His part, will anyone venture to maintain that He ought to have sent sick people away unhealed, when He could heal them with a word? "But such acts obscured His real greatness." This is simply not true. They were the natural vehicles by which His real greatness was made perceptible to the gross hearts of thousands who could have perceived no greatness that was not made vivid for them by some visible sign. As the physical sufferings of Christ upon the cross have conveyed to mankind (although they have not always known it) the sense of some deeper, invisible, and indefinable suffering, the conception of which, without the sight of that visible suffering, could never have entered into the hearts of men, so it has been with the acts of healing performed by Jesus. Men, who scarcely knew they had souls, have drawn near to Him as the great Healer, and, learning by degrees to see in Him somewhat more than the mere Healer of the body, have learned to see in themselves somewhat more than mere flesh. If Christ had not worked "signs," how could the Christian faith have lasted through the dark ages, and which of us would now be worshipping Him and acknowledging His "real greatness?"

I contend therefore that Christ not only did work signs of healing—for this is certain—but also that He did nothing unworthy of Himself and nothing contrary to science in working them. Moreover, by these signs He committed His followers for ever to a care for the physical as well as the moral welfare of mankind; He secured them (as far as He could) against all superstitious shapes of asceticism; He pledged them to regard health as a divine gift, and disease as an evil, and to believe that we are not to crouch before the evils of Nature, but to contend against them with the divine aid, being confident that they are nothing but transitory accidents.

Turning for a moment to the Epistles of St. Paul, we shall see at once how very soberly the Spirit of Christ taught the followers of Christ to estimate their powers of instantaneous healing. St. Paul appears to have taken for granted, as a matter of course, not only in himself, but also in many other believers, the power of working signs and acts of healing, but he places it after wisdom, knowledge, and faith. No doubt he may not have been aware of the naturalness of his extraordinary power; but, estimating it as supernatural, or, if you will, as unnatural, he nevertheless declares that though he could "remove mountains" yet had not love, he would be nothing. Indeed in a certain sense St. Paul acknowledges that this very gift of healing is natural, when he attributes it to the same Spirit who gives some the power of declaring God's will, others the power of teaching, and others the power of governing. The gift of healing was therefore regarded by him as but one among many gifts which we should call natural, and as being by no means the greatest of those gifts: "Are all apostles? Are all prophets? Are all teachers? Are all workers of miracles? Have all the gifts of healing? Do all speak with tongues? Do all interpret? But covet earnestly the best gifts; and yet show I unto you a more excellent way. Though I speak with the tongues of men and of angels, and have not charity, I am become as sounding brass or a tinkling cymbal." What language could more convincingly prove the authenticity of "signs" in the early Church, or more soberly and scientifically—and spiritually—estimate them at their true spiritual value?

Again, there is something very suggestive of the scientific condition of mind in the sobriety with which Jesus recognized what we should call the drift of circumstances, and conformed His course to it. When the Apostles return from their missionary journey, He recognizes the failure of the Kingdom of God to reveal itself to the wise and prudent, and sees in it the will of God. When the shadow of unpopularity begins to fall upon Him, and failure and death loom not far off, He does not at first court death, but suffers homelessness and exile for a time till He has ascertained that the seed of faith has been sown, and His work so far advanced that it will not perish. But as soon as St. Peter's confession makes it clear that the new Church is founded, He at once recognizes that His hour is come, and sets His face toward Jerusalem. Lastly, on the eve of His death, when the certainty of ultimate triumph is broken in upon by the thought of the terrible trial through which He must pass on His way to victory, He even subjects His own prayers to the restraints of *possibility*, "*If* it be *possible*, let this cup pass from Me." What can be a stronger corroboration of the willingness of Jesus to learn by experience, and what is more scientific than this habit of mind? Lest anyone should shrink through reverence from attributing such a quality to the Saviour, we may remind ourselves that it is insisted on both by the Evangelist who speaks of Jesus "growing in wisdom," and by the writer of the Epistle to the Hebrews, who tells us that Jesus, "Though He were a Son, yet learned obedience by the things which He suffered." Now all this would prove nothing in the case of a worldly, scheming, unscrupulous founder of a religion; but in One confessedly unworldly and unselfish, who spoke of Himself as the Son of God, and who acted and taught as though His whole life were a continuous vision of heavenly things, such a willingness to learn argues an absence of fanaticism and a truly scientific sobriety.

We pass to the sayings of Jesus, and here we must expect to be confronted with an apparent discrepancy between two classes of utterances. In the one class Jesus insists upon the *may be*, in the other He recognizes the *must*. For example, He tells a man that "all things are possible for him that believeth;" He declares that "with God all things are possible;" and that "if two or three of you shall agree on earth as touching anything that they shall ask, it shall be done for them of My Father which is in heaven." In the other class of utterances He declares that "it must needs be that offences will come," and that this or that is "given" or "not given." How are we to explain the apparent contradiction? I answer, by bearing in mind that when Jesus says "all things are possible," in the first place He always implies those things which He considered most real and most difficult, such as the invisible acts of repentance and forgiveness, and entrance into the kingdom of God; and in the next place He always implies the addition—"for him that believeth." Very often the context clearly shows that in these utterances Jesus is thinking not of material, but of spiritual operations. For example, the promise above quoted, relative to prayer, immediately follows a discourse concerning forgiveness; and the intention of it is to emphasize in the strongest way the social power to be exercised by the new Church in the forgiveness of sins. Considered in this light, the asseveration that "all things are possible" is simply an intense assurance that the superhuman task of forgiving sins (so much more difficult, as it seemed to Christ, than the uprooting of a tree or the subversion of a mountain!) should be made possible for men by faith in the Father. This follows at once from the nature of faith. Faith means insight. If two or three of the disciples met together in faith, Jesus promised to them a special influence of the spirit of fellowship, which should illumine their faith or insight with a special brightness, so that they should, as it were, see the Father's will, and, seeing it, be guided to pray, not for the impossible, but for the possible. Nay, more, just as we co-operate with God habitually by action, so Jesus seems to have contemplated our co-operating with God by prayer, so as to produce results not reflecting on ourselves alone. But in any case the prayer of faith must be fulfilled, not perhaps in the way expected, but, if not, then in a better and more satisfying way.

If this explanation of the saying "all things are possible" seems to my readers a very thin and unsatisfying extenuation of very forcible words, I can only say that may perhaps be because we are not sufficiently alive to the reality of invisible things, and do not discern how much nobler and harder it is to forgive a sin in the perfection in which Christ forgave sins, than to uproot a tree or subvert a mountain. But passing by that consideration for the present, let me ask what other explanation can be given of this famous promise? Can it be said that it is a late interpolation? But whose interest could it be to interpolate a passage fraught with such obvious difficulty? Or did Jesus mean the promise literally and unconditionally? But how could He mean to make a promise which would not only be immoral and arbitrary and utterly unlike the whole tenor of His life, but, moreover, could be immediately tested and belied? Two of His disciples appear, indeed, so far to have misunderstood Him as to be induced by these words to come to Him asking for the places of honour near His throne. But what was the reply of Jesus? "It shall be given to those for whom it has been prepared." Does not this answer in itself contain by implication a sufficient proof that the promise was intended to be spiritually, not literally construed?

Let us now pass to the predictions of Jesus. Of all of them it may be said that, however much they may look forward to the far-off joyful *will be,* they recognize the intervention of the painful *must be*. Again, they are not narrow, eccentric, and particular, like the predictions of a fanatic, who reads himself into the future. They are true prophecies, based upon prophetic intuition into the laws of the universe.

No one has ever spoken more strongly than Jesus of the power of prayer, yet no one has been more free from the fault described by Plato as that of "feigning things like unto one's prayers." He sowed the seed broadcast, but He predicted that much of it would be utterly wasted, and little would ultimately come to full perfection, saying that to some it is given to understand the things of the kingdom of God, but to others "it is not given." He cried woe unto the world because of offences; but all His pity did not prevent Him from seeing that "it must needs be that offences will come." He wept over Jerusalem, but He pronounced its doom in accordance with the eternal law; it must perish because it knew not the time of its visitation. He longed—can we doubt it?—for the time when the final and blessed *will be* should swallow up the painful intervening *must;* but He sternly asserted the necessity of the intervention, wars and rumours of wars, and great tribulation, "these things *must first be.*" Moreover He distinctly declared that the sequence of spiritual events was illustrable by the sequences of material Nature: they followed, He said, as the shower follows the cloud, or as heat follows the south wind, and might be conjectured as one conjectures the arrival of spring from the budding of the trees. Why were people so blind and dull as not to discern the inevitability of spiritual as well as material laws? Surely the teachers of Israel must be able to see this, unless they wilfully shut their eyes to it. Certainly, if they did not see it, they were worse than fools, they were hypocrites: "Ye hypocrites, ye can discern the face of the sky and of the earth; but how is it that ye do not discern this time?" Is not this recognition of the inevitable sequence of cause and effect in the spiritual world eminently characteristic of the scientific spirit?

Regarded from the miraculous point of view, the predictions of Jesus are deficient because they enter into no striking or verifiable detail, the verification of which would increase the wonder at the coincidence of the result with the predictions; but this very deficiency makes them more scientifically acceptable. To those who desire to regard Jesus as human it cannot fail to be most welcome that He should base His predictions on the general laws and tendencies of things, and that, although He predicted a Day of the Lord, He Himself expressly said that the exact time of it was not known to Him. Passing over one or two apparent exceptions of minor importance, I will refer here to one alone, which is by far the most important, I mean the prophecy about the date of His resurrection.[1] Now here, undoubtedly, we seem to be confronted with an unnatural prediction such as would rather tend to shake than strengthen our faith in the Son of Man. That He should predict His resurrection seems natural and fit; for that fore-knowledge could be based upon the certainty that death could not triumph over Him, and that His spirit must continue His incomplete work; but the mention of the "third day"

---

[1] The reference to Jonah (Matthew xii. 40) appears to be not an utterance of Jesus, but the result of a later misconception of the "sign of Jonah."

is a stumbling-block. It is true that the narrative of the Gospels lays evident stress upon the date, and that the early Church did the same : but, so far from bringing conviction home to modern minds, that might rather suggest the possibility of some early modification of the prediction in conformity with the subsequent fact. There are, however, some words in the prophecy of Hosea which may perhaps remove the difficulty without supposing that our Lord's words were in any material respect materially altered by the narrative; the words are these, " Come and let us return unto the Lord : for He hath torn, and He will heal us; He hath smitten, and He will bind us up. *After two days will He revive us; in the third day He will raise us up, and we shall live in His sight.*" Now we know how constantly Jesus declared that He came to fulfil the law and the prophets, how He identified Himself with the Suffering Messiah to whom the prophecies pointed, and how constantly He used extracts from the prophecies to illustrate His own career. We have therefore only to suppose—surely not an improbable hypothesis—that Jesus used these words of Hosea to describe His own future certain resurrection, and the difficulty in the way of sceptics is at once removed. The subsequent misinterpretation of the prophecy is easily explicable on the ground of the early tendency to fasten upon every symptom of thaumaturgy in the life of Christ.

Turning now to the rule of life laid down by Christ for His disciples, we may ask, Is there anything unscientific or fanatical in that ? He certainly makes great promises to His followers; but does He promise anything that He could not naturally perform ? He promises them rest and peace, and every heavenly blessing. He assures them that if men will do God's will and act as His children, they will find themselves completely in harmony with Nature, and they cannot possibly suffer harm. They may be slain, but that is nothing: God will not suffer a hair of their heads to be injured. Therefore instead of wearing out their souls about the fine things and necessary things of life, let men take their natural course, as the birds do and the flowers do, and let them be sure that the Father in heaven would care for His human children no less than for birds and flowers. But what was, what is, the natural course for men? The natural course is to seek first the kingdom of God, that is, to aim always at doing the high will within us, not the low will within us. In detail the natural course might vary, but the principle would always remain the same. To seek first the kingdom of God did not necessarily imply giving up one's handicraft or trade, leaving one's home, selling one's wealth, depending upon others for one's daily bread. It might imply all or any of these things, but it did not necessarily: such minor details must be determined by the Spirit. The plain duty of man remained in any case always the same, to seek first the kingdom of God. If that involved giving up lands and home and parents, God would give in this life a hundredfold, now in this time, houses and brethren, and sisters, and mothers, and children, and lands with persecutions, and in the world to come eternal life.

Where is the fanaticism, where is there anything in the slightest degree unscientific in all this? What is this but the blessing pronounced by our own poet upon those minds which, being harmoniously wedded to the universe, are able

> " To hold fit converse with the spiritual world :
> Such minds are truly from the Deity,
> For they are powers, and hence the highest bliss
> That flesh can know is theirs, the consciousness
> Of Whom they are, habitually infused
> Through every image and through every thought,
> And all affections by communion raised
> From earth to heaven."

Surely no one will maintain in the face of obvious consequent absurdities that Christ claimed for His disciples any exemption from the Laws of Nature, or made any but conditional promises, the fulfilment of which followed naturally upon the fulfilment of the conditions, as effect follows upon cause. Even the most superficial glance at the two promises quoted above will show that they could not be intended to be taken literally. No amount of wilful determination to misunderstand the character of Christ can carry a sceptic to the point of supposing that He intended to promise His disciples literally " in this life a hundredfold brethren, and sisters, and mothers ; " and the addition in St. Mark's Gospel, " with persecutions," renders the meaning obviously this, that in return for the loss of the common earthly blessings of life, God would bestow upon the disciples a hundredfold the happiness derivable from those blessings even now in this present life. Again, how is it possible to give a literal interpretation to the promise, " Not a hair of your head shall perish," when in the same breath we find " Some of you shall they cause to be put to death " ? It cannot be too often repeated that the mind of Jesus was ever moving amid eternal and invisible realities, of which this visible world furnishes but imperfect and relatively unreal counterparts. He regarded Himself as at every moment in His life working with the Father. Whatever He did on earth He *saw* simultaneously done by the Father in heaven. "The Son," He said,[1] "can do nothing of Himself but what He seeth the Father do.... I can of Mine own self do nothing." Just as Wordsworth, though a profound lover of visible Nature, loved and worshipped through the visible unreality an invisible and real Nature, so, and in a far higher sense, it may be said of Jesus of Nazareth, that while He had the eye of an artist or of a man of science for the beauty and order of visible things, He had also the eye of a seer which, rove where it might, discerned the realities of things—

> "An eye
> Which from a tree, a stone, a withered leaf
> To the broad ocean and the azure heavens,
> Spangled with kindred multitudes of stars,
> Could find no surface where its power might sleep."

Hence when Jesus spoke of bread, wine, water, fire, harvest, seed, leaven, birth, life, death, resurrection, baptism, the blind, the deaf, the lame, He had continually in His mind the Bread of Life, the Wine of the Kingdom of God, the Water of Everlasting Life, the purifying and destroying Fire of the Wrath of God, the Harvest of Righteousness, the Seed of the Word of God, the silent and wholesome influence of the Kingdom, or the stealthy and pernicious influence of Hypocrisy, the Birth into the

[1] The result of many years of study devoted to the "Common Tradition" of the first Three Gospels (and I set out with something of a prejudice against the Fourth) has led me to the conclusion that, although it may be in many parts non-historic, the Fourth Gospel rightly interprets the character of Christ.

Family of God—and, in a word, the spiritual realities, and not the mere earthly unrealities, corresponding to all human names.

This consideration would bring us once more to the subject touched on above, I mean the misunderstanding of Christ by His disciples, and the effect of this misunderstanding in colouring the narratives of miracles in the Gospels. But reserving any remarks on that subject for an Appendix, we content ourselves for the present with claiming this all events, that, whether sceptics agree with us or not in our explanation of the origin of the miraculous part of the narrative of the Gospels, they shall not urge the miraculous element against us as any proof that Christ "had no attitude at all towards science, and never dreamed of it." They cannot at one and the same time allege that Christ worked no miracles, and yet bring forward what they believe to be false narratives of miracles wrongly imputed to Him, as proofs that His influence was unfavourable to science. I believe it can be demonstrated—but if it cannot, it can readily be conceived—that Christ's influence was antithaumaturgic and scientific; that the thaumaturgic and unscientific misconception of parts of his life was not due to His teaching, but in spite of it; and that such a misconception would have inevitably gathered round the life of any great Reformer in Israel. Unless therefore men can prove that Christ is responsible for the belief in thaumaturgy, they have no right to assume it. What they must do must be to fall back upon that part of the narrative which is natural and credible, and to draw their inferences from that. Now we have attempted to show that, in all this part of the narrative,

Christ's words and acts reveal a spirit, both morally and intellectually eminently favourable to science.

Only contrast the tenor of Mohammed's precepts with those of Christ, and we shall see more clearly how very anti-scientific Christ's influence *might* have been, but—fortunately for Christendom—was not. The religion of Mohammed abounds with minute and servile ritual, which pervades all life, infecting and weakening the intellect as well as the moral sense. Christ told His disciples that they need not fast till the days of fasting and sorrow came naturally upon them. Mohammed marked out a defined period for the most rigorous abstinence, and made the fast in the month Ramadhan, one of the five pillars of the religion of Islam.[1] Christ said that the inside, not the outside, was to be purified. "Alas for the soles of their feet," cried Mohammed at the sight of some who had neglected that part of their body in their ablutions, "for verily they shall be burned in the fire of hell." Christ taught us that wheresoever we are gathered together in prayer, He is in the midst of us, and that neither in Gerizim, nor in Jerusalem, but in the Spirit, we are to worship the Father. Mohammed set up pilgrimages as another of the "five pillars" of religion, and enacted a fixed proportion between prayers in different places, so that a prayer in a mosque was worth twenty-five prayers at home, and it needed one hundred thousand prayers in one's own house to equal the merit of a single prayer in the sacred place at Mecca. Christ expressly warned His disciples that His work was incomplete, and

[1] See page 70 in *Islam under the Arabs*, by Major Osborn, to whom I am also indebted for the following details.

that He could bequeath to them not a law, but a Spirit, to guide them into all truth ; Mohammed, as though to bar all future growth of thought, makes God declare, " as a code in the Arabic tongue, we have sent down the Koran ; " and, still further to bind His disciples, he declared that the very words and syllables of the book were directly inspired by God, and written down, in some cases, by himself, acting unintelligently as the mere pen of the Almighty. Mohammed was servilely copied by his disciples in every minute particular of his life : there is no trace of such a servility in the conduct of the earliest followers of Christ. The very voice and intonation of the Prophet in reading the Koran seemed a matter to be studied by the disciples of Mohammed : " In what voice," said one of the companions to Ayesha, " did the Prophet read the Koran at night ? Did he read it in a loud voice, or did he read it in a low voice ?" And upon Ayesha's replying that the Prophet read sometimes in a loud and sometimes in a low voice, the companion exclaimed in rapture, " Praise be to God, who hath made religion so spacious and unconfined ! " Compare this gratitude for small mercies with the religion—surely far better entitled to be called "spacious and unconfined "—of that apostle who declared that Christ dwells in our hearts through faith, and that " though we have known Christ after the flesh, yet now henceforth we know Him no more."

In fine, if the scientific man expressly wanted a religion invented for his benefit and encouragement, I do not know how he could invent a religion better adapted for his purpose than the natural worship of Christ. It liberates him from all immoral fear of truth, and teaches him to love truth for its own sake, and to believe in the ultimate kindness of truth; yet at the same time it teaches him not to neglect the intervening steps on the path to Truth, and warns him that those steps, though painful, are inevitable, and that no one can claim that exemption from them which Christ Himself did not claim. It bids him become a little child with all a child's hopefulness and trustfulness, and with the exploring, aspiring spirit characteristic of the young, but at the same time with that "single eye" of childhood, which, when it sees a sight for the first time, takes in all that it sees, but adds nothing that it does not see. It encourages peace, sobriety, self-control, and discourages those passions which most frequently divert from or distort the truth. Lastly, it expressly forbids us to stand still, it denies our indolence the luxury of servilely obeying a rigid code, and it encourages us to hope that we are all possessed with a spirit not only of light, but of life, which will enable us to grow in grace and in knowledge.

"Still, though it may be admitted that Christ's influence was favourable to science, it cannot be shown that He in any way recognized it or had any attitude towards it. There is no evidence at all to prove that He even foresaw the wonderful development of science and the degree to which it would affect human life." Those who make this objection would do well to state what Christ ought to have done in their opinion, and what amount of recognition of science would have satisfied their requirements. It cannot seriously be maintained that Christ ought to have introduced, or even predicted, the scientific discoveries which were destined to be made in the course of centuries ; that He should have anticipated Newton in the discovery of the law of gravitation, that He should have rectified the notions of history or of physiology current among His countrymen. Such a monstrosity would have been as portentously unmeaning as the introduction of philology, or geology, or the English language, two thousand years before its time. What then would they desire that the best and most perfect of teachers should have done, if it had been His express object to lead mankind to science ? Consider the circumstances of mankind, and then ask whether any teacher could have done better than Christ did for science as well as for morality.

When Christ entered the world He found art decrepit and science stationary. And why ? Because morality, the basis of art and science, was decrepit. The world was in the condition of a clever boy at school, who has been pushed forward a little too fast, and has accumulated rather more of knowledge and mechanical habit than is proportioned to his original power. When a good teacher finds a boy in this condition, he knows well enough that a break must be made in the pupil's studies. The boy has learned, it may be, to produce fifth-rate verses with a fatal facility, and to write out his mathematical book-work with such ease that he does not give himself the trouble of thinking about it. Now what such a boy wants is, not more knowledge of verses, nor more knowledge of mathematical book-work, but to go back again to first principles and to be made to think simply. He must be emancipated from conventionalism and begin again from the beginning like a little child. The best thing for a boy at such a crisis is, very often an illness for a few weeks. The break in his studies, so far from being a hindrance, is a help; for what Bacon says about men is true also of boys, "Let not a man force a habit upon himself with a perpetual continuance: but with some intermission. For both the pause reinforceth the new onset; and if a man that is not perfect be ever in practice, he shall as well practise his errors as his abilities."

Now in precisely the same condition Christ found the world. Imitativeness had long succeeded originality in Greece, and was soon to succeed it in Rome, if indeed Rome was ever original. Conventionalism flourished because faith in truth was extinct. "What is truth?" said the cynical world of antiquity, and would not stay for an answer. The course adopted therefore by the great Teacher of the world was to put the world back for a while in science and art, and to give it a course of morality. Such a course was needed for two reasons. In the first place, morality was needed as a basis for science and art; and in the second place, the "pause" in science and art was necessary to "reinforce the new onset" in science and art. Such a course commends itself to all who know anything of teaching, and it commends itself also by its success. Those therefore who infer from Christ's supposed non-recognition of science that He "never dreamed of it," appear to me to draw an inference not justified by what we know of the art of teaching, not justified by what we know of the scientific success resulting from Christ's teaching, and least of all justified by what we know of the great Teacher Himself, who declared that all earthly blessings should in the end be added to those that sought the

Kingdom of God, and who promised us a Spirit that should guide mankind unto all truth. Why should it be supposed that when Christ spoke of "all truth," He did not mean "all truth"? By "truth" Christ always meant "knowledge of the Father," and so far as science widens our knowledge of Him, so far Christ included science in His promise.

"Then, after all, history is mistaken, and it was not the Church of Christ that in former times condemned and silenced Galileo, and in later times has set itself against the discoveries of geology." No, it was not the Church of Christ. It was Ecclesiasticism; it was Religious Conservatism; it was the legal formal spirit of Pharisaism, again and again reappearing and destined to reappear within the circle of those who call themselves Christ's followers: it was Christianity, if you will, but certainly it was not Christ, nor men acting in Christ's spirit. The spirit of Christ was in Galileo, not in Galileo's persecutors. The spirit of Christ was in Copernicus, and Kepler, and Newton: it was to some extent in all the great seekers after truth who lived among the old Egyptians, and Greeks, and Romans, in the days before the Incarnation; it is even more present in many modern seekers after truth who reject Him because they have never understood Him, but who, in worshipping goodness and truth, unconsciously worship Him. The spirit of Christ has been powerful everywhere —how could it be otherwise?—freeing men from fears, prejudices, distrusts, giving them hope, simplicity, patience, humility, and a passion for truth, and thus leading mankind up to new scientific knowledge as well as to spiritual truth. Poorly indeed have the nations

THE TRUE SPIRIT OF SCIENCE. 327

of Christendom fulfilled their Master's precept to "seek first the kingdom of God"! The next century may see perhaps some approximation, a little less pitiable, towards obedience to that divine precept: and then, no doubt, obedience will bring its promised consequence. But even as it is, such inadequate deliverance from the darkness of superstition and fear as has yet been attained has resulted in an inevitable and consequent dispersion of scientific error. So far as the kingdom of God has been honestly sought, so far "all other things" have been added to mankind.

Yet while we recognize the benefit accruing to science from Christ's teaching, let us also thankfully acknowledge the benefit accruing to mankind from Christ's subordination of science to that ampler knowledge to which He gave the name of the Truth. Science has her part to play in the world's development; but she will play it best when she plays it humbly, remembering that her province is but an infinitesimal portion of the vast globe of knowledge, and that she is not worthy so much as to touch the hem of the garment of Morality, in whose steps she must tread as a servant, or from whom she will deviate only to stray into by-paths of arrogance and error.

CHAPTER XX.

THE TRUE SPIRIT OF ART.

BUT even if it be conceded that the Spirit of Jesus is favourable to science, it will be urged that there is still a deficiency. We shall be told that, though Jesus taught us how to live in the Good, and perhaps conducted us on the way to living in the Whole, yet He did not teach us how to live in the Beautiful : " Towards Art, at all events, Jesus had no sort of attitude." Here again in this second extraordinary misappreciation of the character of Christ we may trace the overshadowing of Christ Himself by Catholicism or Christianity, and it will be easy to show that the Spirit of Christ is the true Spirit of Art.

When we speak of art in this sense, we include, I suppose, none but the arts that produce beauty, whether in form, colour, sound, or thought ; and by art I presume we mean the exercise of the artistic faculty and the appreciation of artistic work. Now what does our artist want of us ? What will he have us do that the disciples of Jesus of Nazareth would not naturally do ? Perhaps he will tell us that he would have us admire beauty unaffectedly ; we are to be absorbed in it. He will even add, in his hyperbolical way, that we are to "worship" beauty. Well, if by bidding us worship beauty he means to inculcate on us that ecstatic admiring habit of mind in which Wordsworth approaches Nature—as, for example, when his heart "leaps up" at the sight of the rainbow in the sky—that is precisely the attitude towards beauty which is inculcated by Christ.

Let us consider somewhat more in detail the artistic spirit. In the first place, I presume, it will be admitted that it is a mark of the artistic spirit to delight in the truth of nature, and not the rules and precepts of men. Another mark is to be intensely unconventional. Rules and unities, and all the shackles of conventionalism, art cannot away with; they are an abomination unto it. As morality hardens into formality beneath law (in the Pauline sense), so art becomes lifeless and criticisms perverse beneath the shade of conventionalism. The withering influence of rules and unities manifests itself in such criticisms as that of Frederic the Great, "A dispassionate judge will acknowledge that the *Henriade* is superior to the poems of Homer."[1] The artist tells us with something like passion that it is a sin to substitute the rules of men for the worship of nature. But does not Christ, in the same spirit, protest against the Pharisees for "teaching for doctrine the commandments of men"? The whole of the life of Christ and the whole of the teaching of St. Paul go to prove this, if anything, that men are to be henceforth not under a law, but under a spirit: does not the artist in the same way declare that Nature is not to be servilely copied, but that we are to enter into her spirit by the free worship

[1] See "Natural Religion," *Macmillan's Magazine*, October 1876.

of the heart? Again, if the artist declares that no amount of mere overlaid information can ever compensate for the absence of the inner love of beauty, and that the hand is useless where the heart is dead, does not Christ also declare that the inside, not the outside, of the platter is to be cleansed, that a corrupt tree cannot bring forth good fruit, and that it is only from the treasure of a good heart that a man can bring forth good things? The artist is speaking of art, and Christ is speaking of morality, but the principle in either case is the same. The Samaritan woman represents the vulgar deference to authority or conventionalism, "Our fathers worshipped in this mountain, and ye say that in Jerusalem is the place where men ought to worship;" here are two conflicting authorities or conventionalities, and the question for her is, Which is to be obeyed? But Jesus represents at once true art and true morality in putting them both aside. "Woman, believe me, the hour cometh when ye shall neither in this mountain, nor yet at Jerusalem, worship the Father. God is a Spirit, and they that worship Him must worship Him in spirit and in truth."

Closely akin to the Philistinism which is represented by the sincere admiration of conventionalism, there comes the insincere repetition of conventionalities for interested purposes. This is hypocrisy, and is alike hateful both in morality and in art. The worship of Nature, says the artist, is to be not at second-hand, but at first-hand. There is something almost æsthetically as well as morally sinful in the man who would wait to admire a picture or a poem till he has ascertained what the great ones say about it. An artistic nation will not be one in which an oligarchy of taste dictates admiration to the rabble, but one in which "they shall no longer say each man to his brother, know the Beautiful, but they shall all know it, from the least to the greatest." Now by what teacher in the world, I would ask, was the insincere repetition of rules and conventionalities ever so fiercely attacked as by Jesus of Nazareth? Who ever, as He did, held up to scorn the sin of saying that a thing is right when you know it in your heart to be wrong? But in thus condemning hypocrisy and recommending truth, Christ was condemning all hypocrisy and recommending all truth : and the spirit of truth extends no less to art than it does to science and to goodness.

Let us consider other characteristics of the artistic spirit. While the artist is to be absorbed in beauty, he is not to lose sanity and self-control. He has, after all, his laws. They are the "exceeding broad" commandments of the spirit, and not of the letter of art. Notwithstanding he must not suffer his freedom to degenerate into lawlessness. He is to be "passionate"— to quote the well-known dictum of Milton—and he is to be "sensuous;" but he is also to be "simple," and he cannot be simple, if he is narrow, and eccentric, and crotchetty, straying into little private eddies and backwaters of his own, quite away from the current of human thought. Again, the artist is to have an eye for the quiet things and the little things in Nature, as well as for her larger and more ostentatious acts. Both these characteristics may be traced in the life of Jesus, and both would naturally result from the influence of His Spirit. The sobriety of Jesus has often been remarked on and contrasted with the uncontrolled fanaticism of other religious teachers. It appears in the high value which He sets upon rest, "Come unto Me ye that are weary and heavy laden, and I will give you *rest;*" in the tact with which He adapts His precepts to His disciples, calling one to take up the cross, but sending another home to his friends; in the gentleness and considerateness with which He treats His followers, and, above all, in His recognition, described above, of the inevitable *must*. Even more obvious than His sobriety is His love for whatever is despised and neglected. What St. Paul says about God's preferring the weak things of this world to overcome the strong, and the foolish things of this world to overcome the weak, admirably illustrates Christ's way of looking at Nature. In His message to John the Baptist, describing the signs of His work, He places highest in the climax, not the opening of the eyes of the blind,[1] nor the unstopping of the ears of the deaf, but the preaching of the Gospel to the poor. What is highly esteemed by men, He pronounces to be abomination in the eyes of God. The splendour of Solomon is not to be compared with the beauty of a flower. Not a sparrow falls to the ground without the knowledge of the Father. Little children are His especial delight, "They do always behold the face of My Father which is in heaven." He is never tired of inculcating the quietness of the spiritual process of redemption. Now it is the leaven in bread, now it is a wind or breath, breathing one knows not whence or whither, now it is the corn-seed rotting quietly in the

---

[1] Some of these expressions were possibly metaphorical; but the climax is still noteworthy.

ground while the husbandman sleeps and rises, night and day, till the seed "springs and grows up, he knoweth not how."

But it is in protesting against the brutal, bestial turn of mind which looks at the world as a great pig-stye, and on the ideal life as a continuous enjoyment of superabundant pig-wash, that Christ's influence on art is most clearly discerned. A life of this kind is described by St. Paul as a life "after the flesh," and he warns us that those who sow to the flesh shall of the flesh reap corruption. In the same spirit Christ describes such a life as a losing of the soul, and as having for its natural haven Gehenna, or the valley of Hinnom, or Hell. Gehenna, or the valley of Hinnom, was said to serve the purpose of being a receptacle for the refuse of Jerusalem; and such men as these were simply so much carrion, without salt to keep them untainted, fit for nothing but to be cast out as refuse from the New Jerusalem.

Now this bestial life "after the flesh," is it not as hateful to art as to morality? Is it not true in art as well as in morality, that men may prefer making money to worship? Do we not hear even in the present day that art is too often polluted because artists stoop to inferior work, or to slovenly work, for the sake of money? Against this low utilitarianism, hostile alike to morality and art, Jesus protests with almost as much vehemence as against hypocrisy. What a picture is drawn of the discomfited fool cut off in the midst of his plans of endless gorging! The parable of Dives and Lazarus may not perhaps come to us direct from Jesus Himself, but it represents faithfully His general attitude towards those who were replete with selfish pleasures, who hungered and thirsted after nothing higher, and who had received all that their souls desired, "*their* good things."

But it will be said, "These last words let out the secret you are so carefully suppressing, and reveal the fundamental deficiency of Christ's system. The object of art is to give pleasure; now Jesus not only does not encourage the pursuit of pleasure; He sets His face rigorously against it. The simple fact that one has been rich, or received 'good things' in this life is enough to secure endless torment in the next. This alone is proof enough that Christ's system is radically hostile to art." I reply that this unwarrantable assertion is due partly to a misunderstanding of Christ's words, and partly, once more, to the preponderance of Christianity over Christ. On the one hand we do not sufficiently understand how, when Christ spoke of hunger and thirst, of being full, and empty, being rich and being poor, He had in His mind spiritual, not material, conditions. To say therefore that a man had had "*his* good things" in this life would be equivalent to saying that he had what he wanted, and that he had no further aspirations. Undoubtedly Christ would have pronounced woe upon such a man. But what believer in art or goodness will say that Christ was wrong? What future can await one who has no aspirations that need a future for their fulfilment?

Surely a glance at Christ's life is enough to disprove the notion that He despised the physical welfare and pleasures of men, or that He thought it a merit to be unhappy. It was the Pharisees, not He, that treated pain as being of little account. To cure disease Jesus was ready to break the Sabbath. It is in connection with this readiness that we understand the meaning of His famous saying, that "the Sabbath was made for man." He meant that this (and He implied that every other) religious ordinance was intended to develop man's *whole* nature, and not merely the religious element. It was equivalent to saying, in modern phrase, religion is intended to develop the artistic and scientific as well as the moral side of humanity. It is true that He exhorted His followers to be contented with a minimum of material comforts, and forbade them on their first missionary journey to encumber themselves with baggage, or even to make themselves independent of hospitality. But in the first place this was a special order, afterwards abrogated; and in the second place, He told them to do this, not for the purpose of making themselves uncomfortable (which would have been asceticism), but simply in order to enable them to do their work more effectually. Instead of shunning festivity, He seems to have courted it, and many of His familiar illustrations are drawn from banquets and wedding-feasts, insomuch that His enemies attacked Him as "a gluttonous man and a wine-bibber." When the laxity of His disciples in the matter of fasting gave offence to some, He peremptorily refused to institute formal fasts. Days of sorrow and parting would come, He declared, when fasting would be natural; then and then only should His disciples fast. At the very moment when He advises them to be content with food and raiment, He shows by His manner that His object is to make His followers happy, not unhappy. They shall have everything they really want. He says, "Seek ye first the Kingdom of God, and all these things shall be added unto you;" and again, "Be not distracted about the morrow, sufficient unto the day is the evil thereof." What have we here but the artistic advice of the Epicurean poet—

> "Dona presentis cape lætus horæ et
> Linque severa"—

except indeed that Jesus welcomed the flying pleasure not as being "the gift of the present hour," but rather as the gift of the Father "who knoweth that we have need of these things." Surely all this points to one conclusion, that, although Jesus was "a Man of sorrows and acquainted with grief," yet beneath the sorrow He possessed an illimitable depth of peace and rest. Angelic thoughts ministered to Him in solitude, and heavenly food was supplied to Him. "I have meat to eat that ye know not of," He said to His disciples. The "meat" was what modern thought would call "communion with Nature;" but Christ, more truly, called it communion with God. Of Him, far more truly than of any human being may it be said, that He knew how to sorrow with men, because He knew also what it was to be at peace with the universe:

> "—In himself,
> Happy and quiet in his cheerfulness,
> He had no painful pressure from without,
> That made him turn aside from wretchedness
> With coward fears. He could afford to suffer
> With those whom he saw suffer."

Thus, then, regarded from every point of view, the influence of Jesus appears to be eminently favourable to the artistic spirit. It encourages simplicity and naturalness, and makes war against conventionalism and hypocrisy, whether in morality or in art. It encourages a passionate love of nature as being the manifestation of the Father; and it makes war both against the bestiality which would wallow in the world as a slough, and against the faithlessness which would criticize the universe as a mere machine. Again, it discourages ostentation and sensationalism, and encourages a love of the little things and a respect for the quiet processes in Nature. Lastly, it diffuses that profound peace, that calm consciousness of being on the side of truth, beauty, and goodness, which is equally favourable to science, to art, and to morality, and which should therefore enable the genuine worshipper of Christ to surpass the worshippers of all other religions in carrying into effect the advice of Goethe, " to live resolutely in the Whole, the Beautiful, and the Good."[1]

Those who cry out " We will have no religion but art : we do not care for the Good ; give us only the Beautiful," appear to be lamentably ignorant of the indissoluble dependence of art upon religion. The very art of the Greeks, which they would fain so servilely copy, and which they regard as a protest against religion, on the contrary, sprang out of religion. Both the Greek drama and the Greek art of sculpture point back to religion, not only as their cause, but also as their inspiring motive. It was not only that religion necessitated choral worship

[1] See "Natural Religion," for which I am indebted to many suggestions as to the relations between true Christianity and art. So far as I can gather, the author appears to regard the worship of Christ as supplemented by the worship of science and of art. I should rather regard the due homage paid to science and art as a *part* of the due worship of Christ. Hence, where the author of " Natural Religion " speaks of the " victory of the modern spirit " (in obtaining due recognition for science and art), I should rather speak of the victory of Christ over Catholicism, or over Christianity.

z

and images of stone; religion also inspired the Greek poets and sculptors with their divinest and most immortal conceptions. Had Phidias, do we suppose, no divine ideal of

> " chaste austerity
> And noble grace that dashed brute violence
> With sudden adoration and blank awe,"

when he wrought his statue of the " unconquered virgin " of Athens ? As soon as Greek art shook itself free from religion, sculpture fell from its pinnacle of dignity, and degenerated into prettinesses and elegances, and the tragedies of Æschylus and Sophocles made way for the comedies of Menander. At the time when Christ came into the world the fall of art was almost consummated. Dramatic art, the arts of sculpture and of painting, even the art of poetry (in spite of the apparent contradiction of the Augustan poets)—all were dead or on the point of dying. The arts which had been once the servants and interpreting priests unto the gods, had now degenerated till they had become mere panders to the vilest sensualities of men. There was but one reason to account for the death of art: art was dying because religion was dead. Christ came to give the world a new religion; and in revivifying religion, it was an absolute necessity, a law of human nature, that He should ultimately revivify art.

It is true that the earliest Christianity, naturally and indeed necessarily, assumed an antagonistic attitude towards pleasure. After Christ's death, when the Bridegroom had been taken away, the time of " fasting " predicted by Him came upon the Church. Many of the disciples were slain: almost all were persecuted and exposed to continual hardships, sufferings, and fears. Daily expecting the advent of the Son of Man as Judge of mankind seated upon the clouds, the Early Church had no leisure to look to earth and the pleasures of life on earth. The earthly pleasures of painting and sculpture, music and the dance, were in these days inextricably bound up with pagan worship, pagan processions, sacrifices, festivities; consequently they came to be shunned as deadly snares. By degrees, when art crept back into the Church as an instrument of worship, the Christian artist naturally desired to exalt the physical weakness by which the Church had triumphed over pagan strength, and to represent the morbid rather than the healthy side of men's physical nature. All this is true, and no one denies that early Christianity was (temporarily) unfavourable to art; but how can it be said that Christ was responsible for this? If it be maintained that He should have foreseen such an error in His followers, I would point to what has been said above,[1] and to what will be said hereafter, about illusions, and I would suggest that in all probability it was good for truth (in art as well as morality) that Greece should have been forgotten for a time, and no less good that Greece should be disinterred at the Renaissance. If Grecian art had remained conspicuous, the world would probably have given itself to a base and retrogressive imitativeness; if it had remained buried, the Spirit of Christ would have lacked its fittest shape of protest against the asceticism for which Christianity, and not Christ, was to blame.

The old Greek and Roman poets, as we have seen, looked at nature from a utilitarian point of view: grass,

[1] See Chapters V. and XXI.

trees, harbours, rivers, and lakes were all pleasant to the eye only in proportion to their convenience for the uses of mankind. As soon as the Dryads and Naiads had been banished from the woods and streams—and they were banished, or nearly banished, at the time of the birth of Christ—the world was reduced for the pagans to a large uninteresting machine. But Christ repeopled the earth, for His disciples, with that spiritual life which it was losing for the Greeks and Romans. For Him the flowers of the field and the birds of the air were the nurslings of God, the harvest was His gift, and the seed-time His promise: the rain and the sunshine, shed equally upon the just and unjust, were the messengers of His all-embracing love. This feeling has found expression in modern poetry and in modern thought. The sky, the seas, the earth, and the flowers of the field are all brought once more by Christian literature into sympathy with the human race. The rocks and forests that caused repugnance and horror to the old Roman mind suggest to us thoughts of a beauty and greatness more than earthly, and inexpressible aspirations towards One whom we adore as the Creator.

The evolutionists tell us that the insects have been busy for ages, guided by the spirit of beauty, heightening and varying the colours of the flowers of the field: but the spirit of Christ has been still more efficaciously busy at the same task. To Horace the rose is the scented plaything of the hour's revel; at most a fresh-plucked violet or hyacinth may suggest the untimely fall of a young warrior: but to Wordsworth—yes, even to Waller and Herrick—the meanest flower that blows comes as a messenger from God laden with thoughts too deep for tears.

Man, as well as nature, has shared in the "larger æther and the purple light," with which the Spirit of Christ has clothed all visible things. The mere physical beauty of the naked human form, it is true, will never be revealed to Englishmen as it was revealed to the Greeks of old. But that is a local advantage, depending, in part at least, on climate and on custom. The Greek sculptors sculptured what they saw daily in the palæstra, the racecourse, the theatre, the procession : and no nation can reproduce their sculptures till it can see the same sights. But to compensate for this want we have a higher gift. The Greeks studied beauty of form, but we have received the appreciation of beauty of expression. The Grecian custom of hiding the faces of their actors in masks, well illustrates the difference between all Grecian and modern art. The former is a faultless mask ; the latter is a human face, not faultless, but living and endowed with thought and passion. If success in art were confined to the representation of the beauty of the human form, then art would at once become narrow and national. But, as it is, wherever there is human life, there are possibilities of art infinitely surpassing the prodigies of the Parthenon. To attempt servilely to copy the Greek sculpture and the Greek drama is an artistic crime. It is putting the new wine into the old bottles ; it is serving authority instead of nature ; it is teaching the precepts of men for the commandments of God. The result is, and must be, failure. The servile sculpture is wood or wax-work, and the servile drama reminds one of nothing but an attempt to write Greek Iambics with the particles left out. Against such an error the Spirit of Christ protests no less emphatically than the spirit of art, warning us that such slavish copying is not childlike, and therefore not consonant with the laws of the family of God, and bidding us contrast the artificial and servile method of the author of *Sejanus* with the free, Christian handling of the poet whom Milton loves as "Fancy's child."[1] The Spirit of Christ bids the artist in every nation on every part of the globe, take courage in the confidence that his own nation and his own land will furnish him with materials enough, if he, for his part, can but bring to bear upon them the artistic eye and hand.

Our cathedrals, our great musicians, our painters and poets, all bear witness to the artistic influence of the Spirit of Christ, and inculcate on us the lesson of the True Spirit of Art, that no true artist should be ashamed of his own nation or his own times. The hour has come when, not on the Acropolis, nor on the Capitol, but in every nation the beauty of truth is to be worshipped. The mind of the true artist drinks in at every pore the spirit of his own age, and gains from the inspiration of the present the results of years of an uninspired grubbing amid the records of the past. The art of Greece was short-lived. Necessarily: for one cannot go on for ever finding

---

[1] Those writers who despise the applause of their countrymen at large, and find comfort in the praise of a small circle of highly educated or deeply read admirers, may do well to remember that Ben Jonson found the same comfort and encouragement in his pedantry—

"When in the Globe's fair ring, our world's best stage,
  I saw Sejanus set with that rich foil,
  I look'd the author should have borne the spoil
Of conquest from the writers of the age:
But when I view'd the people's beastly rage,
  Bent to confound thy grave and learned toil,
  That cost thee so much sweat and so much oil,
My indignation I could hardly assuage."

endless variety in the representation of the muscles of a Hercules, or the pose of an Apollo. There is a limit to the possible and sculpturable attitudes even of Gods and Goddesses, when one has ceased to believe in them. But there is no limit to the hues and shades of *thought:* and the Spirit of Christ has thrown open an illimitable field for art in placing *thought* among her provinces.

Mere physical strength and beauty being duly subordinated, and all the pushing, fussy qualities of the mind being thrown back into their proper place by the Spirit of Christ—the quiet, unobtrusive processes, pity and gentleness, sympathy and sorrow, humility and resignation, now receive something approaching to their due attention. Consider hence how "spacious and unconfined" has art been made by Christ! A bent old man and a wizened old woman are not attractive sights as compared with the Apollo Belvidere, and to a Greek artist such decrepit figures would furnish no material. The dramatist who sought to touch the Athenian heart by the spectacle of the rags and crusts of beggarly old age was sneered at for his folly. Blind old Œdipus, triumphantly avenging himself in death, and winning the fame of a demigod as he sinks into his mysterious grave, might indeed command the attention of an Athenian audience; but no artist before the descent of the Spirit of Christ could have written thus of commonplace old age: "I at least hardly ever look at a bent old man or a wizened old woman but I see also with my mind's eye that Past, of which they are the shrunken remnant; and the unfinished romance of rosy cheeks and bright eyes seems sometimes of feeble interest and significance compared with that drama of hope and love which has long ago reached its catastrophe, and left the poor soul like a dim and dusty stage, with all its sweet garden-scenes and fair perspectives overturned and thrust out of sight." The Jews rejected sinners, the Greeks rejected commonplace people; but the Christian artist, looking from commonplace people up to Christ, asks whether there is not " a pathos in their very insignificance, in our comparison of their dim and narrow existence with the glorious possibilities of the human nature which they share." Yes, and let us add, Is there not a joy in our comparison of their dim and narrow existence with the glorious Ideal to which they shall be hereafter conformed? By this pathos and by this joy Christ has so cleansed for us the visible world that the Christian artist can " call nothing common or unclean," but has all nature for his home.

CHAPTER XXI.

THE TRUE REVELATION OF DEATH.

THE FIRST PART.

The doctrine of the resurrection of Christ, the great hope of many faithful Christians, has in these days become a stumbling-block to many sceptics, who would perhaps believe in Christ but for this doctrine. Throughout His life they can follow Christ with us, joining in our love and reverence for Him; but, after His crucifixion, they feel they must part company with us. "This doctrine," they say, "we cannot accept: yet, without it, we feel that Christ's faith was a delusion and Christ's life a mistake: consequently we cannot believe in Him. We wish we could, but we cannot bring ourselves to believe that one actually dead rose from the grave, and was touched and handled by friends, and then, retaining His body, ascended into heaven. Scarcely any evidence would induce us to believe this: but the evidence of the Gospels certainly cannot."

Well, one thing we will promise our objectors, that in this chapter we will not ask them to take one step beyond the path prescribed by evidence, or to believe anything in the least unnatural. We will rest upon nothing but facts or demonstrable inferences. In a word, we will act like Positivists—or rather, I should say, like true Positivists; for, whereas most Positivists take into consideration all facts great and small, always excepting the character and influence of Christ, we, while endeavouring to imitate their reverent appreciation of facts, will try to avoid their error, and not to exclude from consideration the greatest fact in the history of humanity.

What are the facts then, as they must be admitted by all to be—by all at least who can bring to the study of the Greek Testament some little scholarship, but also some little knowledge of human nature? The facts, stated impartially, are these:—"In the time of Tiberius Cæsar, about a generation after the suppression of the insurrection of Judas of Galilee by the Romans, there came forward a new leader of the Galileans named Jesus of Nazareth. He held the same views as Judas, so far as concerned the proclamation of the independence and imminent redemption of Israel, and the equality of all members of the nation: but he advocated them in a manner entirely new, and he introduced other sweeping reforms. The nation, or the great bulk of it, rapturously welcomed his first attempts at reform, which were aided, with the populace at all events, by a power that he shared with many of the reputed prophets and reformers of Israel, a power of instantaneously healing disease. But very soon the new leader became unpopular. He appeared to aim at nothing less than sweeping away the whole of the Mosaic law; he spoke, at first more vaguely, afterwards with more and more of definiteness, of breaking down the barriers between Israel and the Gentiles. He alienated the literary and clerical classes by courting the society of the loose livers and the heterodox and the traitorous 'publicans,' and by making unprovoked attacks upon their cherished law and its conventionalisms. He alienated the free-thinkers of the day, and the Prince of Galilee among them, by setting up a standard, stricter than ever was set up before, of morality based upon inner righteousness. He alienated the Galileans by absolutely refusing to take up arms and by pertinaciously resisting their efforts to force him to place himself at their head. His growing unpopularity culminated when the last of the prophets, John, who had vainly striven to rouse him to action, perished in prison by the hand of the executioner, without a single attempt on the part of Jesus to rescue him. Lastly he alienated his own disciples by using language which was in some cases absolutely unintelligible to them, but which, where they could understand it, appeared paradoxical, incredible, repulsive. Thus by every step that he took he seemed deliberately to court failure.

"But the remarkable characteristic of his public career—or at all events of all but the very first portion of it—appeared to be this, that he *did* court failure. Over and over again he spoke of his failure as a certainty. Towards the close of his life he even spoke of his death as a certainty. Yet amid all these predictions of imminent failure and death, he seemed to retain his conviction of the certainty of ultimate success. He predicted troubles and wars, but in the end he declared that Israel would be redeemed. Jerusalem, he said, must be destroyed and the temple of Herod must fall; but he pointed the hopes of his disciples forward to a new and regenerate Jerusalem, to a new temple built upon an immovable rock, against which the gates of hell should not prevail. By that new temple he appeared to indicate a regenerate and compact society or church, including the whole human race, which was to be consecrated to God by an indwelling spirit of filial love. But all this great success was to be obtained, in some mysterious way, out of his failure and out of his death. Of death indeed Jesus always spoke as being a light matter—at least whenever it meant not spiritual but physical death. He declared to his disciples that, although some of them should be slain, nevertheless God would not suffer a hair of their heads to be harmed. Of himself he said that though he must die, yet in some way his death should subserve the interests of mankind. Looking on all men, but pre-eminently on himself, as the Son of God, he spoke as though he were certain that not only would his work be continued after his death by his Father, but also he himself must remain even after death, still the Son, still living and working with the Father. Quoting an old prophecy which declared that, if one would but turn to the Lord, the Lord would raise up and *cause to live on the third day*, Jesus applied the prophecy to himself, and declared that on the third day he too would rise again.

" From every point of view, failure seemed to stare him in the face, but more especially from the unintelligent and unappreciative nature of his immediate followers. The spiritual empire which he contemplated over the hearts of the whole human race, was not so much as dreamed of by them. The simplest metaphorical expressions appeared to be beyond their comprehension. His aversion to violence, and his plans of success through failure, were equally unintelligible. When he spoke of his immediate death, they were disturbed and scandalized, and actually remonstrated with him for thus playing with their feelings. He shrank from violence as from the touch of Satan; they were ready to call down fire on a whole village of Samaritans to revenge an insult to their master. He was for all-inclusiveness; they were for excluding, not only all but children of Abraham, but even those children of Abraham who would not follow with them. He, in the crisis which was then coming on the world, looked upon wealth and power as snares and temptations; they wrangled in his very presence for the future dignities and emoluments of the new kingdom. He spoke of humility as the sole path to greatness, and regarded himself as the servant of mankind; they looked forward to domination, not as servants, but as lords. He loved children and all that was child-like and lowly; they would fain have driven children from his presence, and repelled and scandalized those whom Christ called his 'little ones.' He looked to the heart and to the invisible motive of an action, and saw treasures of charity in the widow's mite; they praised the great gifts of the rich. They admired what was ostentatious and materially grand, as, for example, the magnificent structure of the Herodian temple; he turned from the building with horror as being tainted with blood, consecrated to formalism and hypocrisy, and destined to a speedy and desirable destruction. In a word, he was spiritual, they material; he moved in heaven, they on earth. During the whole of the public career of Jesus a great gulf lay between him and the very disciples whom he had chosen to continue his work.

"As his death approached, the gulf widened. His disciples continued to show themselves at best not much above ordinary men, and, at the worst, occasionally gross and selfish. One of them Jesus suspected of intending desertion, and indeed predicted his follower's treason. St. Peter, it is true, in the hour when Jesus found his fortunes at the lowest (if we except the eve of his death), openly professed his faith in Jesus as Redeemer of Israel and the Son of the living God. But it appeared to be a kind of heaven-sent flash of intuition rather than a steady and continuous perception of Christ's plans of spiritual empire; for, the next moment, the same disciple expostulated with his master on his prediction of his death, and was rebuked by Jesus as a minister of Satan. Nevertheless, this flash of conviction in one of his disciples so far moved Jesus that he predicted that in the strength of that conviction his new society should be founded and should prosper for ever; and with this hope he at once set out for Jerusalem and death.

"Still the gulf between himself and his disciples widened. Even on that last fatal journey to Jerusalem, when the unwonted splendour of his countenance, as he moved to his doom, had dazzled and awed his followers,[1] even then they dreamed of nothing but conquests and division of great spoils. 'Lo! we have left all and followed thee: what shall we have therefore?'—such is the question that the first confessor of the Messiah is not ashamed to ask of the Prince of Israel, for whom he

[1] St. Mark x. 32.

is shortly to fight, as he thinks, and to whom he may render services that ought to receive their just reward. The same spirit actuates the other disciples: two of them ask for the place of honour in the court of the new king; the rest, in the same spirit, resent the petition. So late as a few hours before Christ's arrest the apostles are disputing among themselves who is to have pre-eminence in the kingdom that was to be established before a week had expired. Effort after effort was made by Jesus to bring the painful truth home to the callous hearts of his disciples. In one of our narratives he is said to have striven to quell their quarrels and inspire them with his spirit by attiring himself as a slave and washing their feet. But all our narratives appear to agree that the culminating effort was put forth in a kind of funeral feast, in which Christ at once celebrated his approaching death and bequeathed his last legacy to his disciples. After all other efforts had been found fruitless, Jesus appears to have deemed it hopeless to prepare his disciples for their future struggles with the world by leaving them any more precepts, or anything in the shape of a definite code. He was determined to trust to his influence and to nothing else. Sometimes he seems to have spoken of a Comforter, sometimes of a Spirit of God, sometimes of himself or his presence as the future help of his followers. This feeling he summed up and expressed in a form which he instituted as a perpetual commemoration of himself, to be observed for ever by his future society. In the course of his last meal with his disciples, handing bread and wine to them, he bade them partake of it, and, in partaking it, partake of his body and his blood. The body and blood of

Jesus was to be for his followers in all future time their perpetual food, their perpetual bond of union.

"This last effort failed like the rest. One of those who shared in this very funeral feast consummated his plans of treason fresh from participating in the sacred bread and wine. When Jesus predicted to the rest the approaching trial, they answered with idle protestations; when he prepared them for danger, they only vexed his heart by their old literalism, producing 'two swords' as evidences of their readiness to defend him. To resort to the sword was in the judgment of Jesus nothing else than to resort to Satan: but it was useless to argue with them further. Weary of all expostulation, he exclaimed, 'It is enough,' and turned away to meet his fate. His disciples, utterly unable to appreciate their master's state of mind, could not so much as watch with him through his night of agonising expectation.

"When he was arrested, indeed, the fire of their love for him blazed up for a moment, and St. Peter drew his sword and wounded one of the aggressors. But the very act was calculated to shake the confidence of Jesus in the whole of his life-work. He rejected the offer of such aid as condemned by the curse of God, and surrendered himself without resistance. Then at once there fell upon his followers a sense that they had been completely deceived in him. When the Roman soldiers laid hands on their leader and dragged him away, and there came down no fire from God, and the legions of angels did not descend from Heaven, then it seemed that Jesus was not the Redeemer of Israel in whom they had trusted. Leaving him to his fate, they appeared to be leaving not their former Master, but the powerless phantom of the prince who had lately entered Jerusalem as a prince enters his capital. At once they all forsook him and fled; the apostle who had drawn the sword denied all knowledge of his Master; they made no effort to rescue him, and when he died on the cross and was buried, they gave themselves up to mourning and despair. Thus a life of failure seemed to have culminated for Jesus in a fruitless death.

"But now a few days afterwards we find everything changed. Even though it may be admitted that the change may not have taken place so shortly afterwards as our narratives indicate, yet, at all events, it must have taken place soon afterwards. And what a change! These Galilean peasants, loyal and affectionate, it is true, but by all accounts lately so gross, narrow, unspiritual, and destitute of all originality, now suddenly come forward as the proclaimers of a new religion, and as the regenerators, first of their nation, and ultimately of the whole world. These illiterate fishermen, who had lately been abashed by the logic of a few censorious scribes, now boldly confront the rulers of Israel, and, while defending themselves before the tribunals of the greatest, find the right words flow from their lips without an effort. These recent recreants, who had deserted or denied their Master in his extremity, now brave death, and meet death without a token of fear. These ambitious and quarrelsome followers, who had before, even in their best moments, been infected with some taint of selfishness, thinking of wealth and empire, now have no thought except to do their Master's will and to show forth his glory. These materialist Jews who but a few days ago had been able to understand no power but that of material force, no success but what was visible and immediate, no redemption but the mere emancipation of Israel from the Roman yoke, with full license to impose the yoke in her turn upon the world—now enter into all the spiritual plans and purposes of Jesus, and have, in a few days, without him learned that which with him they could never learn. The new religion that they proclaim is the same pure and spiritual religion that Jesus proclaimed—a worship of God as a Father through Jesus of Nazareth as His son, resulting in a brotherhood of men. Though at first confined, as was natural, to the followers of the law of Moses, it very speedily extended to others, and the extension was ratified by the whole body. It spreads and is prosecuted: it spreads in spite of persecution; it converts one of the foremost of its persecutors; and within a generation after the death of Jesus his followers are found scattered over the whole of the Roman empire.

"Lastly, if it be asked by what process did the religion of Christ thus overrun the world, we are not left in doubt for the answer. A few letters written by some of the earliest followers of Christ are still extant, and they are our most valuable evidence for determining how the world was converted. This cannot be too constantly borne in mind. It is not to the Gospels but to the Epistles that we must look if we wish to see Christianity in its first glow of vigorous life conquering the world. The Gospels were written afterwards for the satisfaction and edification of the Church; but the world was converted without the Gospels. The Epistles exhibit the Church in the process of converting the world, not appealing to a document as a Gospel, but to the Gospel as a power commending itself to the consciences of mankind by its innate righteousness, and by the 'signs' that everywhere followed its proclamation. These letters were not formal compositions, still less apologies intended to convince those who were outside the Church. They are familiar, we may almost say in some cases casual communications—a few of which happen to have been preserved out of a very large number—intended often for special churches or persons, and to meet special questions or difficulties, stating little formally, and taking for granted much; documents, therefore, beyond suspicion of being forged or interpolated—to any great extent at all events—for polemical purposes. The exact authorship or date of each letter is a matter of little importance. It is enough for us that, as a whole, they faithfully exhibit for us the spirit of the Church of Christ in the first century, and that some of them exhibit it as it was within a generation after the death of Christ. To the Epistles, therefore, we shall naturally look as the best representative of the spirit that prevailed among the followers of Christ a few years after his death.

"Now regarded in a natural way as the effect of some cause, the Epistles point to one of the most powerful and heart-changing causes that ever influenced mankind. As we turn from page to page we ask, quite regardless of German disputations as to genuineness and authorship, 'Where in the world did these men get this teaching from?' An able advocate of the morality of the Talmud, whose premature death must be lamented by all students of the Bible, has collected into a most interesting essay a long list of moral sayings, wise maxims, and delicate proverbs extracted from the Talmud, all of which breathe a spirit of pure benevolence; but (not to say that from the same source there could be collected no small number of frivolous and anti-gentile utterances) there is wanting in the long list of excellent sayings collected by Mr. Deutsch that fervid force of spiritual enthusiasm which characterises most of the Epistles. The whole string of gems gathered by that essayist cannot compare with one single chapter of the great persecutor of the Church in which he hymns the praises of 'Charity.' It is not in the Talmud (so far as it has been popularised) that we can find the spirit which inspires St. Paul to write 'one man esteemeth one day above another; another esteemeth every day alike. Let every man be fully persuaded in his own mind. He that regardeth the day, regardeth it unto the Lord; and he that regardeth not the day, to the Lord he doth regard it.'

"But if the originating cause of the Epistles is not to be found in contemporary literature of Israel, still less is it to be found in the literature of the West. The double-mindedness and depression of the contemporary Western philosophers afford a noteworthy contrast to the straightforward confidence of the apostles. Strabo Varro, and Seneca all agree in distinguishing between the religion of philosophers and the religion fit for the mob. 'The multitude of women,' says Strabo, 'and the entire mass of the common people, cannot be led to piety by the doctrines of philosophy; to effect this therefore superstition is necessary, which may call in the aid of myths and tales of wonder.'[1] Anger and vengeance are,

[1] Strabo, quoted by Neander, in the Introduction to his *Church History*.

it is true, deprecated; but it is because they are unphilosophical and undignified, not because they are cruel or wrong. As a natural consequence, a contempt for the poor and humble, and of course for slaves, breathes through the literature of the day. As for any hopes of reform, or of forgiveness, in science, or art, or politics, or religion, there is no trace of it. Even in Horace's time, the great consolation of the wise man is that God himself cannot unshape past pleasures or unmake the joys of the happy yesterday : 'Fortune, exultant in her bustling cruelty and persistent in playing out her insolent game, casts her fitful honours now on this, now on that favourite,' if she deserts us, there is nothing for the wise man but patience and honest poverty. But the prevailing gloom finds its deepest expression later on in the well-known saying of Pliny, that 'man is full of desires and wants that reach to infinity, and can never be satisfied. His nature is a lie—uniting the greatest poverty with the greatest pride. Among such great evils the greatest good that God has bestowed on man is the power of taking his own life.'[1] Where indeed in heaven or earth could men look for succour? From heaven the philosophers had banished the gods, and on earth the 'present god' was a Nero or a Caligula. If there were gods in heaven they were unjust or idle, and inferior to a good man :—

' Victrix causa deis placuit sed victa Catoni.'

"It is like stepping from night into noon-day to turn from this literature to the Epistles of the New Testa-

[1] *Ibid.*

ment. Everywhere there is hope, life, progress, morality, truth. There is no distinction among the Christians between the religion of the philosophers and the religion of the poor. 'God has chosen the poor in this world rich in faith,' says one writer, and another declares of Jesus himself that 'though he was rich, yet for your sakes he became poor, that ye through his poverty might become rich.' Slavery is abrogated—at all events in the eyes of God—and at the same blow falls Strabo's distinction between religion for women and religion for philosophers, 'For ye are all the children of God by faith in Christ Jesus . . . . there is neither Jew nor Greek, there is neither bond nor free, there is neither male nor female; for ye are all one in Christ Jesus.' 'Vengeance' is to be replaced by kindness, myriads of sins are to be 'covered' by charity or love. To Pliny, who believes that men are inferior to swine, the groanings of the human aspiring heart are a lie; to St. Paul they point to a profound truth, 'And because ye are sons, God hath sent forth the spirit of his son into your hearts, crying, Abba, father.' Lucan appeals from the justice of the gods to the justice of a patriotic suicide; St. Paul exults in earthly injustice and persecution as the scene of heaven-sent triumphs, 'nay, in all these things we are more than conquerors through him that loved us. For I am persuaded that neither death, nor life, nor angels, nor principalities, nor powers, nor things present, nor things to come, nor height nor depth, nor any other creature shall be able to separate us from the love of God which is in Christ Jesus our Lord.' But the culminating miracle in the spiritual miracles with which the Epistles abound is found in that sublime hymn in which, as St. Peter inaugurated the introduction of faith, so St. Paul inaugurates the introduction of what may be called a new power into the world—the power of love, or charity. This is to be the regenerating principle of mankind. Above force and valour, above cunning, skill, and wisdom, above prophecies and mysteries and knowledge, yes, even above faith and hope, charity is erected by the foremost follower of Christ as the 'abiding' or eternal virtue, which, by its quiet processes, is to redeem the world. 'Charity suffereth long, and is kind; charity envieth not; charity vaunteth not itself, is not puffed up, doth not behave herself unseemly, seeketh not her own, is not easily provoked, thinketh no evil, rejoiceth not in iniquity, but rejoiceth in the truth; beareth all things, believeth all things, hopeth all things, endureth all things. Charity never faileth. And now abideth faith, hope, charity, these three; but the greatest of these is charity.' Of all the miracles or signs said to have been wrought by the disciples of Jesus, there is none equal to this hymn of charity, written in the reign of Nero, none that so forcibly reminds us of Christ's prediction, that his disciples 'should do greater works than he himself had done, because he went to the Father.'"

Such are the undisputed facts of the close of Christ's life, and the change in the hearts of His disciples after His death, which caused the spread of the Christian religion.[1] The question we now have to ask is this,

---

[1] I take for granted that there *was* a change, and that the mis-appreciation of Jesus by His 'disciples is a historical fact. If anyone chooses to deny this, and can believe that the disciples invented incidents and discourses, and a whole narrative of lies, on purpose to give the impression that the

"What was the cause of this change in the hearts of the disciples of Jesus?" If anyone admits the change, but says, "There was no cause for it"—such a man appears to me to admit a miracle: for I know scarcely any miracle in the records of the miraculous that would be a greater miracle than the production of a change so marvellous and so world-reaching in its effects, without any definite cause. A man who can believe in this miracle, may at least be expected to be consistent, and to find no difficulty in believing in the rest of the miracles of the Old and New Testaments.

If any man admits the change, and admits that there must have been some cause for it, must he not also admit that the cause, in some way or other, must have been connected with the conviction of the disciples that Jesus of Nazareth had, in some sense or other, risen from the dead? Internal and external evidence leads irresistibly to this conclusion. On the one hand, the disciples continually protested their belief in Christ's resurrection; St. Paul makes it the corner-stone of his teaching; the assailants or critics of the Church from the earliest times regarded it as an accepted dogma of the followers of Christ; and—most important of all—the life of Christ is inexplicable without the supposition that He anticipated His resurrection; again the earliest narratives of His life attribute to Him prophecies of it which are almost certainly genuine, and which, even if not genuine, bear witness to the prevalent belief in the resurrection from the earliest times; lastly, it is not possible, on any other

Apostles were dull, gross, selfish, and timorous, while in reality they were wise, faithful, and brave, I should regard such a person as so singularly credulous that it would matter little what he believed.

hypothesis, to suppose that the disciples could have been lifted from hopelessness to confidence, from despair to successful energy.

But it will be urged, " Believing that Jesus of Nazareth had risen from the dead, is not a proof that Jesus had risen. It has been suggested that the supposed death of Jesus upon the cross may have been nothing but a swoon. Another suggestion is that the belief in the resurrection of Jesus was caused by apparitions. You must dispose of both of these suggestions before you can call upon us to believe that Jesus really did rise from the dead." These two suggestions appear to me to stand on an entirely different footing, and not to be mentionable in the same breath. The hypothesis that Jesus may have recovered from a swoon, and afterwards, presenting Himself to His disciples, may have deluded them into a belief that He had actually risen from the dead, I should reject as absolutely incompatible with any historical appreciation of His life and character. It is inconceivable that Jesus of Nazareth should have condescended to play the part of an impostor and have buried the rest of His life in obscurity in order that He might regenerate the world by a lie. Or, if it is said that there might have been no intention of deceit, but that He might have died soon afterwards, the objection is obvious that the death of Jesus of Nazareth could never have been kept secret from His disciples. Besides, the solution is manifestly inadequate to the requirements of the problem. What we want to have explained is, how the hearts of the disciples became inspired with a spiritual insight and force, in the strength of which they conquered the world. How could their spiritual insight have been thus quickened by the spectacle of the feeble form of their Master creeping from a grave only to die after just presenting Himself to their gaze? What was there in such an unsatisfying and depressing sight, followed by another and an unmistakable death—that could not have been concealed from them—to destroy their materialism at a blow, and to enable Peter to stand up in the presence of Israel and say, "The God of Abraham and of Isaac and of Jacob, the God of our fathers hath glorified His Son Jesus"?[1]

Having disposed of the hypothesis of a fictitious death, we ought now to pass to the other hypothesis, that of an apparition. But before doing this let us consider the evidence that convinced in old times a man who was very unwilling to be convinced that Jesus had actually risen from the dead. The sight and voice which convinced St. Paul of the resurrection of Jesus appear to me to be historical facts of which there can be no reasonable doubt. Even if we grant that the details in the Acts of the Apostles may not be exactly accurate (though I believe they are), yet St. Paul's reference to his vision of Jesus in his letter to the Corinthians, combined with the necessity of some such cause to explain the effect, establishes the vision as a historical fact. "Well, but the vision was natural, not supernatural: it was the result of previous thoughts, doubts, and fears; it did not convert St. Paul; he was half converted before." Let it be so; I am quite disposed to admit it. Absolute demonstration is out of the question, for we have

---

[1] Of course it may be objected that the speeches in the Acts of the Apostles cannot be accepted as authentic; but these words will be accepted by all as the best and shortest summary of the feeling of the early followers of Jesus.

no sufficient record of the thoughts of St. Paul before
the seeing of the vision, and, in particular, of the effect
produced upon him by the martyrdom of St. Stephen:
but it is at least probable that St. Paul, in the midst
of his course of persecution, had felt and resisted the
growing conviction that Jesus was the Messiah.

Let us then review the narrative of the appearance of
Jesus to St. Paul, regarded as a natural occurrence. The
words of the vision, "It is hard for thee to kick
against the pricks," clearly point to a state of mind
in which, as an ox rebels against the goad, so St.
Paul was struggling against the prick or sting of conscience which was goading him to avow that he had
been persecuting the Righteous One. If it was so, then
there is nothing improbable in the supposition that the
death and vision of St. Stephen may have powerfully
contributed to the vision of St. Paul. Almost any
persecutor, much more one so honest and truth-seeking
and so open to religious impressions as St. Paul, would
have been moved as he gazed upon the brightening face
of the martyr, who looked up steadfastly into heaven
and saw the glory of God and Jesus standing on the
right hand of God, and then died appealing to that
same Jesus to receive his spirit and to forgive his
enemies. The thought of the bare possibility that the
martyr might be right was first perhaps flung like a
wind-wafted seed into the persecutor's heart; and there
perhaps it lay, dormant, but not dead, while he strove to
stifle it in action. But it was not stifled. It was growing, and round it were gathering a thousand fostering
influences; all his hitherto suppressed discontentments
and dissatisfactions with the dry pedantry of Rabbinical

traditions ; all the old childish and youthful yearnings after a world-wide domination, wider than David's kingdom, to be exercised by the children of faithful Abraham ; all the divine possibilities of redemption wide as the world, of peace and righteousness greater than any law could give—all of which might in some new strange way be realized if only that dying heretic, looking up in his last agony, *did* see Jesus of Nazareth in heaven. Change of scene for the purposes of new persecution, so far from drowning, made more audible the growing voice of conscience during the leisure of a long journey, which gave him time to revolve recent events. Again and again there rose before him doubts and perplexities which he had thought subdued, the stubbornness of these Galileans, the strangeness of their faith, their reported cures and miracles, their confident assurance that their Leader had been raised from the dead, their piety and the self-devotion of their lives, and Stephen's face, contrasting perhaps with the faces of some who stoned him, his thrilling forgiveness, his steadfast gaze—at what ? At the face and form of Him who in the noontide glare of an eastern sun, now suddenly at the appointed time flashed in upon the traveller with a more than earthly brightness, depriving him of sight, prostrating his soul, and realising his direst fears, his sublimest hopes. All this again, if you will, is natural ; let it be as natural as the flash of thought which, times without number, has revealed the meaning and purpose of a dead father's life to a reckless and ungrateful son. But though it is natural in kind, it is supernatural in degree—as far above our nature as the heaven is above the earth, as Christ is above the level of a common man. If indeed the vision of Christ to St. Paul was natural, then must not even a sceptic be driven to exclaim in wonder, " What must have been the character, what the moral and spiritual force of Him who could so inspire His followers with His own spirit that by their mere reflection of His brightness they could produce naturally, and in strict accordance with the ordinary sequence of cause and effect, a vision of the glory of their departed Master in the heart of His bitterest persecutor ? "

Take another undoubted historical fact shewing the highly-wrought condition of the minds of the followers of Christ after His death, and the effects, to us scarcely credible, produced in a natural way by His Spirit upon them. Some days after the crucifixion, when the disciples were assembled together, the whole assembly is said to have begun to speak in sounds past their own control. Jews understanding many different languages, entering the room, heard these Galileans (who knew no language but Aramaic and Greek) expressing themselves in the tongues and dialects of the far distant countries in which they themselves had been born and reared. The same inarticulate sounds, not really language but the unintelligible ejaculations of excited worshippers, interpreted by sympathy, made themselves intelligible to many different hearers, who seemed to be hearing each his own dialect or *patois*, the familiar accents of his nursery.

If to anyone this account seems incredible, let him soberly consider the references to a similar phenomenon in the Epistles of St. Paul, where we find the apostle speaking of it as an habitual occurrence in the Church of Corinth, and this not in eulogy, but in terms of depreciation. At that time the power had come to be formalized, and was in danger of being abused. Not all that heard the inarticulate languages could then understand them, but there were certain persons who had a recognized gift of special sympathy with the utterers of these strange sounds, and a power of interpreting them to others. Stronger testimony than this dispassionate, critical, almost depreciative evidence of the apostle thus indirectly given, could scarcely be demanded; and, however explained, the gift of tongues must be accepted as a historical fact. If it be replied that it admits of a natural explanation, we grant this at once. Only we ask, What must have been the nature of the man who could thus by His influence after death so knit the hearts of His followers together in the bonds of affection for Him and one another, that, in the first years after His departure, His disciples found themselves driven at times to use in their worship a new language that was really no language, yet made intelligible by sympathy?

CHAPTER XXII.

THE TRUE REVELATION OF DEATH.

THE SECOND PART.

AND now to return to the question, "What was the cause that produced the change in the hearts of the Apostles?" Almost all will answer, "The conviction of His resurrection;" but some will say that the conviction was based upon objective realities, others will say that the conviction was purely subjective. I must confess, that the mere conviction that Christ had risen from the dead, whether that conviction were based upon the touch of the Lord's body, or upon a sight of His intangible form, does not seem to me sufficient to account for the change in the Apostles. It accounts for their new boldness, but it does not account for their new spiritual insight. To me it seems therefore, that many people who fight on the one side for what may be called the tangible, on the other side for what may be called the intangible, resurrection, sometimes drop out of sight the essence of Christ's true resurrection, which consisted in a rising again in the hearts of His disciples through the power of His Spirit. Whichever theory therefore, of Christ's resurrection may be ultimately adopted, it ought never to be forgotten that the outward and visible manifestations of Jesus, whether tangible or intangible, were but the signs of an inward and invisible resurrection of the purified image of Jesus in the hearts of the Apostles, in virtue of which inward and spiritual resurrection, they were enabled to enter into the meaning of His past life and act in His Spirit for the future.

One cannot glance through the Epistles of St. Paul without seeing that the source and origin of all his spiritual life is expressed in the passionate utterance, "The love of Christ constraineth us." Elsewhere, he speaks of dying to the world and being crucified with Christ. Sometimes he speaks of being "in Christ," but quite as often he declares that Christ is in him. Christ dwells in the heart of each of His followers, through faith, he tells us. In other words, the spirit of this world is driven out of the heart, and the faithful believer is possessed by the Spirit of Christ. This is the true resurrection of Christ for men, and it is the natural result of the faith that Christ is not dead, but lives for ever in the bosom of the Father; but to see a mere vision, or even to have touched the body of the Lord Jesus, without faith in Him, would have been no true, because no spiritual resurrection. I myself believe that, besides the spiritual resurrection, there were also visible manifestations of Jesus, which were partly the signs and partly the causes, of the spiritual resurrection in the hearts of the disciples; but it seems to me quite possible to believe in the objective reality of the spiritual resurrection, while rejecting the truth of every narrative of a substantial or visionary resurrection.

Some of my readers will feel impatient of what will appear to them very subtle and superfluous distinctions. "The resurrection," they will say, "is a cardinal dogma; you ought not to split hairs about it. You ought to confess plainly, 'Christ never rose, but I will shew you that Christ is still our Master.'" But I cannot confess that Christ never rose, for the simple reason that I believe Christ *did* rise. If, instead of saying "Christ rose," I were to say, "Christ did not rise from the dead, but though He did not rise, His influence was, and is, still exerted upon His disciples," I should be saying what I believe to be false, instead of what I believe to be true. If Christ was not really living and working in the hearts of His followers after His death, then His life becomes a fanatical delusion (or at best an illusion containing no proportionate core of truth), and the conversion of the Roman Empire becomes an effect without a cause. And why am I to give up the words in which Christ Himself predicted His own triumph over death, simply because modern materialists choose to say that there is no reality or truth in any but a material resurrection? These materialists will ask us next to give up the use of the words in which we declare that "we feed upon the body and blood of Christ"—because forsooth there "is no real feeding." Now, just as Protestants declare that they feed upon Christ's body and blood, not, on the one hand, because they believe in transubstantiation, nor, on the other hand, merely because they desire to retain a formulary long current in the Church, but because they feel that these words of Christ were used by Him in a spiritual sense and best express that spiritual meaning—so, and for the same reason, believers in Christ's spiritual resurrection should not allow themselves to be induced to use any other words than those in which Christ Himself predicted that He would rise from the dead. All that can be fairly demanded is that, as we are using the word in a spiritual and not in a material sense, we should explain our use of the word so that no one may be deceived. This having been done, there is no further ground for complaint. The whole question turns on this, whether what is spiritual is real. I maintain it is not only real, but the only thing that is worth calling real. But there are some persons to whom Christ's spiritual body and blood, or Christ dwelling in St. Paul's heart through faith, seems not so "real" as a pound of visible and tangible flesh.

But it may be urged, "We know that, when Christ spoke of His body and blood, He was using metaphorical language; but on the other hand, when He spoke of rising from the dead, He must have meant it literally." Why so? Whence this arbitrary distinction? Have any of my readers seriously considered what was in the mind of Jesus when He applied to Himself the prophecy of Hosea, "After two days will He revive us; on the third day He will raise us up, and we shall live in His sight"[1]? Perhaps some have been in the habit of thinking that Jesus definitely contemplated the uprising of His bodily frame from the tomb, and that He definitely fixed "the third day" for the date of that uprising. But how unspiritual, how utterly unlike

---

[1] I put aside the reference to Jonah in the whale, as an obvious interpolation, which breaks the flow of the "original tradition," in which the passage has been inserted.

Jesus must all this seem! Once more let me beg my readers to recall Christ's constant habit of using in a spiritual sense the terms bread, leaven, meat, water, life, death, and the other words denoting material objects. He who spoke of His flesh and blood and body always spiritually, and so persistently that He perplexed and alienated many of His most devoted followers, can it seriously be supposed that He predicted a resurrection of His mere flesh and corporal frame? "The flesh profiteth nothing," said Jesus; "it is the Spirit that quickeneth." How true, and how applicable to the present case! What could the mere resurrection of Christ's bodily frame have done for the disciples without the influx of His Spirit into their hearts? There is a certain correspondence and proportion between the Last Supper and the resurrection. Just as the last supper sums up the objects of Christ's life, so the resurrection sums up the fulfilment of those objects. Now the objects of Christ's life are included in this— giving His flesh and blood to His disciples; and the resurrection fulfilled these objects by assuring to them for ever the perpetual and undisturbed possession of the flesh and blood of the Lord. But how; tangibly? No, but spiritually, dwelling in their hearts through faith. Then, as this undoubtedly—at least in the belief of Protestants—was the meaning of Christ's words in the Last Supper, and as this spiritual use of words has been repeatedly shown to be a marked and constant characteristic of Christ, is it not at least likely also that this and no other was the meaning of the prediction of the resurrection, and that the words of Jesus require a spiritual, not a fleshly interpretation?

When the position of those who believe in the spiritual resurrection is once defined and understood, it will then be readily acknowledged that the exact material details of the manner in which Christ may have manifested Himself to His disciples are comparatively unimportant. The belief in some outward and visible sign of the Resurrection will then seem rather demanded by an intellectual than by a moral necessity, rather to explain the phenomena than in order to satisfy one's own craving for evidence that Christ did really rise. The real reason for believing that the disciples either saw Christ after His death or were in some other unusual way convinced that He lived, is this, that without some such manifestation, the spiritual resurrection and the subsequent conversion of the world is almost too great a miracle. Unless the disciples were convinced by the evidence of their senses that Christ rose from the dead, we cannot understand how it was that in so short a time they were raised from despair to confidence, and how it was that from the earliest period the disciples constantly asserted that they had seen their risen Master. Again, if Jesus predicted that He would rise from the dead, then it is nearly certain that the disciples—interpreting His prediction as they almost invariably interpreted His words, in a material sense—would have found it almost impossible to rise to the height of confidence which they actually attained, had they not witnessed some sensible manifestation of Jesus which appeared to demonstrate that their Master's predictions were not false. Moreover the hypothesis of the stimulus of such visible manifestations of Christ's spiritual resurrection is completely in accordance with what we know of many other men, whether in Israel or out of Israel, who have been nerved to do great spiritual deeds. For Moses, for Isaiah, for Samuel, for St. Paul, the divine errand for which they were being prepared has required, as a culminating shock in the process of preparation, a temporary breaking down of the walls of sense, and an appropriate revelation of things invisible, in the strength of which they have gone forth to fight the battle of faith in things unseen against the incredulous world. If we believe, as I believe, that all these visions were natural, that does not in the least prevent, rather it encourages, the belief that they were God-sent and real. To these arguments we may add the great number of accounts of the appearance of Christ recorded in the Gospels, which, although we are not able to lay stress upon the minute details of each separately, yet by their varieties and divergences appear to confute the supposition of collusion and to reveal unmistakably beneath the surface of divergent detail a solid stratum of historical fact.[1] Lastly, the hypothesis of some visible

---

[1] It may seem that I am pursuing a very arbitrary course in neglecting the evidence of the Gospels to the tangible resurrection of Christ. I do not desire here to enter into my reasons for not laying stress upon that evidence. But sceptics who think that evidence not only false but incompatible with the honesty of the narrators, may do well to refer to the Appendix.

It may perhaps, however, be necessary to state that the "Original Tradition" which is common to the first three Gospels, contains no record of any appearance of Jesus to the disciples, nor even a statement that the sepulchre was found empty. The "Original Tradition" ends in these words:—

(1) Matthew : ἀπεκύλισε . . . . ζητεῖτε . . . . οὐκ ἔστιν ὧδε, ἠγέρθη . . . . εἰς τὴν Γαλιλαίαν.

(2) Mark : $\genfrac{}{}{0pt}{}{ἀπο}{ἀνα}$} κεκύλισται . . . . ζητεῖτε . . . . ἠγέρθη οὐκ ἔστιν ὧδε . . . . εἰς τὴν Γαλιλαίαν.

(3) Luke : ἀποκεκυλισμένον . . . . ζητεῖτε . . . . οὐκ ἔστιν ὧδε ἀλλὰ ἠγέρθη . . . . ἐν τῇ Γαλιλαίᾳ.

manifestations of Christ's presence after death appears necessitated, not only by the evidence of the Gospels, but by the direct testimony of St. Paul. While mentioning the appearances of Jesus to himself, St. Paul adds as part of the Gospel which he had delivered to the Corinthians, accounts of repeated appearances of Jesus to the other Apostles and disciples. "He was seen of Cephas, then of the twelve; after that he was seen of above five hundred brethren at once; of whom the greater part remain unto this present, but some are fallen asleep. After that, he was seen of James, then of all the Apostles. And last of all he was seen of me also, as of me born out of due time."

In accordance with this view, it would seem to me that the manifestations of Jesus did not appear to the disciples till they, like St. Paul, had been prepared to receive them. What the spectacle of Stephen's death, and the subsequent journey to Damascus, had done for St. Paul, that the spectacle of the crucifixion and the subsequent period of wretched bereavement and despair had done for the eleven Apostles. Those intolerable hours between the death of Jesus and His first manifestation to His disciples were not wasted. What Shakespeare predicts of the power of the ordinary revelation of death, was in Jesus finding its highest fulfilment:

> "The idea of his life shall sweetly creep
> Into their study of imagination,
> And every lovely organ of his life
> Shall come apparell'd in more precious habit,
> More moving-delicate, and full of life,
> Into the eye and prospect of their souls
> Than when he lived indeed."

Not now as a King, or Conqueror, or Dispenser of

rewards, but for Himself and for His own sake, as the very bread and life of their souls, they longed and yearned for the dead Friend whom yesterday they had seen expiring on the cross. The death of Jesus did for His disciples even more effectually what had been done before by the spectacle of His apparent failure and disappointment when He was an exile in Cæsarea. As then before, so now again, they ceased to trust Him for His wonders and greatness, and were thrown back upon their trust in His goodness, in Himself. The vacant cross from which their Master had just been taken down addressed them as it were in their Master's stead, and once again put the familiar question, "Whom say ye that the Son of Man is?" What reply had St. Peter and the other disciples to make now? Could they still say, "Thou art the Christ, the Son of the Living God?" Facts forbade it : and yet if He was not the Christ, what was He? Was it possible that one so supremely righteous, and wise, and unselfish could have thrown His life away for naught? If He was not one with God, of what nature must God be to have any point of discord between Himself and One so good, so loving, and so absolutely unselfish? But again, if He was one with God, then surely He could not perish : God could not leave His soul in the land of darkness. Death must not, could not, for ever hold Him. He must be still living, still waiting to lead them.

At this crisis Jesus manifested Himself first to one, then to others, of His disciples. Let the details of the manifestations remain in abeyance; but let thus much, at least be admitted by all, that for all the practical purposes of a living presence, Christ's manifestations of

Himself after death had even more influence upon His disciples than His actual presence in the flesh. So it is, as we have seen, to some extent, with the influence of ordinary men after their death, especially where they have died before their time, as we phrase it, with some earnest wishes, some good and great plans unfulfilled, leaving with the survivor the feeling that he did not while they were living appreciate the departed. How much more, then, must this have been natural over the grave of Jesus of Nazareth! And if, in some cases, the deaths of ordinary men are followed by apparitions impressing the survivors with a sense of their presence, how much more may it be expected that the sorrowing disciples of such a one as Jesus should receive the most vivid manifestations of their Master's continued presence! Indeed, having regard to what Jesus was at the very lowest estimate that can be formed by the most sceptical, and considering the influence He must have acquired over His disciples, the hopes He had raised in them, the sense of ingratitude that He must have left behind Him in their hearts, the feeling of a life and work truncated, one is tempted to say that the wonder would have been, not in His appearing to His disciples, but in His failing to appear.

That the women should have been the first to carry the tidings of His resurrection, and that the apostle who denied his Master should be the first, or one of the first, to see Him, seems in accordance with the theory that the appearances of Jesus did not violate natural laws. Again, as long as the disciples remained unconvinced and inactive, it was natural that the celebration of the Lord's Supper should be frequently marked by such appearances; but by degrees, as the disciples realised the unceasing spiritual presence of the Lord Jesus with them, these visible manifestations became more and more unnecessary and causeless; and therefore day by day, when He vanished upward from their gaze, it was natural that they should see Him depart with less and less of pain and regret. Equally natural was it that at last (when the time for action came, and the full hearts of the disciples, bursting with the new spiritual power poured into them by their Master's Spirit, went forth, to battle against the empire), they should see the form of Jesus ascending to heaven with a voice predicting His future triumph over the world.

But it may be urged that all, or almost all, the admitted apparitions of the dead have appeared, not to many persons together, but to one. Now, on the contrary, almost all the manifestations of Jesus after death appeared, not to one disciple, but to many. In answer to this, let it be remembered that, if the manifestations of Jesus were natural, they must naturally and necessarily correspond to the cause that produced them. As Jesus of Nazareth differed from other men, so the results of His influence, if manifested by visions or voices in a natural way, must proportionately differ from the ordinary apparitions of the ordinary dead. Now His love for His disciples, and theirs for Him, differed in one important respect from the ordinary love of child for father, or brother for brother. The love of the Apostles for the Lord Jesus was, if it may be so called, a social love; it did not thrive on solitude, but on union and fellowship. He taught them to regard their loving one another as the inseparable sign of their love for Him. Whenever they met together the little group of disciples was meaningless without Him. The sense of a common sorrow, common yearnings and necessities, all looking for satisfaction to one familiar form, prepared the way for the appearance of that form. Wherever two or three of His disciples were gathered together, Christ had before promised His special Presence. That promise in itself, by the hopes it might excite, might go far to prepare the way for its fulfilment. Let it be remembered also that, in one of the manifestations, some of the disciples are expressly said to have "doubted" at first, and that no manifestation at all (with the exception of the vision of St. Paul, of which we have spoken above) was granted to the enemies of Christ, or to non-believers; or, in fact, to anyone who was not prepared by faith, or at least by love, to welcome the manifestation. All these considerations indicate that, whatever may have been the nature of Christ's appearances to His disciples, they were at all events guided by some spiritual law, and were not of that arbitrary kind which at once repels belief. If they had been mere "miracles," that is, wonders intended for the purposes of demonstration, and wholly independent of the faith of the spectators, how much more miraculous and demonstrative would have been a single public manifestation vouchsafed to the assembled enemies of Christ!

But an objector may urge, "I do not see what you gain by extorting from me the admission, that an unsubstantial apparition of Christ may have appeared, or I will even say *did* appear, to His disciples." I should reply that, such apparitions appearing to more than one person at a time, and appearing repeatedly, would demonstrate even to a sceptic the impression made by the personality of Christ upon His disciples, and would prepare the sceptic to anticipate a great work, reserved for the influence of Christ in after time. For at present, I find many sceptics putting Christ calmly on one side, and saying "We know nothing about him. He is to us no more than *the real or ideal founder of Christianity.* It was St. Paul, not Christ, that really Christianized mankind." I reply, "According to your own admission Christ was not only a power in His life-time, but also an extraordinary power after His death, and may be reasonably expected to be an extraordinary power for ages to come."

The fact that the visions of the eleven Apostles may have been as natural as the vision of St. Paul does not militate against their truthfulness. If they partook (like the visions of Isaiah and of all Seers) of the nature of illusion, that is but the necessary characteristic of all truth revealed from God to men, and does not militate against the supposition that the visions were objective (if God is objective), and that they were sent by God to men. I do not lay stress upon the apparitions of Jesus as constituting His real resurrection : far from it. But I submit that they are a noteworthy testimony to the invisible forces which were working for Him after His death. Love, hope, faith, and reverence are the invisible allies of Jesus in the hearts of men : and it is these powers that raise Him up invisibly in our hearts : but the visible manifestations of Christ to His disciples are not insignificant indications of that invisible resurrection ; and they bear witness that on every side in human nature Christ left friends behind Him, even in the frail flesh and blood and brains of His followers as well as in the depths of their affections.

Yet in conclusion I would reiterate with all the emphasis in my power that the real resurrection of Christ is spiritual and not sensible. The sensible resurrection of Christ has been declared to be rather an intellectual than a moral necessity. But faith in the spiritual resurrection of Christ, as predicted by Himself, appears to be morally as well as intellectually a necessary article of faith for every one who is acquainted with the phenomena of Christianity. Intellectually the resurrection appears necessary to explain what it was that regenerated eleven materialist Jews and enabled them to regenerate a worn-out world; what it was that inspired another, a former persecutor of the Church, a Hebrew of the Hebrews, a zealot of the law, to cast aside law and nation, and in the days of Nero to hymn the praises of all-conquering charity. But morally and spiritually also the resurrection seems necessary, because to suppose that Jesus was disappointed and deceived partake of the nature of a sin. Nay, even if Jesus had never predicted any resurrection, and had never manifested Himself after death to His disciples by any signs either visible or tangible, I still think it would be what the Latins would call *nefas* to suppose that He was not now ruling on high and seated at the right hand of God.

But an objector may urge that the whole of the facts may be admitted and explained without any belief in the immortality of the soul, and consequently in the separate existence of the Spirit of Jesus after death. "What you say about the effects absolutely requiring the operation of the Spirit of Jesus as a cause, can be met thus. Put 'influence' instead of spirit. You yourself have shown us how the dead are idealised and their influence is intensified by death. We adopt your theory, and we say that what you call the spirit of Christ was nothing but intensified influence, nothing but Shakespeare's '*idea* of his life,' creeping into the imagination of the sorrowing disciples. Thus, you see, we accept all your facts, but explain them differently." To such objectors I should reply, "Nothing can, in the nature of things, demonstrate to you (in the ordinary sense of the word 'demonstrate,' as applied to logical proof) that the souls of men have an independent existence after death. But if you are not entirely impervious to such proofs as are consistent with the course of nature, surely the faith of Jesus in His own ultimate triumph over the world, justified as it was by success, may fairly induce you to look to Him as something of an authority in matters of this undemonstrable nature. You admit that He was the greatest man that ever lived, if greatness is to be measured by the uplifting of one's fellow men. You admit that He wrought this uplifting not by violence, nor by policy, but by His "influence," exerted through a life of suffering and death. Surely so powerful a personality does not influence men by accident or by lies. Is it not possible, then, is it not likely, that this man is more in harmony with truth and facts than you and I, and that we are not likely to find any other authority so well entitled to be trusted about whatever may await us after this present life? And until we can find a better authority, can we act more wisely than in accepting Him as our truest guide, and His language as our truest language? But if we use His language, then, instead of speaking about His influence after death, we shall prefer to speak of His spirit, His presence, or Himself. But still further, even if you say "it may be so, but we cannot feel sure," even then I would ask you whether you ought to speak of this "influence" in the past tense as a mere transitory power operating for a few days or years after Christ died; whether it has not been uplifting mankind for eighteen centuries; whether it is not uplifting us now; whether it or something like it—an influence of love—has not been uplifting mankind before the birth of Christ, since man was first created; and lastly, whether we can find in heaven or earth anything more admirable, more productive of love, trust, and awe, than this sublime "influence," as it was expressed in its highest form by Jesus of Nazareth. But if you admit that there has been and is nothing in the world more productive of love, trust, and awe than the "influence" of Jesus after death on mankind, then, whether you know it or not, and whether you call it influence, or spirit, or Jesus, then I claim you as a worshipper of Christ, in whose presence—

> "You stand,
> Adore, and worship, when you know it not,
> Pious beyond the intention of your thought,
> Devout above the meaning of your will."

The reasonableness and fitness and naturalness of the phenomena of the resurrection may be well illustrated, if we will imagine for a moment that the course of

Christ's life had been other than it was. Imagine then—though the hypothesis is distressingly unnatural —that Christ had not died upon the cross; that He lived to see His empire extended over the civilised world, and that, after seeing the records of His life, His precepts, speeches, and conversations transmitted to posterity, He passed away from the midst of mankind. Humanly speaking, we may almost say that, upon such an hypothesis, there could have been no visible manifestations of Christ's presence after death, perhaps even no spiritual resurrection except in heaven with the Father, no resurrection at all on earth in the hearts of His followers. Codes, biographies, pictures, statues, the grateful sense of fulfilment and satisfied gratitude would have filled the place of those unsatisfied yearnings which made Jesus visible after death to the sorrowing Apostles. Now have we ever thought how much we should have missed if the course of things had run thus?—how poor and inadequate a substitute the records of a hundred biographies and the most complete of codes would have furnished in the place of that indwelling image of the Crucified One which flashed upon Saul of Tarsus, and which for eighteen hundred years has been inspiring the hearts of the lowly, the suffering, the down-trodden, and the desolate? Where, then, would mankind have looked for the great Revelation that the failures of God are stronger than the successes of men, that suffering is stronger than vengeance, that forgiveness is stronger than sin, that all evil is conquerable by good, and that death itself—strange paradox!—can be so conquered by dying that it may be made the step to ascend to a higher and nobler life?

For this is what Christ's resurrection amounts to. It is the true revelation of death as the servant of life; and it explains the meaning of that which has been since the creation of life the great riddle of the universe. Thus regarded, it takes its place naturally as the central point in the history of the world, and presents itself not only as the justification of past aspirations, but also as an emblem and earnest of a future when all death shall be swallowed up in life. Let us try for a moment to look at the resurrection in this way, as a stage in the progress of mankind, and let us see how this great fact would naturally appear to a believer in the theory of evolution.

Going back in imagination to the first beginnings of creation, we find ourselves obliged to conceive of two things, Force and Matter. Under the influence of Force we see this planet of ours assuming shape and solidity, and passing from its first gaseous mass to a fluid mass, and from a fluid to a solid, till at last, becoming habitable, it becomes the home of life and of life's shadow—death. In this series of dissolving views we see wave after wave of created living things called into being and blotted out of being, and each following wave seems to beat higher than the preceding one, upon the shore of Force. Vegetable life, rounded off by hardly discernible shades of increasing vitality, passes upward into animal life; animal life itself rises in an ascending scale of perfection in its organization, till man appears, bringing with him, in time, righteousness, and with righteousness, the shadow of righteousness, or sin.

Until man came into the world, death, the shadow of life, was not felt to be an evil, and sin, the shadow of righteousness, had no existence. But as man rose higher and higher in the scale of force, ascending from the lower and animal forces first to the mental forces—such as attention, memory, judgment, and forethought—and next to the moral forces—such as love and pity—then death and sin came to be more and more hateful in their nature and paralysing in their influence. In the vegetable world, and almost equally in the world of animals, death had been deprived of its sting by the absence of forethought and memory. There was no fear of death in the living; there were no sad memories of the dead in the hearts of the survivors. Death also had clearly contributed to the progress of life as a whole; for by means of death the lower organisms had been swept away to make room for the higher. But now with forethought came the fear of death upon the living, and with memory came the bitterness of sorrow for the death of the departed.

While men were (if they ever were) in the stage of animals, death must have worked as well for them as it had worked for their lower companions in life. It must have forwarded progress by the struggle ending in the survival of the fittest, and can have produced no sense of hardship. But as men rose in the scale of Force, becoming discontented with the lower forms of it, such as violence, cunning, and skill, and feeling their way towards the higher forms of it, such as reason, faith, hope, and love—death became darker as life gained in brightness, and the darkness and inexplicableness of death and sin threw a cloud over heaven and earth, taking all the sweet freshness out of existence, and leaving men hopeless and motiveless. Men had looked up before appealingly to the invisible forces of the world, and had been led by dreams and visions, by the faces of their children and their parents, by the glories of the sun and moon and stars, to frame for themselves rulers of the world, human, yet divine, who would mend what was wrong in another life beyond the grave. But they had not enough of moral force in them to devise things in consonance with the great Force of the universe; and consequently, in the hour of need, the aërial fabric of the Olympian palace with its aërial tenants vanished like a rainbow, and with it seemed to have vanished all motive for action in mankind.

At this crisis there came into the world a Man who embodied in Himself all those hidden and higher forces of life, towards which the ancient world had been groping its way—righteousness, pity, faith, love, forgiveness. This Man planned and executed a new project for the development of the human race, which He called redemption. Trampling under foot violence and craft, He proclaimed the supremacy of love. He Himself lived a life of suffering and love for the oppressed, and submitted to a humiliating death. But He predicted that by dying He would conquer death, and that He would not only rise up from the grave, but also would lift up all mankind with Himself. All took place as He had predicted. He died, but He rose again, and after death He was found to be infinitely more powerful than when He lived. Stamping his followers with His character, this Man predicted that He would introduce into the world a new and conquering race, a new type of humanity, which, as He said, should conquer all others, and, by a new and spiritual law of the survival of the fittest, should inherit the world. This, too, has been verified, and at this moment those who worship this Man as the supreme expression of the Force that controls the world are acknowledged to be the only progressive portion of humanity, and can be shown to owe their progress to their worship of Him and to their acceptance of His character. This Man, or Force, has pervaded and regenerated every province of life, science, and art, and politics no less than morality; and it is only a question of time when the masses of the poor will recognize Him as the one true Reformer of life, and will unite in His name to destroy poverty and war. The integuments of illusion which enclosed and preserved His spiritual teaching have, some of them, perished already, and many more are likely soon to perish; but His words, as He himself predicted, abide and must abide for ever. His words may be summed up in this: the great Force of the world is a Father of men, and the great evolution or progress of humanity is a process of conformation of human children to the divine Father. With this Force or Father Jesus declared Himself to be at one; and He taught us that we could approach God the Father through Himself as the Son. Further He led us to believe that, as the children of God, we shall have an eternal existence, over which death can have no power, promising us not a mere "diffused presence" in the hearts of such as may survive us, but an eternal faculty of loving and being consciously loved by our Father in heaven. In the strength of this spiritual hope bequeathed to us by Jesus of Nazareth, humanity has forced its way upwards through the ruins of falling civilizations, and seems, at the present day, only entering upon a new stage of accelerated ascent.

Does not all this strange story of a progressing world bear witness to something more than a mere blind whirlpool or eddy of fate, and attest to "something of great constancy"? The existence of the great heroes and poets of humanity—Homer and Moses, Isaiah and Socrates, Dante and Shakespeare—developed according to the theory of evolution, consistently and regularly, by innumerable stages of ascent, from the slime and the ooze—might even in itself seem to protest against the notion that men are nothing more than casually improved brutes? But when, in the middle of the strange story of progress, we are confronted with the appearance of Jesus of Nazareth summing up in Himself the regenerating forces of the world, and predicting and achieving a new and higher regeneration by those same natural forces supremely expressed by Himself, then do not facts themselves, as well as our own responsive aspirations, seem to bear evidence that Jesus of Nazareth was not mistaken?—that He at all events cannot be a casual appearance, or a sport of fate?—but that the Force which has been all along at work in the creation and development of things has been, not a chance, but a Will, and this Will a righteous Will, and that Jesus of Nazareth is at one with that Will? Unless, indeed, we have an *à priori* determination that God shall always be, for us, the Unknowable; and unless by constant effort and practice we have hardened ourselves against all proof of the existence of anything except what we can see and touch, I hardly know how we can look upon the sufferings and predictions and triumphs of Jesus without a conviction that in these deeds we discern God's handiwork, and that in the doer of them we discern God's Son. And if Christ's work is God's, then in that portion of it which is most manifestly divine we must always place the Resurrection. For what science has done for us to interpret death in the animal world, that and much more has Jesus done to interpret death for us in the world of humanity. For whereas science shews us death in the animal world subserving the progress of the animal races, Jesus shews us death in the human world, not only subserving the human race at large, but also the dying individual; and He encourages us to look upon the future existence of the spirits of the blessed dead not as a mere diffused subjective presence in the hearts of the survivors, but as an everlasting and individual life in the bosom of God the Father, of which higher life the life of earthly influence is nothing but an inferior emblem.

Surely he must be a credulous, a very credulous man, who can believe that so great a work as that of Jesus of Nazareth has been achieved as the result of accidents, or delusions, or impostures. It is hard, it is almost impossible to conceive how His deliberate plans of failure and death and resurrection could have succeeded, had He not had a divine intuition into the laws of the universe and a deep harmony with the aspirations and necessities of men. By such intuition I conceive that Jesus triumphed, and by it He is destined to triumph for all time. For though absent from us He has the universe still as His friend; and the pulses of inanimate nature beat responsively to the voices of His ever-present Gospel. The sunshine and the rain suggesting His revelation of God's free love; the mysterious wind breathing whence and whither we know not, reminding us of His spirit of goodness; the quiet processes of earth, with its budding trees and growing harvests recalling the quiet processes by which He introduced the Kingdom of Heaven; the amplitude of sky placing before us the illimitable power of the Son of God seated at the right hand of the Father; the faces of trustful children and of loving parents preaching over again His Gospel of the sonship of men and the fatherhood of God; the births and deaths, the joys and sorrows of men re-enacting in miniature and inspiring in each succeeding generation the spirit of His life—all these are His allies:

> "He has left behind
> Powers that will work for Him, air, earth, and skies.
> There's not a breathing of the common mind
> That will forget Him. He has great allies,
> His friends are exultations, agonies,
> And love and man's unconquerable mind."

CHAPTER XXIII.

THE PAST WORSHIP OF CHRIST.

THE Christian as well as the Jewish Church has been subject to its illusions, and these from the very earliest period in its history. The Apostles, during our Lord's life on earth, lived in one continuous illusion. The language that most naturally expressed His thoughts was to them bewildering and inexplicable, and up to the moment of His death they had no notion of His mission. We have seen that many of those lessons which we call Christ's Parables and Metaphors, were to Him the expressions of actual truth. It was no Metaphor when He described Himself as the Bread of Life. When he spoke of Eternal Life, He did not mean the indefinitely protracted act of breathing, but that inner life which results from human nature partaking of the Bread of God. When He spoke of death He saw not mere cessation of corporal action, but a paralysis of the soul; and the raising of the dead suggested to Him the human soul emerging from the fetters of sin. To Him deafness and dumbness, lameness and blindness, all the diseases and all the sufferings of men were rather inwardly than outwardly viewed, as diseases of the soul leading to diseases of the body. He saw few visions: but all His life was one continuous vision. Where others saw a flash of lightning He saw Satan fall from heaven; when He saw a harvest white for the reaper, it was the harvest of souls; with Him leaven meant the subtle-spreading influence of man among men, working sometimes for good, sometimes for ill; the seed was the invisible Word of God sown in the hearts of men; fire was the purifying and destructive influence that destroyed and purified imperfect humanity; wind was the invisible breath of God, whispering His messages to mankind, or sometimes winnowing good from evil in the individual heart, or in the family, or in the nation; a fruitless leafy tree was a religious hypocrite; a mountain was a stupendous sin irremoveable except by the leverage of a divine upheaval; a straying sheep, or even a coin upon the floor, suggested the vision of a lost but still precious human soul waiting for the divine search. A critic—who, if acuteness without reverence could have guided a man to the meaning of Christ's life, would have been His best interpreter—has ventured to condemn the character of our Lord (as portrayed in the Gospel of St. John) for taking pleasure in mystifying opponents with enigmas. Such a criticism indicates a singular misappreciation of facts. Christ, like the ancient prophets, had the prophetic gift of sight: He was a Seer as well as a Messiah, and He spoke of what He saw. The spiritual processes that are to us invisible and unreal were to Him visible, and the only realities, and, as such, they were described by Him. Had He used any other language, He would have stooped to the lower level of His disciples instead of raising them to His level. He was aware that

His disciples, though partially imbued with His Spirit, did not understand His words; but what then? Any revelation from God to men must necessarily be imperfect and involved in illusion, if the revelation is to be adapted to its recipients. Better present bewilderment, leading to future real knowledge, than a complacent trust in a partial and stationary semblance of knowledge. What He said and did they knew not now, but they should know hereafter. While Jesus lived on earth the Apostles were of the earth, and their only conceptions of reality were earthy. Their twelve promised thrones would in a few months be set up for them—so they hoped—in twelve provinces of Palestine, and they would oust the Herods and the Pilates. That was an error, but it was an illusion, not a delusion. For the hope led to good, and was the necessary earthly integument of that subsequent spiritual hope which has been fulfilled not in Palestine, but in Christendom. St. Peter is visibly recognized as the Patron Saint in Rome, St. Paul in London; and even where no monuments of stone constitute for them a visible memorial, the spiritual children of Abraham recognize the invisible judgment of the Apostles of Christ. The life of Jesus of Nazareth was—apparently —a delusion for one; but for the eleven it was the most divine of illusions.

To the last, the Apostles and the early Church remained under the illusion that Christ's coming was near at hand. Some utility in the illusion is obvious. It is not easy to see how the Jews and Gentiles of the early Church could have been uplifted to such a height above the bustle and stir of earth, or how they would have had strength to persevere in their up-hill battle against the opposing world, had they known that more than nineteen centuries must pass away before their Master would visibly return. But besides its utility, this illusion contained a truth. Christ did " come," in many places and at many times, during the first and second centuries of the Church. Wherever His Spirit purified the world, whatever corner of the earth His Spirit convinced of sin, wherever the Gospel raised the standard of morality and made men judge themselves more truly, there, in the only true sense of the word, and in Christ's own sense of the word, Christ " came." We indeed still look forward to a final " coming," when every eye shall look on Christ as the Judge of the world : but even when that day arrives, it will probably be no visible " coming " that we shall witness. None the less really, Christ will come into the souls of men, and repentant mankind shall acknowledge Him alone as their true Judge and exalt Him in their hearts, beholding Him seated at the right hand of God. Here, then, although the early Christians were under an illusion as regards the clothing of their hope, yet we do not believe them to have been deceived in the hope itself.

If we pass on to the later illusions of the Christian Church, against some of which we Protestants feel bound specially to protest, we shall yet gladly acknowledge that these, too, have served a divine purpose, and contained a divine truth. Consider, for a moment, beneath what a mass of ancient heathen traditional superstitions the Christian faith was in danger of being overwhelmed, when Paganism surrendered to Christianity ;

the beautiful heathenish customs, feasts, and rites, more eloquently corrupting than a thousand philosophic apologies; the heathen modes of religious thought, the heathen religious phrases and technical terms, such as "expiation," "sacrifice," and the like, all of which, when adopted by the Church, were sure (as words always do) to begin by being the servants, but to end by being the tyrants, of thought; the heathen notions of incarnation and of the intercourse between gods and men; the prevalent ignorance of natural laws, and spiritual laws, and laws of any kind, except the *fiat* of power. Then bear in mind the influence of the barbarians on the Church; the impossibility of making a Clovis understand the theology of St. Paul, or even sympathize with the filial type of righteousness which was revealed to the world by Christ; the incompatibility in the barbaric mind between forgiveness and resentment, gentleness and manliness, humility and nobility; the apparent necessity of definite teaching, definite substantial rewards, and still more definite punishments, for any religion that might hope to control the conquerors of the empire. Lastly, consider the attitude of the Church; how, in those dark days, the best and most unselfish spirits of the times, fleeing from universal lust and bloodshed, immured themselves in solitude, apart from the blessed influences of social life, apart from the Revelation of the Family and of the State, casting from them as profane the innocent joys of life, struggling for the very existence of the Church against the sea of barbarism around them. Give but a thought to all these opposing and corrupting elements, and it will no longer seem strange if the seed of the Faith of Christ should lie for some ten or twenty centuries apparently dormant or decaying, while really changing its nature only to spring up into a higher life.

Take, for example, the adoration of the Mother of the Lord. From this, more than from any other error of the early Church, we shrink as being an open breach of God's commandments. Yet surely it cannot be denied that many barbarous tribes to whom the loving nature of Christ would have been incomprehensible—at all events as Christ was then preached—found a more natural object of worship in the more intelligible tenderness of the Virgin Mother of God. At the best, it is sad to think that the character of Jesus should have been perverted into that of an avenging Judge, a mysterious Sufferer whose sufferings were only so far comprehensible that they clearly gave Him a right to execute vengeance on all mankind. It is a terrible thought that between Jesus the Mediator and the terrified world, the Virgin should have stepped in as a necessary second Mediator. Yet, in some degree, do not almost all Christians, even of the present day, commit the same *kind* of idolatry? In the secrecy of our hearts we all nourish a faith in some kind of bridge or ladder between us and Christ—the Church, the Sacraments, the Bible, something or other that will enable us to keep off that too awful proximity which makes us cry, "Depart from me, for I am a sinful man, O Lord." It may be that many of our modern idolatries are far more pernicious than Mariolatry was in old times. In worshipping the purity, love, and tenderness of the Mother, those idolatrous Christians were worshipping the very attributes that were inherent in her divine Son. The illusion which resulted in the adoration of the love of the Virgin for her Child, like a husk hardened against the influence of the weather, preserved in barbarous times the almost forgotten truth that God is Love.

Take again the belief in transubstantiation, in the mechanical efficacy of sacerdotal forgiveness, and in a material hell: all these were, in some sense, illusions, for they all contained germs of truth.

The Frankish king who would fain have been present with his brave Franks at Calvary that he might have rescued the Saviour from the ignominy of the cross—how could he have understood the sublime language of the Old Testament, or its rehabilitation in the New: "Man shall not live by bread alone, but by every word that proceedeth out of the mouth of God"? Still less could he have understood that the soul as well as the body needs its nutriment, and that Christ is the spiritual food of the human race. But to the help of his sensuous faith there came, in the mercy of God, bread seen and tasted, wine poured out and drunk, the body and blood of God visible on the altar. Here then was an awe-inspiring wonder, heaven brought down to earth daily by the priest's hand. Through this plain, striking, and oft-repeated rite of superstition there flowed into the hearts of men, mixed with much error, a great and divine truth. Here, as elsewhere, the old rule prevailed. Those that had, to them there was added, and from those that had not, was taken away even that which they had. By the faith in the body and blood of God the utterly gross, sensuous, and evil-loving were made yet grosser, and encouraged in evil-doing by the hope of impunity: but those who had some germ of spiritual life found themselves raised by the Sacrament of Christ into an indefinable consciousness of communion with Him as the Sustainer and Nourisher of their souls. Again, the servile faith in the mechanical efficacy of merely officially pronounced forgiveness, even at the very time when it was producing, as its natural fruit, the sale of Indulgences, did, nevertheless, serve to keep alive in the hearts of men (who would not have recognized forgiveness as a mere spiritual and invisible faculty) the belief that they were not left by God to remain at one dead level of morality, but that men over men have power for good, and that God had given authority to the Son of Man on earth to forgive sins. Lastly, the belief in a material heaven and a material hell must surely be thought to represent a true faith proportioned to the ages in which it was entertained. What the body is to the mind, that the old material hell was to our present conceptions of God's purifying punishments. Therefore in barbarous times—when there was no possibility of bringing home to the minds of men the invisible pains and fires of self-reproach, repentance, and remorse—the fiction of the material flames of hell exerted on Christendom an influence not wholly for evil, because it at least bore witness to the justice of God, and to some sequence of punishment on wickedness, even on the wickedness of the great.

The same rule applies to the whole history of the Christian Church. It is a series of illusions; and each illusion contains, with some error, its modicum of truth. The illusions of the Church ought no more to make us despair of ultimately attaining the truth, than the illusions of babyhood ought to cause despair of truth to mature men. In each of these illusions there is the same law and the same proportion. Each arises from our inability to express Christ intelligibly to our souls. Christ is the Real Word: the illusions of the Church are Metaphors—not lies, but Metaphors—by which we rise higher and higher to the Reality. The use of Metaphors is to set invisible things visibly before us, and this the illusions of the Church have done. But the danger of Metaphors is that they impose fetters upon thought, as though they were really true. It is the essence of every good Metaphor to be (literally taken) wholly false; but the Illusions or Metaphors of the Church have too often, and too long commended themselves to Christendom as though they were literally true. If it seems at any time strange that God should deliberately subject His children to intellectual errors, let it at least be remembered that the capacity of error is one great prerogative of the human race, distinguishing it from beasts. Beasts make few or no mistakes and little or no progress: men err and progress proportionately. And intellectual error—what is it after all as compared with moral rectitude! It is like an error of spelling in a great epic. Steadfastly let us bear in mind the great Revelation conveyed in Pascal's sublime proportion, "What the body is to the intellect, that the intellect is to the Spirit:" this is a key that will unlock the doors of many chambers of mysteries in our Father's House.

CHAPTER XXIV.

THE PRESENT WORSHIP OF CHRIST.

CHILDREN still have their illusions; mankind, in its childhood, had its illusions; the great nations of the world, the Greeks, the Romans, even the Children of Israel, were trained by illusion; the Church of Christ in the middle and earliest ages, yes, even the apostles of the Lord themselves, have not been free from the universal training of illusion; can we then hope that we of the Church of England, alone of all the world, are likely to be preserved from the common fate? We cannot think so. But admitting that we are certainly under illusions at this present time, what are we to do? Are we, like precocious children aping their elders, to affect doubts and suspicions that we do not feel? Who could approve of the unnatural disillusion of a child of three years old, who should have already learned to compare his parents with others, and to criticize instead of blindly reverencing? Such disillusion would probably, if analysed, be found to be based not upon facts so much as upon a rooted selfishness, blinding the child to what is good in others besides himself. And so with us, we shall not reach the truth by determining to believe that everything deceives

THE PRESENT WORSHIP OF CHRIST. 401

us; we shall not arrive at our seasonable disillusion through obstinate declarations that we will free ourselves from all danger of illusion by believing nothing. To believe nothing would be the worst of delusions, far worse than any of the illusions that we so anxiously avoid. But the right course is that we should simply accept the whole truth so far as we can gather it from every source, not shutting our eyes to anything because it happens to be new, not accepting anything because it is old; or perhaps, as we ought to word it for some too restless spirits in these days, not shutting our eyes to anything because it is old, nor accepting anything merely because it is new. In this spirit we shall leave our illusions behind us when, and not till when, God has prepared us to receive the truths they severally contain. Against what dangers, then, looking to past history, ought we in England now specially to be on our guard? Surely against this danger, which in some shape or form has been the great pervading peril of Christendom from the first—the danger of substituting for the invisible Christ some other visible Mediator between ourselves and God, or, in other words, the danger of believing too much in the things that are seen, and too little in the things that are not seen.

Take one of these modern perils. We may be superior to that belief in the magical nature of the sacraments, which finds expression in transubstantiation; but are we not unduly influenced sometimes by the quasi-mediatorial nature of the visible Church? The Church—I mean the visible, imperfect Church, not the ideal Church—is, without doubt, one, and perhaps the highest one, among many visible means by which God represents

Christ to us. The Church should be a window in the walls of the world, through which we are to look on Christ. But if, instead of looking straight to Christ through the Church as through a transparent medium, we choose, in our dread of high ideals and our preference for familiar imperfections, to place behind that medium the intercepting stratum of our own earthiness, then straightway the visible Church becomes a mere mirror to throw back upon us the reflection of our own gross selves; then all the ordinances and rites and services and spheres of useful action within the pale of the Church forthwith degenerate, and the polluted temple of Christ becomes nothing better than a mere asylum, constructed to shelter servile outcasts fleeing from the punishing hand of offended righteousness. Tinged by our selfish sensuousness, Christ Himself ceases to be a Man, and becomes a Scheme of Salvation. It is in this superstitious, lazy spirit that a faithless soul is tempted to shift from himself the responsibility of using the God-given faculties of conscience and reason under cover of an appeal to a vast number of imperfect beings like oneself: "*Securus judicat orbis terrarum.*"

How lazy and how degrading a subterfuge! As Adam shifted the blame on Eve, so at the judgment-day we are to shift the blame on our society, be it what it may, our sect, our nation, our Church, the Church of humanity, the common sense of all generations: "The Church deceived me, and I did eat!" Ah! how much nobler that spirit of solitary strength standing out against an opposing world in the might of the unbending consciousness of right, which extracted praise even from the imperial and Epicurean poet beholding—

> "—cuncta terrarum subacta
> Præter atrocem animum Catonis."

The spirit of acquiescence which befits young children still in the circle of the family, which once befitted Christians in the dark and middle ages when learning and judgment were beyond their reach, and which even now may befit uneducated Christians so long as they are placed in the same disabling circumstances, does not, in these days, justify an educated man in closing his eyes against the errors of the Church as revealed by history, or in rejecting the teachings of science and criticism simply that he may have the satisfaction of repeating the same thoughts in the same syllables as are shouted by the largest crowd he can find. Against the danger of being induced to blink the truth by the desire of such "security" as this, every man of sense and spirit will resolutely guard.

A second danger, perhaps more common, has been the substitution of the Bible for Christ. In the great struggle of the Reformation it was natural that the written "Word of God" should be appealed to by Protestants as a standard higher and more trustworthy than the decision of any church-council. But men went beyond this. Breaking with the infallible Church, but still in the old, faithless way craving for some infallible and visible guide beside the Spirit of Christ, the Reformed Churches would fain have fastened infallibility upon the mass of inspired literature, product of many different minds and ages, known to us by the name of the Bible. The tradition of the old illusion has still left its mark in England : and to this day there are some who conscientiously believe that not a single historical inaccuracy, much less intellectual error or moral imperfection, is to be found in all the pages of the Scriptures. Such an illusion may, at present—more shame for the prevailing ignorance—do little harm to the simple cottager poring reverently over the Sacred Volume, and superstitiously accepting every word of it as literally exactly true : *he* does no violence to his intellect, he forces himself to reject no other revelation of God, he stifles no voice of conscience. But with the educated man it is otherwise. He knows that, in all early literature, narratives recording supernatural events are to be accepted with suspicion, and that many such narratives, without any desire to deceive, record what is natural as being supernatural, merely because the laws of nature were not then recognized. He knows that both the Old and New Testament—as though Providence had expressly intended to guard us against the idolatry of a book—contain not less, but more, variations than the MSS. of classical authors ; and, further, that several passages in the New Testament, as well as in the Old, are demonstrably interpolated. Lastly, he knows that criticism has not yet concluded its investigations in this direction, and that, if men were to base their faith in Christ on the exact accuracy of every detail in each of the Gospels, many years might not elapse before basis and superstructure alike would be utterly destroyed. Knowing all this, the educated man who persuades himself to act as though he believed in the old illusion of the infallibility of the Scriptures, is guilty of an error, for him quite as dangerous and degrading as the illusion he has discarded of the infallibility of the visible Church.

It is best to be plain as to the nature of this self-imposed delusion in educated men. It is very often of the same kind as the self-imposed delusion of the Pharisees with reference to the law. Facts told the Scribes, their hearts at times told them, that the law was not perfect, not a finality. But the thought of the imperfection of the law was so distressing to them, so very inconvenient, that they repressed it. Without the old lamp for their feet, whither might they not wander? Who could suppose that Jehovah would thus destroy the light He had Himself given, and leave His people guideless and in the dark? For, as to the misty shifting testimony of conscience, what was it that it should for a moment be compared with the definite testimony of an unchanging law? Not to speak of the loss of their own *status* and occupation as the interpreters of the law and depositories of traditional comment, the destruction or merging of the law in any new dispensation was too bewildering to be thought of. Hence they refused to think of it, and, if the thought would rise, they hardened their hearts against it; they taught against, and acted against, the law of conscience, wherever it came into collision with the law of Moses. So doing, they were branded by Christ with the terrible name of hypocrites: but might not some of us also incur this same charge if Christ were now moving as a man among us? As the veil of nationalism was upon the hearts of the teachers of the Jews whenever the law was read, so is the veil perchance on our hearts too, the veil of sectarianism, or ecclesiasticism, or sensualism, or rationalism, some shape or other of selfish prejudice obscuring our insight into truth. To us the latest, as well as to the earliest disciples of Christ, is addressed that awful warning: "Beware of the leaven of the Pharisees and Sadducees, which is hypocrisy."

But there is another kind of veil on our hearts, besides the veil, of self-will, self-interest, and servile dread of a vague and unfamiliar future. It is the veil of our fleshly and earthy prejudice. Be as unselfish as we may, we cannot help attaching too much importance to "the things that do appear," too little to unseen things. It is not anthropomorphism that we need fear, but rather the worship of the lower and grosser parts of human nature, and respect for those things that appeal to it; the danger of confusing heavenly realities with earthly metaphors; the terribly cramping power of language, which should be the servant, but too often becomes the master, of thought. The poetic descriptions of a material heaven and material punishments, the pictures of paradise, the plans and maps of hell and purgatory, have done their work in preserving and intensifying faith in the justice of God and in the inevitable punishment of sin: but they have also done harm in partly concealing the spiritual truth which they have enclosed. It is time now for us to discard the husk and to fix our thoughts on the fruit. The only heaven is the perfect fruition of the fatherhood of God; the only hell is the consciousness that we are averted from Him; the only purgatory is the scorching, yet attracting sense of His intolerable light, by which our half-unwilling selves are to be drawn in to be absorbed, destroyed, and live again in

Him. The grosser views too prevalent about the joys of the future heaven, in their artificial assumptions encourage all sorts of artificial theories about the way in which those joys may be gained or lost. Hence springs in the better sort of minds incredulity and disbelief in any future, but in the lower sort a positive distaste for spiritual life, and some such unfitness for the true heaven as is expressed in the following imaginary lament of a disappointed saint arriving at the portals of paradise:—

> "No train of angels at the gate!
> No glories on my vision fall!
> No blaze of pomp, no regal state!
> And is this heaven? And is this all?"

The conception of a material hell is a far greater stumbling-block than the illusion of a material heaven. The time has indeed passed when educated men could try to coerce others or could allow others to coerce them into rectitude, by such detailed descriptions of the several punishments of hell as we find in Dante's *Inferno*. We revolt nowadays against the lake of burning pitch, the draughts of molten gold, the showers of scorching snow, the fiends with prongs and pincers, and all the rest of the old apparatus of hellish horror. None the less are we haunted by the thoughts of them, and the spectre often works one of two evil results. Either we transfer our terrors from a material to an immaterial hell, and continue to believe that there may be, after all, such horrors (only immaterial), so malignant, so fiendish, so wastefully vengeful—in which case we lose all trust in God, and drop into slaves in His presence: or else we throw up belief in a future punishment of any kind at all, in which case we lower our sense of God's justice, and with it our sense of His mercy; and, in the end, discarding our belief in heaven as well as in hell, we give up all thought of the future, all hopes and fears of immortality.

It is high time to preach heaven and hell to men anew, as states rather than places, inevitable and natural; spiritual in deed, supernatural if you like, but natural too, as natural as the law of gravitation. The change that will pass over each one of us at death may be a sudden and a striking one, as striking as the change of the chrysalis into the butterfly; but, as the nature and substance of the chrysalis caused and shaped the substance and form of the butterfly, so that there is not on the wings of the fresh-born fluttering insect a single spot or shade of colour which is not the inevitable and predetermined result of past causes, so with the soul of man, what we shall be will depend upon what we were and are; and, even in heaven, our earthly acts and words and thoughts, and even the sins washed by the purifying blood of Christ, will in some shape still appear colouring our individual existence, and moulding the nature of our heavenly service.

But we must preach the true hell as well as the true heaven. It is difficult to describe the wholesome influence that the just fear of a natural hell would exert upon the minds of Englishmen. We in this country are known as a law-loving people: we abhor the thought of arbitrary or capricious punishment. Consequently, when we interpret literally passages of Scripture which represent the Judge as sitting on the white throne with the whole world at His bar, and, at a word, summoning

one portion to the joys of heaven and banishing another
to the fires of hell, our minds revolt against a species of
judgment which seems to put on one side the countless
shades of righteousness and unrighteousness and the
countless extenuations or aggravations of circumstances,
of which no English judge would fail to take account.
But, if we would analyse the true meaning of ideal
judgment and ideal punishment, then, instead of hastily
and presumptuously rejecting, we should accept such
passages with spiritual profit. The ideal judgment is
not a mere utterance of words pronounced by a judge
and followed by legal penalty. For what if your audience
rejects your judgment as partial ? What if the criminal
himself resents it as unjust ? You may coerce his body ;
but, if you have not coerced his mind by your judgment,
you have achieved but a poor triumph, fit for a despot,
not for the ideal judge. The ideal judgment is not a
collection of words, nor a physical pain, but a *thought*.
It is the sense of the contrast between good and evil
and of the condemnation of evil by contrast with good,
passing from the mind of the judge with irresistible force
into the mind not only of the audience, but also of the
criminal himself. Following on this definition of the
ideal judgment is the definition of the ideal punishment.
It is a punishment appropriate, inevitable, acknowledged
to be just by the offender, and executed by him upon himself. Like the ideal judgment, so the ideal punishment
is a *thought*, not a place : it is the above-mentioned
contrast between sin and righteousness awakened for
the first time in the heart of the sinner, a two-edged
sword cleaving the guilty soul in twain, dividing the
light from the darkness in him, and making the darkness

for the first time black and terrible in the consciousness of the dawning light; it is the unsatisfied yearning for purity, the passionate loathing of the sin-tainted self, the knowledge of what might have been, the dreary sense of what is and must be and ought to be now, of what must be and ought to be for ages upon ages, the pitiable prospect of an almost endless struggle; and with all this the stern, irrepressible voice of the self-judging conscience of the sinner, "Yes, this is just, this is merciful; it cannot be otherwise; it is the best for me; it is the best for all." Will not hell come upon us Christians as a new revelation when we have finally disabused ourselves of the old illusion of materialism and have learned to acknowledge that, after all, the justice of the Father of our Lord Jesus Christ is not inferior to justice as it was defined by the greatest of the Greeks, "Giving to every one what is best for him"?

Carrying out consistently the process of spiritualizing our conceptions of Christ, we shall do well to disentangle our faith in Him from every thought that would limit His nature and work by physical and material considerations. When we speak of Him as having ascended into heaven, we obviously must not lay stress upon a mere change of place nor upon a visible transportation of His body, or a semblance of His body, in a vertical direction above the eyes of a number of spectators. I myself believe that the Apostles actually saw the Ascension; but another Christian may disbelieve this, and yet, if he acknowledges that Christ is spiritually exalted in power over the universe and over the hearts of His disciples, he will have attained the real substance of the faith in the Ascension. In the same way Christ's present glory does not consist in the fact that He now occupies a material seat upon the right hand of God, but rather in the perfect spiritual communion which we believe to exist between the Father and the Son. Or, to go still further, the divine Sonship of Jesus of Nazareth does not consist in the fact that Jesus was begotten by a miraculous act the Son of Mary and not of Joseph, but rather in identity of will and in virtue of spiritual sonship such as no other human being can claim. If therefore at any time criticism should prove to demonstration that the earlier chapters of St. Matthew's Gospel and St. Luke's Gospel are not historically accurate, a spiritual believer in Christ would none the less retain his belief that Jesus of Nazareth is the only begotten Son of God.

The man whose faith in Christ, though it may have been nourished and preserved by historical illusions, has grown hardy and strong enough to dispense with any props liable to be shaken by science and criticism, and who can fight all doubts in the strength of his trust in the human personality of Christ—he, and he alone, can feel confident, in these days, that his faith will remain unmoved. So far from trembling at science, such a believer will echo the grand saying of Edward Irving, that every creature, from the archangel in heaven to the worm that crawleth on the ground, doth bear witness unto Christ. The infinite past revealed by geology and history, the millions of years possibly spent in collecting and hardening this planetary globe of ours, the millions more required for furnishing it with vegetable and animal life, and for elaborating that life up to the level of humanity, the dreary ages of supposed savage or semi-human existence, the collisions of conflicting nations, tending to eliminate inferior races, and to develop the higher qualities of humanity—all these will seem to the spiritual believer in Christ to indicate, not too long nor too grand a preparation for the Incarnation of the Son of God. Calmly reviewing the past, he will look forward to the future with equal calmness; for if so many thousands or millions of years were required to prepare the field for the seed of God, well may a few thousands or millions more be required before that seed shall have had time to germinate and fructify.

CHAPTER XXV.

THE FUTURE WORSHIP OF CHRIST.

When natural science and history take their right place in our schools, the change that has been of late years coming over men's minds with relation to Christianity will probably become more rapid and general. The next generation may find themselves altogether unable to believe in the historical accuracy of many parts of the Scriptures which they at present unhesitatingly accept. There will be, perhaps, no sudden revolution in criticism, no new discoveries bearing on the text of the New Testament; but the minds of the youth of England will gradually take a different turn, and exactly the former convictions will no longer be possible. The lock being altered, the old key will no longer turn in it. What then will happen will depend greatly upon the manner in which the teachers of Christian truth prepare to meet the impending change.

Some teachers may resolve to make no preparation except increased industry in inculcating the old doctrines and in exposing deviations from them. *Stare super antiquas vias*, may seem to them the sole watchword in the face of impending revolution. Others may think that the right course is to begin at once to place before the young a complete scheme of sceptical assaults, with their several appropriate refutations. Neither course is free from objection. As for " standing on the old ways," be it remembered that Time, the great innovator, never stands still, so that if we wish to keep things the same relatively to their surroundings, we must needs be perpetually making changes. If the generations progress, the modes of teaching the truth and the shapes and forms that truth will assume must progress also, however the truth may remain unchanged. "Antiquity deserveth that reverence that men should make a stand thereupon, and discover what is the best way." True; but the author continues, " But when the discovery is well taken, then to make progression." The second, or polemic course, is open to the obvious charge that it tends to concentrate the attention of the young too much upon polemics, too little on religion, too much on dogmatic Christianity, too little on Christ.

The course I should myself adopt in teaching the young, would be rather to endeavour to make Christ in His human nature appear to them admirable, lovable, adorable, and, in a word, so naturally necessary to their souls, that in after days, if they found themselves obliged to give up certain historical beliefs, they would still retain their faith in Christ, because that faith was based, not upon minute details of history, but upon the inherent necessities and aspirations of their own hearts. While studiously refraining from saying anything that might shake the faith of the young in those relatively unimportant parts of the Scriptures about which one might be compelled to suspend one's judgment, or which may appear on good grounds not authentic, it would be quite possible to find in the Scriptures an inexhaustible material for the purposes of positive instruction tending to faith in Christ, so that no danger need be anticipated of any cramping limitations that might make the teaching of the Scriptures a forced and unnatural lesson.

If the next generation is not, in this or some similar way, prepared to lay hold on Christ, it seems likely that the present defection from Him will speedily be increased. Some few souls of special spiritual insight having penetrated by the divine grace beyond Christianity to Christ Himself, will have been drawn by Him into a region where logic and doubt cannot enter: but for the majority a fiery trial is in store. Young men will find themselves called upon to join one of two camps, the camp of Reason, or the camp of a Christianity that will (rightly or wrongly) appear to them essentially unreasonable. According to their dispositions they will make their several choices, some giving up Reason, and probably finding a refuge in the Church of Rome; others, and these perhaps the majority, giving up Christianity.

Now, without underrating the effect on the imagination produced by the grand and continuous history of the Church of Rome, it may still be doubted whether that Church is likely to retain a permanent hold upon men trained in our public schools, in our universities, and in the political institutions of free England. Still more doubtful is it whether men gifted by Nature with faculties of love, trust, and awe, can long tolerate life without any higher object to call forth these faculties than the men and women in their society. On both classes Christ, if presented as an object of worship in virtue of His humanity, might exercise a novel and powerful attraction. More especially might He influence those who still believe in a God and have not yet rejected Christ, but are in danger of doing so because they are told that they cannot be Christians without believing in many things that they regard as impossible and unnatural. "Here," they will say, "is a new religion, offering us a noble and natural object of worship, offering us perfect peace, freedom from doubts, freedom from theological wranglings. Why should we not worship Christ? Nay, we do worship Him: for there is no one in the world, sceptics though we are, for whom we entertain more love and trust and awe, than for Him: and if these three feelings constitute worship, then have we been needlessly estranging ourselves from Christ, being in fact ready to worship Him, even when we thought we were rejecting Him. We have lost much by ceasing to think of Him as our example, our sacrifice, the sustenance of our souls; we have lost much by feeling unable to work consciously for Him, to profess ourselves His servants, to confess Him as our Lord, our King. There is not much in a name, but there is something; and we have lost something by not calling ourselves Christians. Why too should we absent ourselves from the prayers and services of the Church? Surely there is little, even in the Creeds themselves, in which we cannot join. Do we not believe that Christ is the Son of God, and One with God? Do we not believe that He is now on God's right hand, and that He is and will be the Judge of mankind? Do we not believe that He offered Himself up as a sacrifice for men, and that He manifested Himself after death to His disciples, and that

His Spirit guided and guides the Church? All this we spiritually believe. Others believe it materially; but their material belief is only so far worth anything as it includes the spiritual belief which we hold. In reality, therefore, and in spirit, we are in harmony with those who are called orthodox. Let us then neither separate ourselves from them, nor insist upon making a new sect or a new form of worship. If either party ought to make concessions, we ought to concede: for they stand, in name at all events, upon the old ways; and our faith is safer and stronger than theirs.

Let us assume that some such a spirit as this will come over the next or some future generation; and let us ask what, on this assumption, would be the result, and what future would be in store for Christianity? The first apparent result would seem to be a return to the principles of the very earliest Church, in which Christ was everything, and Christianity, as yet, nothing. The Person of Christ would assume quite new proportions, and the Christian religion would be seen to consist in nothing else but allegiance to Him. Some would retain the old material beliefs, others would discard them, others would suspend their judgment about them; but in all alike the feeling of loyalty to the King of Salvation would so overshadow all details of the forms of religious faith that the latter would be felt to be of infinitely less importance than the former, not to be fought about, nor wrangled about—interesting, no doubt, and fully deserving of the attention and investigation of historians, scholars, and physiologists, but in no way whatever affecting the vital rooted allegiance of the heart for Christ. The Church of Christ would once more become what it was

E E

proclaimed to be by Christ Himself; not a close theological club, excluding all but those who will sign certain theological conventions and bye-laws, but a kingdom inviting to the privileges of citizenship all those who feel for Christ more love, trust, and awe than for any other human being. The worship and service of Christ will become far more natural and inviting than it is now, and far more attractive to those who are outside the Church. Addressing non-believers, the Church will say—not, " Here is our theological club, we invite you to enter it. Our bye-laws can be demonstrated almost with the same cogency as Euclid : accept them, and you shall be made comfortable for life and for all time after ; reject them, and you shall be tortured for all eternity"— but rather, " Here is the Kingdom of God : we citizens of it find a great peace in it and a wonderful help toward well-doing in serving God as He has been revealed to us by Jesus of Nazareth, whom we regard as His Eternal Son. Do you not also feel drawn towards Jesus ? Do you not feel the need of Someone to love, and trust, and reverence ? Can you point to anyone who can be a worthier object of such feelings ? If you cannot, come into our kingdom. We welcome all comers as citizens, we impose no intellectual conditions, we recognize the restrictions of no laws. We do not ask you to believe a number of dogmas or material facts *about* Christ : all we ask is that you should believe *in* Christ as the supreme object of love, trust, and awe. Even if you cannot do this, but can only wish to do it, we still ask you to attend our meetings for worship and for service : for we find that in the fellowship of united, though imperfect worship, there is a strange power knitting Christians together and making Christ more intelligible to them. Come, if you will, then, as half-citizens till you feel yourselves able to claim the rights of our full franchise. Only come." In response to such an appeal it seems to me that thousands of educated men in England and in India, now aliens from Christ, would crowd back into the Church.

In the New Church there will be much more leisure for faith in Christ than there is in the Church at present. As things are, how common is it to hear five-sixths of a sermon or a theological treatise devoted to proving that everybody else but the speaker or writer is wrong, and, of the remaining sixth, five-sixths again devoted to proving that the writer's sect or church is right, and nothing but the beggarly residue left to illustrate Christ and to make Him manifest to the hearts of men! But in the future we may hope that all this will be changed. Three hundred years ago Bacon anticipated increased leisure for science from " the consumption of all that can be said in controversies of religion, which have so much diverted men from other sciences." That, indeed, was a lamentably unscientific prediction: for how was it possible that men could desist from spinning their interminable cobwebs of religious controversy as long as they considered that on the issue of the controversies hung eternal life or death? The more trifling or the more insoluble was the problem, the more bitter and interminable the controversy was sure to be, because it must needs be waged without possibility of appeal to any scientific standard. But now, as men come to estimate religious polemics at their true insignificance and religious faith at its true worth, religious polemics may be trusted to vanish, not for lack of matter, but for lack of interest in it, or rather owing to the absorbing and overshadowing interest of higher thoughts. When once the invisible processes of forgiveness, sacrifice, faith, imputation of righteousness, and justification by faith are recognized as natural, no less than the law of gravitation, then people, instead of wrangling about them, will accept them as actions of a spiritual force, and will make this their main question, "How can we live such lives as to obtain means of doing Christ better service than we are doing at present? How can we best draw others in to the kingdom of God?" The principles of science being now accepted, the business of scientific men is to act upon them, and to make fresh discoveries; just so will it be with religion. The principles of religion being accepted, the age of polemics will be supplanted by the age of action and discovery. Then at last, with better grounds perhaps, we may look for the fulfilment of Bacon's prediction, slightly modified, and may hope for a disregard of all that can ever be said in controversies of Christianity which have so much diverted men from Christ and Christian action.

Heaven and hell, in the New Church, looked on as Christ looked on them, will more powerfully influence human conduct. It will be felt that heaven means doing God's will, means sincerity, means doing good work, whether it pays well or badly, means a hatred of all things mean and ignoble and a love of all that is high and pure, means a sense of mission and communion with sources not one's own of more than human light and purity and truth: and, feeling this, men will think more of these blessings and less of money and amusements, and sensual gratifications, and social so-called pleasures and attractions. Blake in his single squalid room, Fox in his leather breeches sitting by night in a hollow oak, or sleeping in a hedge-bottom, but endowed with the consciousness of heaven-sent gifts and tasks, will then seem nearer to heaven, dearer to the hearts of the living, and destined to be dearer to the hearts of posterity than many a complacent poet or popular historian, or even the greatest of those successful politicians, skilled not in things, but in the way of putting things, [illegible] of statesmanship have consistently carried out Bacon's advice to the selfish statesman, "Let him not trouble himself too laboriously to sound into any matter deeply, or to execute anything exactly: but let him make himself cunning rather in the humours and drifts of persons than in the nature of business and affairs."

When once men recognize—in the scientific spirit of Christ—the intervening *must be* as well as the far-off *will be*, and the continuity between earth and heaven or earth and hell, then all life will become at once grander and vaster, more religious and yet more sane. The joys and sorrows and duties of earth will all become ampler and fuller, in the recognition of their limitless consequences. A new nobility will fall upon the simplest relations between human beings. The ties of the family will be strengthened, ennobled, and purified. The old Roman leaven in us, which makes us still look down on petty trades and on some kinds of occupations, will be quite driven out: and the most menial service will then be, socially as well as ecclesiastically, recognized as service done to Christ, and therefore essentially noble.

Even that cruellest and hardest of all physical evils to endure, the long and weary waiting of the sick man amid the increasing pains of a lingering death—how much more bearable will it appear when it is felt that every drop in the cup of suffering has been blessed by Christ, and is, according to His will and according to the laws of the world, that is, the will of the Father, moulding and strengthening the soul of the sufferer for an eternity of nobler work hereafter, perchance to be the guardian angel of some nation or some planet, or to be a world-inspiring poet, teaching in yet higher strains to yet more countless multitudes the lesson taught us by Milton:—

"They also serve who only stand and wait."

The new and purified fear of hell will produce a new and increased hatred of sin, not only a hatred of great and striking sinful actions, such as murder, robbery, and the like, but something approaching to Christ's horror of the sinful *state*, the "life of the flesh," as St. Paul calls it—or, as we call it nowadays, the life of selfishness. Men will no longer ask, "How far may I enjoy myself without regard to my fellow-creatures, and yet gain heaven?" or, "What definite sins must I avoid so that I may just escape hell?"—but they will say to themselves, "So far as I am selfish and worldly, no abstinence from definite sinful acts can avail me: so far as I am selfish, I am in hell already and treasuring up future punishments of hell for future ages. God, I know, will conform me unto His image in the end; but woe unto me if I protract His task. Whether after death I meet my loved ones, the dear, the innocent, the pure, the great souls and minds of all past ages, in close communion with Jesus Himself, or whether, after death, I pass to I know not what condition or region of cold, unsatisfied, far-off longing for all that is good and bright— this has been placed by God in my power; and every thought and word and deed of to-day will shape my destiny, by shaping my character, to the uttermost ages of the future." Men will no longer shrink like slaves from the supposed tortures of God, nor will they defy them, like freemen resisting a despot. They will accept in accordance with a divine order, and they will regulate their lives accordingly. Instead of being an endless, arbitrary torture, it will be a limited and appropriate punishment: but it will be natural and inevitable, and belief in the natural justice of God will be found a far more powerful moral agent on the human mind than belief in an unnatural vengeance.

Then by degrees there will arise in the New Church a new estimate—Christ's estimate—of the great things and small things of life. As the poet tells us of Lazarus that after he had risen from the dead he moved about the visible world in a different way from common men, like one seeing things invisible, startled and shocked at apparent trifles, and indifferent to many grand and striking incidents, so will it be with all upon whom the invisible-seeing Spirit of Christ has once passed. Not only will men seek more after righteousness and less after luxury and wealth; but they will also be roused to a new sense of beauty and culture, and to a new appreciation of Art and Science, recognizing in them two hands from the Father, whereby He is moulding His immortal children for unending destinies. Once more will Art be studied in the old religious spirit, yet not now in any bondage to materialism or to conventional dogma, but with the sense that in Art, as in Morality, the Spirit of God will ever lead us into new fields if we will ever follow like little children. Art and Science as well as religion, will be regarded as civilising influences, with which the state is bound to encompass each of its future citizens. As we grow in the knowledge of the human mind, educational methods will be better understood, better practised, and more easily and surely communicated to future teachers. Then, and not till then, education will reach its standard, and produce its legitimate results. Pleasures will become simpler and purer, and at the same time less costly, and the State will be enabled to give the very poorest of its children such a training as will enable rich and poor to meet together on a common footing, no longer divided by gulfs of difference in knowledge, and taste, and thought.

The Congregation can hardly fail to become, in the New Church, a far more social influence than it is at present. When once the social spirit of Christ has taken hold of men, and the nature of the true worship is understood, then that great law of fellowship upon which Christ based His promise, that wherever two or three are gathered together there He would be present— will be more fully understood and more widely acted on. Prayer and verbal praise will seem a very small part indeed of worship, a very unsatisfying manner of expressing allegiance. The same Spirit that impelled many to assemble for prayer would probably impel many to remain, or assemble again for work; and philanthropy, in a thousand new shapes as well as in the old shapes, would be universally recognized as a true and almost necessary form of congregational service. Thus the reproach of selfishness brought against the English life might be wiped out, and the Congregation, supplying in this way the link at present missing for the English people, might fill the chasm between the life of the family and the life of the nation, and might do for England what the πόλις did for the Greeks. Poor-laws would everywhere be supplanted by congregational benevolence, working through personal, not official, kindness, and bringing naturally on society that double blessing which always falls on mercy. But the congregational efforts would not stop short at alms-giving. If ever, in addition to the Grecian sense of beauty, the Roman sense of order, the Jewish sense of holiness, and the English sense of growth and continuity, the spirit of Christian philanthropy and the spiritual yet scientific conception of earthly life as the natural preparation for an eternal life, should ever take root in our hearts, it would then be felt that the Church—and in the Church the congregation—has a far nobler work before it than any that we have yet contemplated. The Church will triumph over the world, not by renouncing the world, but by consecrating the world to the service of Christ. Ministers of religion will no longer set this life against the next, earth against heaven, earthly joys against heavenly joys. The object will be to train the body, mind, and spirit of every citizen of this country so as to prepare each for the kingdom of God, by removing excessive temptations to evil, by supplying helps and encouragements to good: and among these helps and encouragements will be the capacity of each for receiving, and causing to others, the maximum of happiness. Each church in each town or hamlet, besides having its common treasury for external and internal philanthropic purposes, will have its museum, its library, its schools and scholarships, giving to the very poorest children an open career in study, if only they prove themselves worthy of it. At the social and business meetings of the congregation, rich and poor, meeting on terms of more intellectual equality than at present, will hold a freer and more natural intercourse. The standard of social morality being raised, and the conscience being awakened to the claims of the society upon the individual, men will no longer, as at present, make it the object of their lives to accumulate, with all speed, in trade, business, or profession, wealth enough to enable them to retire and to live in idleness. Work will no longer be done so perfunctorily, life will be not subjected to its present unnatural strain, and the holidays and relaxations of life will not be so conventionally dull or so unhealthily unnatural. Men will take a greater pleasure in their daily work, in their homes, in their several towns and neighbourhoods. A man of wealth will feel, and be felt by others, disgraced if he has not done something with his money during his life to leave a beneficial mark upon his neighbourhood. There will be a somewhat closer approximation to the times of ancient Rome, when "men's private incomes were small, but the common treasury ample." Round the Church will cluster much of the art and taste, as well as the philanthropy of the congregation. Each church will be a receptacle of many congregational thank-offerings and memorials, not in the petty style to which we are now accustomed, but on such a scale as to encourage the highest art: and such pictures as "The Light of the World," and the "Finding of Christ in the Temple," instead of being hawked about the kingdom by dealers, will find their way immediately to churches as their natural homes. The public spirit of the congregation will begin with its own immediate neighbourhood, but it will not end there: the nation will also profit from it. Everywhere there will be the growing feeling that it is in such things, vulgar, for a private man to retain for his own use or enjoyment objects of unusual beauty or public utility. Private picture-galleries, museums, and collections will be rare; public collections more numerous and complete. Inequalities of property, and unequal burdens of work and hardship—which we may suppose to have been partly remedied already in our new Church by the diminished temptations and increased pleasures of the life of the poor—will be still further removed as the Spirit of Christ moves men with increasing power. To effect all this there would be no appeal to the constraining force of legislation: it would be the result of quickened conscience, roused to a livelier recognition of neighbourly duty, by a keener sense of allegiance to a common Master.

In the New Church death will no longer be feared. For, when the bugbear of an unjust hell is removed, and the spiritual resurrection of Christ is recognised— like the law of gravitation—as an undeniable fact or law confirmed by daily phenomena, then death will assume its right position as the minister of love, and the servant of eternal life. Then, the fear of death being abolished, the accursed ugliness of mutes and hearses, and the like—which do more now to make death fearful to little children than all St. Paul's Epistles can do to make it not fearful—will be no longer tolerated.[1] Recognizing the continuity between life and death, all will find prayer for the dead reasonable as well as natural and necessary. Even for the bad, as well as the good, it will be felt that there was a sure and certain hope in the life, or in some of the many lives, to come. But the memory of the blessed dead, rooted in the minds of the living by the daily prayers of a lifetime, and dissociated from all the old servile terrors and superstitious pollutions which have desecrated prayer for the dead in the minds of English Protestants, will become, next to Christ, the most powerful uplifting influence in the Christian Church.

All this will come to pass in its due course, for it is the inevitable result of Christ's influence upon men, and it is but a continuation of what has already begun. But the time is not yet. Superstition and self-interest must first have their day, and be tried as the remedies for the evils of mankind, and be found wanting, and be rejected, before the day of the Lord can arrive.

The history of Jesus upon earth may possibly be repeated in the history of His Church. As the Galilean peasants rejected the Messiah who would not assume the

[1] Much of this indeed could be stopped at once if but a few men of standing and piety would, in their wills or other expression of their last wishes, request their friends not to wear mourning for them, and *cause the request to be published with the advertisement of their death*. Not till the survivors are thus protected against the imputation of unfeeling neglect, can a reform be expected.

substantial pomp of a Herod or a Cæsar, so half of Christendom may fall away from Christ when reason no longer allows them to picture the Saviour wreathed in literal flames and sitting aloft upon a material cloud. Again, as the Pharisee rejected the righteousness of God and sought to hide themselves from it in a thicket of legal formalities, so some of us may seek to flee from the judgment of the All-seeing and from the voice of our own consciences, which is His voice, to the covert of forms and dogmas, absolution of priests, or justification by faith, or the efficacy of the sacraments, or the inspiration of the Scriptures—anything, in short, *about* Christ, so as to escape from Christ Himself. But it will not avail us. Science and conscience, working as allies, will go throughout the world stealing into the hearts of men : science will break off the enclosing husks of illusion from the seeds of truth, conscience will commend them to the soil of the human heart, and the tree of the Church will grow anew.

But self-interest is a more dangerous foe, impenetrable to the shafts of science, nay, rather sometimes an ally of science, fighting under her shield ; and it seems impossible that men should learn the lesson of unselfishness except by repeated trials of trust in self-interest, and by repeated disappointments.

Yet until men and nations have learned that self-interest cannot furnish a solid basis for any stable kind of society, Christ cannot "come." Evil, therefore, must come before the good. Rich men must follow, for many a year to come, their foolish chase after a happiness to be bought by money. Class must be arrayed against class in the vain hope of attaining a selfish happiness, the rich by extorting the maximum of labour, the poor by extorting the maximum of pay. Commercial selfishness carried to its legitimate result, must work out its own punishment, and bring on the collapse of trades, stagnation of industries, the ruin perhaps of nations. Nations themselves must play out their cruel game of war; great races must wear one another out beneath the burdens and costs of armaments. All the panaceas but the right one for the evils of humanity will be tried and worked out to their utmost consequences of mischief. Alliances, nationalities, political constitutions, gigantic international trades-unions, leagues against war, leagues against the inconveniences of sin, all these and all other methods of subduing sin from the outside, instead of extinguishing it from the inside in the heart of man, must be tried, and tried often, before the human race will be induced finally to cast them all aside as no true saviours for mankind. Science also, with her enlarged dominion over all material things, must have her day of illusion, and must tempt mankind with her dream of a comfortable existence, in which every man shall have food enough and work enough, as in the traditions of the days of Solomon recorded by the chroniclers of Israel, an existence free from pain and disease, prolonged amid rational and intellectual enjoyments, and brought to a timely close by the painless skill of the physician. Endowed with strange and admirable powers, fortified against pain, fearless of death, exulting year by year in new revelations of knowledge, and in new capacities for pleasure, humanity will seem to some its own best self-sufficing saviour. This dream in its turn must be dreamed out, till men awake, weary of the paradise of science in which, though there is the tree of knowledge, there is no tree of life; though there is no pain, there is sin; though there is no sickness, there is sorrow—sorrow for the loss of friend after friend, sorrow for one's own approaching severance from dear survivors, sorrow made all the more bitter by the new-discovered pleasures of the happy world.

Not till Christ's prophecies have been perfectly fulfilled can the coming of Christ take place. Not till [...] other Christs in vain shall humanity at last turn, self-convicted of [...] appealing in its uttermost despair to the Despised and Rejected of men, whom then, and not till then, every heart shall adore and every eye behold as the one True Judge and Saviour of the World. Exalted to the skies, Christ, with the two-edged sword of His Spirit, shall summon all mankind to His tribunal, dividing and distinguishing good and evil, and pronouncing His irresistible verdict, by which righteousness shall be purified for an eternal life, and evil, self-condemned, shall execute its own irreversible destruction. Then shall come the end of all things, when the whole human race, bringing to a close its weary wanderings and its ignoble servitudes, and leaning on the supporting hand of the Son of Man, shall throw itself in self-surrendering penitence at the foot of the Eternal God, and entering into His palace, shall be surprised to find itself, not in a strange region, but returned to a familiar home. There, in that atmosphere of Truth, summing up in one view all its past existences and all future developments, the human soul shall perceive at last that God works all things well, that illusions have led to knowledge, and sin itself to higher righteousness; and while the harmony of all the ages breathes forth to us the meaning of Time, which is the unutterable Name of God, our hearts shall all confess that the riddle of the perplexing Metaphor of the world was the best preparation for the revelation of the Eternal Word.

APPENDIX.

APPENDIX.

ON A POSSIBLE ORIGIN OF THE MIRACULOUS ELEMENT IN THE NEW TESTAMENT.

To do justice to this subject it would be necessary to take each miracle separately, to examine it in detail, and to shew how it might have originated without a basis of supernatural fact, and yet without any intention on the part of the narrator to deceive. But it is obviously impossible to embody the results of such an investigation in a short Appendix; all that I can do here is briefly to indicate the argument and to give one or two illustrations of it.

But before proceeding to the argument, I must premise that I do not decide against the miraculous element as being incredible simply because it professes to be miraculous. I can quite understand the position of those who hold that the Maker of the world provided from the first that in the history of mankind there should be certain miracle-epochs and miracle-workers, whose works should be contrary indeed to the ordinary laws of Nature, but still in conformity with certain rarely manifested laws of Nature—laws of which at present we know little or nothing, and which might be regarded as a direct manifestation of the divine Will. My difficulty in the way of adopting the theory of miracle-epochs is, that the evidence in favour of it does not appear to be so strong as the evidence in favour of a different theory. The more one studies the history of all ancient nations, the more one finds that antiquity is always the home of the supernatural, and that criticism reduces the supernatural to the natural. When we find this in the history of Greece and of Rome, and of ancient Israel, we are naturally led to infer that similar reasoning might explain the phenomena of the history of the New Testament. "There are difficulties and weak points in every theory about the New Testament miracles:" true, but the difficulties inherent in the literal theory seem to me to be greater than the difficulties attending the theory which I may designate as the Metaphorical Theory.

If the miracles of the New Testament were in these days the basis of belief in Christ with any large number of educated persons, I should feel doubtful about the seasonableness of any remarks of a nature to shake that basis. But my impression is that the very miraculous narratives which through the dark and middle ages of the Church were effective, and perhaps necessary, integuments for the preservation and conveyance of Christ's spiritual truths, are now on the contrary becoming, if they have not already become, serious stumbling-blocks to great masses of educated Christians, hindering them from understanding and from worshipping Christ. To these I address myself; and I beg any who feel their faith in Christ to be bound up with faith in the miraculous element of the Gospels not to read further. It is not for them that I am writing. I am writing for those who reject the whole of the Gospel narrative because they conceive that they are logically bound to reject the whole if they reject the miraculous element; and my object is to shew them that it is possible to reject the miracles, and still to retain one's faith in the *honesty* of the *whole* narrative of the New Testament, and in the *historical accuracy* (liable of course, like the accuracy of other histories, to the deductions of criticism) *of that part of it which is not miraculous.*[1]

---

[1] Under the term "miraculous" I include exact fulfilments of Old Testament prophecies in minute detail, *e.g.* the one in St. Matthew xxi. 2; see below, p. 439.

Before going further let me point out that neither Christ nor the early Church justifies us in laying so much stress as is often laid upon the miracles of Christ. Christ, as we know, distrusted the faith that looked to Him as a mere wonder-worker. Almost all His mighty works (I think it could be shewn that all His mighty works) were acts of healing, which (as I have said above, in the Chapter on the True Spirit of Science,) may be accepted as historically accurate but not supernatural. Many even of these acts of healing are expressly recorded to have been performed in secret; and when He spoke of doing seeming impossible things, and said that His disciples should do greater works than He had done, it is evident ***** ***** ***** (in His spiritual estimate of the relative importance of things) was contemplating, not the subversions of mountains, or the uprooting of fig-trees, but the production of repentance and regeneration by the forgiveness of sins—the most difficult and divinest work imposed by God on men. Again in the early Church we find miracles indeed, but almost invariably works of healing, attributed to Christ, and to His disciples, after Christ's death. The power of working "signs" is placed by St. Paul low in the list of heaven-given graces; and no mention whatever is made in the Epistles of any single miracle performed by Christ. The great cardinal fact of the Resurrection is alone insisted on. The feeding of the five thousand or of the four thousand, the raising of Lazarus, the walking of Christ on the waters, the conversion of water into wine, the discovery of the coin in the fish's mouth, the blasting of the barren fig-tree, or the destruction of the two thousand swine by the evil spirits expelled from the Gadarene demoniacs—of all these striking, picturesque actions, evidently supernatural if true, (which one would have supposed would have appealed everywhere to the imaginations of the poor and uncultivated converts) there is absolutely no mention in the Epistles of the New Testament.

Yet, be it remembered, it is the Epistles that exhibit the Church in the act of arguing, convincing, and converting—

rather than the Gospels. The Gospels, at least as we now have them, seem to have been written for the confirmation of believers in the things in which, as St. Luke says, they had "been instructed;" for the purposes of public and private reading; and, in a word, rather for use in the Church than for use against the world. But when St. Paul is arguing against the legalism of the Judaizers in the Epistle to the Romans, or against those who denied the Resurrection, as in the Epistle to the Corinthians—we seem to see the earliest workings of the Christian mind laid bare to us, and it is interesting to note how very little importance seems to have been attached in those early times to the miracles of Christ. It was Christ Himself (not Christ's miracles) that was the spring of the earliest Christian action, Christ declared to be the Son of God with power—not so much by miracles and signs, though they are occasionally mentioned in general terms—as "according to the Spirit of holiness, by the Resurrection from the dead."

Let no one fear, therefore, that if the unhistorical character of the miraculous element in the New Testament should be demonstrated, we should be left without any historical basis for our faith in Christ. Pervading all the Epistles there is distinctly discernible the presence of the Spirit of the Son of God as it "constrained" St. Paul in the earliest times; and we can seek no better constraining influence. Returning to the Gospels we find that (even if we remove the miraculous element) there remains in them a precious treasure of spiritual life and teaching, which, while it explains the constraining influence that led St. Paul to convert the Gentile world, also supplies to us a firm and solid ground for worshipping in Jesus of Nazareth the Son of Man and the Son of God.

To shew this has been the object of the preceding pages—to shew how we may and must be led to the worship of Christ by purely natural considerations, even though we put aside the miraculous element in His life. But in the course of the book, though I have never, as far as I know, based any argument upon anything miraculous, I have, nevertheless, frequently quoted from our Gospels passages which have none of the miraculous element, and have taken for granted their historical accuracy. Now it is possible that some sceptics may say, "How can you draw the line between what is historically accurate and inaccurate in the Gospels? If the narrators have proved themselves untrustworthy by admitting unhistorical matter into their narrations, does it not follow that the whole of their narrative is impugned?" I answer, "No. If we can shew that all, or a great part, of the miraculous element originated not in any desire to deceive, but in a misconception of metaphor (or, possibly, in a misapplication of prophecy worked out in excess of detail, in an honest conviction that the prophecy must have been fulfilled in every point), then we shall see at once that the miraculous and non-miraculous element stand on quite distinct levels. The suspicion that may prevent us from accepting the former will not apply at all to the latter. That Christ literally drove out devils from a Gadarene demoniac into two thousand swine, we may naturally be unable to believe; but if it can be shewn that the narrators of this story did not invent it, but misunderstood it—then why should our non-belief in this story prevent our believing that Jesus chose twelve apostles, or that He instructed all His disciples to love their enemies, and to do good to those who hated them?"

Christ does not vanish with the miracles—that is my contention. If every miracle in the Gospels (except the acts of healing) be shewn to have arisen from misconception, we still have Christ in the Gospels, in the Epistles, in the past history of the Church, and in facts around us, revealed as the Word of God taking flesh, living, and suffering, and dying for men, and finally rising again, and by His Resurrection uplifting all mankind through His Spirit toward the Father in heaven.

Now therefore, in perfect fearlessness, we may approach our argument, or rather such a meagre sketch of it as can alone be given here. First, then, let me point out that much of the old Greek mythology, which was, in old-fashioned theories, said to be deliberately devised by cunning priests or philosophers, is now shewn to have grown up gradually and imperceptibly as a natural result of a subsequent misconception of early metaphorical language. Thus, the fable that Athene sprang from the head of Zeus, is said with great probability to have been a misunderstanding of the saying, that the Dawn sprang from the East, the forehead of the sky.[1] However scholars may differ among themselves as to the precise explanation of this or that theological story, thus much seems to be certain—that much of the ancient Greek mythology was the result of a misconception of metaphor.

Next, in the ancient history of Israel, we find at least some cases in which miraculous narrative is based on the misconception, not perhaps of metaphor, but of poetic hyperbole. Take, for example, the story of the standing still of the sun at the battle of Beth-horon. No one now believes the literal truth of the statement that "the sun stood still." "Well then," says an uneducated reader, "we must reject the whole of the narrative of the battle of Beth-horon as a lie." Certainly not. It would be as silly to reject the narrative of the battle of Beth-horon, because of the miraculous element in it, as it would be to reject the narrative of the battle of Salamis, because of the well-known tradition that in that battle Athene was visible, stimulating the shrinking Greeks.

If instead of so hasty a rejection, we examine the context of the narrative in the book of Joshua more closely, we may be led to the origin of the miraculous element. There we find the narrator appealing to an extract from an older book: "And the sun stood still, and the moon stayed, until the people had avenged themselves upon their enemies. Is not this written *in the book of Jasher?* So the sun stood still in the midst of heaven, and hasted not to go down about a whole day." Now we have only to suppose that the poetic hyperbole of the ancient extract was mistaken for a literal

[1] Max Müller, *Lectures on the Science of Language*, vol. ii. p. 550.

statement by the later narrator, and then worked out in picturesque detail, and the whole is explained without any necessity for inferring that the narrator intended to deceive. There is no more reason to suppose that the original extract intended to narrate any actual standing still of the sun, than there is reason to suppose that anything more than a thunderstorm and river-flood is referred to in the triumphal song of Deborah, which relates how "the stars in their courses fought against Sisera."

Again a great deal of the so-called miracle in the Old Testament vanishes when we call to mind the Hebrew way of looking at natural phenomena, especially such phenomena as are unusually striking. I remember hearing that, in a petition sent to Sir Moses Montefiore by some Jews in Eastern parts who had suffered severely by a destructive fire, it was stated in perfect good faith that "God had sent down fire from heaven and had burnt up their town:" it was the Hebrew way of expressing what we should have expressed in the words "accidental fire." The same spirit pervades the ancient books of Israel. Above all, in great deliverances of the Chosen People the poets of Israel naturally saw with peculiar clearness the arm of Jehovah revealed: "The help that is done upon earth He doeth it Himself." But whatever Jehovah does must be done in a striking way; there must be no delay; the prophet or man of God through whom He acts must be obeyed at once; the elements must give prompt and fearful obedience. If Moses is delivered and Pharaoh is destroyed by the winds and waters of the Red Sea, or if Joshua is favoured in his passage of the Jordan by the dried-up stream, what seems more natural than that the Jordan should only then suspend its flow when the feet of the priests entered its waters, and that the Red Sea should retire and advance in exact obedience to the outstretched rod of the leader of Israel?

Carrying out these thoughts into detail, we shall see how easy it is to suppose that the picturesque details of the suspension of the Jordan stream during the passage of Joshua may have arisen in part from some actual basis of fact, but in part from the sense that if Jehovah wrought the deliverance, it must have been effected in a startling way, and in part also from some such hyperbolical expression as we find in the Psalms, "The waters saw Thee, O God, the waters saw Thee and were afraid." Again the story of the passage of the Red Sea (undoubtedly in the main authentic) may in the same way have owed some of its detail to similar poetic expressions, describing how "He divided the sea and caused them to pass through, and He made the waters to stand in an heap," but much more to the same feeling described above, that whatever Jehovah wrought must be perfect in dramatic grandeur.

Lastly, to conclude our remarks on the Old Testament miracles with a specimen of the misconception not of hyperbole, but of genuine metaphor, the perplexing signs of Gideon and the fleece—perplexing and almost incredible if taken literally—are perfectly intelligible, if they are but a later version of some early metaphorical expressions, recording how, when the rest of Israel was imbued with terror, the hero Gideon alone was untouched, and when the rest of Israel was heated with over-confidence, Gideon alone retained the coolness of judgment.

"But," it may very reasonably be urged, "the misconceptions mentioned above required a considerable interval of time between the original expressions and the subsequent misconceptions, in order to give rise to the unconscious perversion. Now no very long interval of time, at least none of sufficient length, can be supposed to have elapsed between the works of our Lord and the composition of our existing narratives. Consequently the theory falls to the ground." I shall answer this objection by showing that *even in our Lord's own lifetime* His metaphors (as we call them) were being continually misunderstood and interpreted literally. This is admitted in the clearest manner by our own narratives.

When He bids His disciples beware of the leaven of the

Pharisees and Sadducees, they understand Him to warn them against the sin of eating leavened bread. When He speaks to the woman of Samaria of the true Water, she retorts that "the well is deep." When He tells His disciples that He has meat to eat that they know not of, they ask, "Hath any man brought him aught to eat?" When He speaks of the sleep of Lazarus, the disciples reply, "Lord, if he sleepeth he shall do well." When He describes the second birth, Nicodemus, "the teacher of Israel," finds it possible even in so obvious a metaphor to see a difficulty. When He speaks of the Feast of God, He is constantly supposed by every one to open... dom and a "feast of fat things." When He speaks of giving His flesh and blood for the world, many of His disciples exclaim, "This is a hard saying; who can bear it?" When He bids His disciples sell their garments to buy a sword if they have not one, they answer, "Lord, behold here are two swords"—although it is certain that Jesus could not have meant the words literally. When He speaks of the Temple—meaning the Church, the Temple of Humanity, which was His body—He was supposed to mean the Temple of Herod in Jerusalem. Should it be urged that all but two of these instances are from the Fourth Gospel, we would call special attention to the following group. When He promises to His future society the power of binding and loosing sins, and declares that "if any two of you shall agree on earth as touching anything that they shall ask, it shall be done for them of my Father which is in heaven"—we find the mother of Zebedee's children with her two sons, interpreting the "two or three" with strict literalism, and supposing that the promise may include the privilege of sitting on the right hand and on the left hand of the Messiah's throne. When Jesus touches on the spiritual conditions necessary for spiritual exaltation—the "cup" and the "baptism," the two sons of Zebedee still understand Him literally. The rest of the Apostles, deprecating the ambition of their two companions, nevertheless adopt the same literal interpretation.

Now it is true that many of these misunderstandings are found only in the Fourth Gospel: and some have inferred hence that they are not authentic. But the first three Gospels contain so many cases as to place it beyond doubt that such misconceptions of Jesus by His Disciples were recognized in the earliest times as authentic, and—which is much more important—they indicate misconception as the habitual state of mind of the disciples, and represent Jesus as continually obliged to explain His spiritual meaning, and not unfrequently obliged to rebuke their materialism. Now it is in the highest degree natural that in a later Gospel, the chief object of which was not to narrate facts so much as to draw out the character of Jesus, this habitual misconception on the part of disciples and hearers should receive greater emphasis—as indeed it deserves, for, without it, much of the life of Jesus is scarcely intelligible—and that the writer should lay stress on dialogues illustrating this misconception, rather than on the recognized and received tradition of the words and deeds of Jesus. Bear in mind, also, that the whole of our records of Christ's life could easily be compressed into a few columns of a newspaper, and then consider—in proportion to the mere fragment of biography handed to us—how striking and how numerous are the cases of recorded misconception. But if, in so short a narrative there are so many cases of misunderstanding by the apostles themselves, definitely noted by our narrators, is it very difficult, is it not rather very natural, to suppose that, in the generation succeeding the Apostles, other cases of similar misunderstanding may have sprung up, based upon metaphorical expressions of Christ adopted by the Apostles in their preaching to the Early Church?

I shall now pass to the application of this theory to two or three of the most perplexing miracles in the Gospels. Our choice of the two or three will be determined by considerations so important that they claim the utmost attention.

APPENDIX. 445

The early disciples being, for the most part, unlettered men, it is reasonable to suppose that no formal account of the life of Jesus of Nazareth was at first committed to writing. But from the earliest times there must have been a need, and an employment, of some short account of the "Acts of Jesus," for the instruction of the Church, if not for the conversion of those outside the Church. Such a short narrative would probably be at first oral, and handed down and diffused by oral tradition. It would soon begin to vary slightly in different churches, in Rome, for example, Antioch, and Alexandria, gathering detail with ~~That when~~ ultimately Gospels came to be composed in writing, while inserting much ~~...~~ might vary somewhat with the tendencies of the several churches —the new narratives would incorporate as far as possible in its original form the ancient and venerable tradition which was common to all the churches.

Such are the phenomena that might be naturally expected: and such accordingly are the phenomena that present themselves in the first three Gospels. It is well known to every student of the New Testament that the first three Gospels contain (amid much variation of phrase and many additional incidents peculiar to the individual Gospels), a common thread of incident expressed in phrases so similar as to make it almost a certainty that all three Gospels are based upon some original and common tradition—probably oral—which may be called the "original Gospel." Now, this original Gospel, though it may not have preceded by many years the earliest of the first three Gospels, appears entitled to greater authority than any one or any two of our present Gospels. For the mere fact that the writers of our first three Gospels, writing independently and often divergently, nevertheless agree in incorporating in their narratives the "original Gospel," seems clearly to establish its superior authority, even if we put aside the authority it derives from priority of existence. Any miraculous incident recorded in the original Gospel deserves, therefore, special consideration.

Now setting aside acts of healing (which we have accepted above as not supernatural but historically accurate) we find only six actions that have any claim at all to be called miraculous in the original Gospel. Of these six, three are, the raising of Jairus' daughter, the transfiguration, and an angelic vision and voice declaring to the women at the sepulchre of Jesus —" He is not here, He is risen." As to the first of these, the original Gospel preserves the exact words of Jesus, "She is not dead, but sleepeth." I at once, therefore, accept this as historical, but not supernatural. Similar recoveries are recorded in the Old Testament, and one in modern times has been mentioned by the present Bishop of Orleans as coming within his own experience.

The transfiguration and the vision and voice at the tomb I should accept as being historically accurate and as being "objective" (using the word under protest, as I have explained above), but not as being supernatural, except so far as they sprang from the inconceivably impressive personal influence of Jesus, which was "above our nature." The sceptic will say that, if they are true at all, they are "subjective," but he cannot deny that they may be true. There is nothing in them essentially contrary to the laws of human nature, when human nature is unusually excited and impressed. The same applies to all the three so-called miracles mentioned above; they are not essentially supernatural.

But when we come to the three remaining miracles of the original Gospel, we are confronted with very different phenomena: they are, the stilling of the storm, the destruction of the swine, and the feeding of the five thousand in the wilderness. Nothing can make the two last of these miracles natural. It is not my object, or it would be easily attainable, to shew how difficult it must be to avoid grotesque and repellent suppositions as soon as one endeavours, accepting these two narratives as literal, to answer the question, "How did these things happen?" To these two miracles, therefore, we shall now endeavour to apply the solvent of the metaphorical theory. As to the first of the three, I mean the stilling of the storm, though I myself am almost prepared to accept it as historically accurate, yet I must acknowledge that a balance of probability is in favour of the metaphorical explanation of this miracle also.

Let us deal first with the healing of the Gadarene demoniac and the destruction of the two thousand swine by the exorcised devils. Cases of "possession" were very common during the period of the Gospel history, not only in Palestine, but in other parts of the Roman empire. They are not often found in the early history of nations. The case of Saul is almost unique in

patriotic, simple, and warlike; more self-introspective, melancholy, and superstitious; vicious and lascivious for want of healthful occupation and interest—"possession" became more common.

It appears to have raged like an epidemic in Galilee, and in provinces exposed to the influences of Grecian idolatry and distant from the quieting solemnities of the temple worship; but Judæa seems to have been comparatively free from it;[1] and though the first three evangelists, as long as they speak of Galilee and the north, often allude to them, yet when Jesus journeys southward, they cease mention of them.[2] The mischief was so common as to give rise to various impostures. It became a lucrative profession to cast out devils. A Jewish exorcist is said by Josephus to have cast out an evil spirit in the presence of Vespasian and his officers. The spirit was drawn out from the nostrils of the man possessed by the aid of a certain root applied to his nose, and it was then forced to overthrow a bucket of water in its flight as a proof of its expulsion. Such grotesque impostures have caused many to deny the reality of "possession." But

---

[1] In the same way I believe the dancing mania described by Hecker was a local malady principally confined to the banks of the Rhine.

[2] This may perhaps meet the objection of Strauss, who declares that the omission of any mention of "possession" in the Fourth Gospel arose from the fact that the author was an educated man, and ashamed of recording such absurdities. The Fourth Gospel deals almost entirely with the life of Jesus in Judæa.

though such expressions as "the devil went out of him," are of course metaphorical, yet at the present time there are cases where the shortest and most real description of the patient's state is to say, "a man is not himself," "he is out of himself." By these words we imply that another self has "possession" of the man. The language of the diseased person falls in with this way of speaking. In India, where cases of so-called devil-frenzy are still not uncommon, the "possessed" will tell the inquirers in his quiet moments that he is not responsible for his words or actions in the moment of possession: "*it* makes me do these things," and "it" is a euphemism for "the devil." Somewhat similar is the language, even in England, of those who are possessed with homicidal mania: "When *it* seizes me, I must kill some one, were it only a child."[1] The maniac is "conscious of the horrible nature of the idea, struggles to escape from it, and is miserable with the fear that at any moment it may prove too strong for him."[2]

In this morbid condition, the senses of taste, and sight, and hearing, turn traitors, and confirm the diseased man in the belief that everything is against him, that devils encompass him outside, that devils have established themselves even in his very body. One patient imagines that his stomach is full of toads, or crows, or serpents; another feels himself consumed by an inward fire; a third sees blood-red flames before his eyes; he hears loud roaring noises, or thunderous cannonades; sulphurous flames are in his nostrils; lifeless objects assume life to threaten him, and the pitying face of a friend becomes a grinning demon.[3] Cases have been known where two distinct voices, one bass, representing the moral will, the other falsetto, representing the immoral will, issue in succession from the patient and bear witness to the strife of wills within him.[4] The insane fit ceases sometimes, only to give way to convulsions, which in turn are succeeded by recurring insanity. In these unhappy beings the intellect sometimes retains a

---

[1] Maudsley's *Physiology and Pathology of the Mind*, p. 309.
[2] *Ibid.* p. 310.   [3] *Ibid.* p. 263.   [4] *Ibid.* p. 278.

partial and fitful life, but the moral affections are invariably destroyed. The same irresistible impulse which leads him to devour things materially noxious and hateful, and "in the fury of his heart, when the foul fiend rages, to eat cowdung for sallets, swallow the old rat, and the ditch-dog, the swimming-frog, the toad, the tadpole,"[1] goads him also into everything that is morally repulsive and obscene. The shames and decencies of humanity are removed. A spirit, indeed unclean, takes possession of the man, and he freely indulges the instincts of the animal.

As to the chances of recovery, we are told that if religious excitement, and nothing else, has been the cause of an outbreak, recovery may be anticipated with confidence. But chronic mania and monomania when once established leave very little hope of recovery. In rare instances it may take place under the influence of systematic moral discipline, or in consequence of some shock to the system, which may be due either to the effects of some intercurrent disease, or "to a strong emotional affection."[2]

I think Jesus would have treated many of these modern cases as cases of "possession;" and it seems to me the only adequate description of such men is, to say that they are "possessed" by an unclean spirit. They often deserve, and they gained from Jesus, the most sincere sympathy. Often they are paying the penalty of their own sins, but sometimes also of the sins of others. The drunkenness or vicious excesses of one generation are visited on the second or third, in the form of melancholy, mania, or imbecility. Christ pitied them as he pitied the "sinners." They were to be found, it would seem, in almost every village of Galilee, in every large concourse of persons. Sunk in bestiality, they were at once repelled and attracted when they heard the voice proclaiming forgiveness for the past, light and life for the future, a brotherhood of men, and God a Father seeking the lost sheep of Israel, and caring more for the one lost

[1] Shakespeare's *King Lear*, iii. 4, 134.   [2] Maudsley, p. 419.

than for the ninety-nine safe in the fold. Their lower self, the evil spirit in them, cried out to be left alone in its familiar darkness, their human self implored help: in this distraction they burst out, often in reproaches, the evil spirit gaining the temporary mastery. Then came the voice of the Healer, bringing the "shock" or "emotional affection" sufficient to change the current of a life; and, with a loud cry, accompanied sometimes by convulsions, the man was healed.

Now applying these facts to the case of "possession" under consideration, we see at once how every circumstance tends to show the naturalness of the condition of the Gadarene. As Mary Magdalene was said to have been possessed with seven devils, so this man believed himself to be possessed with a large number, possibly a thousand or two thousand. But the name of the evil spirit was "Legion." Whence this name? "For we are many"—is the reason given by the wretched man himself. But there was another reason beside the number of the evil spirits. If a Syrian—whether Galilean, as is most likely, or a foreigner—felt that he was indeed possessed and dominated by the most powerful and hateful of evil spirits, what name could suggest itself more naturally than the name of that engine of detestable despotism which combined two or three thousand unclean heathens into one compact, irresistible whole, that servant of Satan called a Roman Legion? Again, we have seen that the "possessed" often imagines that his stomach is tenanted by animals, and these, in every case, obscene and hateful. Now what the "ditch-dog" or the "tadpole" was to the madman of Shakespeare's time, that the "swine" were to the true child of Abraham in our Lord's time. There is therefore every probability that this man not only believed himself to be possessed with a legion of devils, but also that he believed these devils to tenant and defile his stomach in the form of swine. Further we have found that "possessed" persons often speak, now in the character of their human self, but also often in the character of the diabolical and unclean self which is oppressing the human self. Bearing this in mind, we turn to the Gospel narrative, and we find the possessed man appealing to our Lord in the name of the unclean spirits, and making some request. What that request was is not so clear, but the same request seems to be expressed in two ways, viz., that the spirits might not be sent "out of the country" (Mark), or "into the *abyss*" (Luke). The meaning of this request seems to be illustrated by the well-known parable of the unclean spirit who takes seven other spirits to return with him into his old home. The traditional feeling on the subject was that the evil spirits disliked to be cast out into the " abyss," the homeless vacancy of space. The body of their temporary [illegible] out they were homeless, until they could obtain a new home. Josephus speaks of them as being "the spirits of bad men entering into the living," and though they injure the body which they occupy, yet the belief seems to have been that an evil spirit hated the disembodied state, and was " loth to leave the body that it loved." One last consideration remains. It seems to have been not uncommon for the "possessed" to see (or think they saw, which is the same thing for our purpose) the exit of the evil spirit manifested by some external visible result. We found above that the professional exorcists took advantage of this natural fancy in the case of the demon who was caused to overturn a bucket of water in its exit. All that we now need is some instance where evil spirits are described as going visibly forth in the shapes of noxious beasts. Such an instance we find in the Arabic Gospel of the Infancy (described by Tischendorf as " an ancient and memorable monument of the superstition of Eastern Christians ") where we read that from a certain youth, upon the mere touch of the swaddling bands of Jesus, " evil spirits began to go forth from his mouth in *the shapes of ravens and serpents."* With all these facts before us, I shall now simply state—leaving it to speak for itself—what I believe to have been the natural basis of fact as it was originally expressed, the misconception of which in after times, when worked out in picturesque detail, led to the amplified supernatural narrative as we find it in our Gospels. "There was a man possessed with evil spirits. The name of the evil spirits was Legion. Now the evil spirits besought the Lord that He would not cast them into the abyss. But the Lord cast out the evil spirits: *and they went forth from his mouth into the abyss, in the shapes of swine.*"

I pass now to the feeding of the five thousand, and as the principle of the Metaphorical Theory is now explained, I shall confine myself to little more than a statement of the supposed original shape from which the subsequent narrative may have sprung. "As the children of Israel in old times fed on the Rock that followed them, and that Rock was Christ, so did the followers of Christ feed upon Him in their wanderings with Him in the wilderness: and He satisfied them with the Bread of Life." A development of this doctrine would declare that Christ broke the bread of life for His disciples, and that the disciples ministered it to the multitude.

But there appears to have been a special form of this teaching (found in the Gospels of St. Matthew, St. Mark and St. John) which connected the incident with our Lord's approaching death, and which perhaps identified the feast with the Last Supper. The key to the connection is found in the true reading of St. Matthew xv. 32, St. Mark viii. 4, which passages contain the description of the feeding, not of the five thousand, but of the four thousand. The right reading is, not "they have now been with me three days," but "*three days still remain to me.*" Compare this with the statement in St. John's narrative of the feeding of the five thousand (vi. 4), "and the passover, a feast of the Jews was nigh;" and it will appear probable that the "three days" of St. Matthew xv. 32, St. Mark viii. 4, mean the interval to elapse *before the passover*, "Three days remain to me *before the passover.*" Now if we turn to Matthew xxvi. 1 (Mark xiv. 1), we find our Lord saying, shortly before His final paschal feast

APPENDIX. 453

with His disciples, "You know that *after two days is the passover, and the Son of Man is betrayed to be crucified.*"

Bearing in mind these facts, we shall find in the second development of the doctrine a possible reference to the Lord's Supper, together with a possible reference to the early conversion of the masses of Christian believers. The bread of life is bestowed upon the Apostles that they may minister it to the Church. According to this supposition the original tradition would be to this effect, "And Jesus called His disciples, and said to them, I have compassion on the multitude, because three days still remain to me before the Passover"—when He was to be offered up for men—" and they have no bread; then He bestowed the Bread upon His Apostles. Afterwards the Apostles in turn bestowed it upon the multitude."

In later times when the narrative had come to be regarded as literally true, it became natural to insert more exact details. Then, if on the one hand the antithesis between the small number of loaves and the large number of persons seemed the most natural point to lay stress on, "five" was a natural number, as being the usual number to express "a few;"[1] and the two fishes may perhaps have represented the two Sacraments.[2] But if, on the other hand, the point was, not the smallness of the amount of the bread, but the perfection of the bread of life, then "seven," the perfect number, seemed more appropriate, and the "few fishes" pass into the background.

Mark also that the *eucharistic* notion in the narrative of the feeding of the four thousand seems implied in the use of the verb *eucharistein* (Matthew xv. 36, Mark viii. 6), while in the feeding of the five thousand both authors use the verb *eulogein*. This duality of thought is expressed in the subsequent narrative of the actual Lord's Supper, where St. Matthew and St. Mark

---

[1] Compare St. Paul's "I would rather speak *five* words with my understanding," (1 Cor. xiv. 19) and " at the rebuke of *five* ye shall flee" (Isaiah xxx. 17).

[2] The "fish' in early Christian times was often used as an emblem of Christ, from the similarity of the first and last letters of *Iethus* and *Iesous*.

(who alone narrate *both* the feeding of the four thousand and that of the five thousand) used the *two* verbs *eucharistein* and *eulogein*, whereas St. Luke, who only narrates the *one* feeding of the five thousand, uses in the description of the Last Supper only *one* verb, *eucharistein*.

As for the picking up of the fragments, the number of the baskets might be twelve or seven, naturally varying according as one desires to lay stress upon the truth that the twelve Apostles, who ministered the bread, themselves received fragments of it proportioned to their number, or the other truth, that the perfect bread, after being ministered to the Church, still remained superabundant (with an abundance typified by the perfect number seven) to supply food for all future wants.

If this explanation seems thin, pedantic and improbable, bear in mind that the choice lies between this and other explanations also highly improbable. If the literal theory is to be accepted, it is in the highest degree difficult to conceive at what stage in the narrative the fishes and loaves were multiplied, whether in the hands of our Lord, or in the hands of the disciples, or in the hands of the multitude. Again, it is hard to see whether the number of the fishes remained the same, the bones and flesh of each being enormously magnified, or whether the fishes remained of the normal size, but fresh individual fishes dead and prepared for eating were suddenly brought into existence. Some such supposition seems required by the literal theory, and in either case the difficulty is very great, especially when we consider that the whole of the miraculous element in the original Gospel (if we except the stilling of the storm, about which we shall speak directly) is now reduced to this single incident, so that, if this vanishes, no vestige of the miraculous remains. Is it likely, one feels driven to ask, that after all the rest of the miraculous has been resolved into the natural, this miracle, so seemingly unnatural, should admit of no similar explanation?

Then again we recall the instances where Christ's spiritual use of the terms "meat," "bread," "flesh," "blood," "water," was misunderstood even in His lifetime. The misunderstanding of His use of the word "leaven" also recurs to our mind and throws a curious light on the apparent misconception of the narrative of the feeding. On one occasion He warned His disciples against the "leaven of the Pharisees." They misunderstood Him as usual, and supposing that He was speaking literally, they said to one another, "It is because we have forgotten to bring bread with us." Upon this Jesus retorted, rebuking their literalism and explaining that, as He had before ministered bread to the multitude in the wilderness when the disciples had gathered up the crumbs and had been satisfied even so, and in that same sense He called upon them to avoid "leaven." Why did they set their minds on earthly bread and earthly leaven when they had with them the all-sufficing bread of eternal life? Could they not yet understand spiritual things, He indignantly asked them; had they no intelligence, was their heart still callous? Having eyes, could they not see, and having ears, could they not hear? And had they not even the power of memory?[1] This appears to be the meaning of Christ's utterance. But later times found in it not a rebuke for literalism but a justification of literalism, and made the tenor of Christ's exhortation to consist in this, that the five loaves produced twelve baskets of fragments and the seven only seven baskets, so that Christ's power to produce food was independent of the amount of the material supply.

As to the narrative of the Stilling of the Storm there are various ways in which it might have arisen. It might, indeed be urged that this act was the result of a harmony between Jesus of Nazareth and Nature, so that He felt the divine impulse to rebuke the wind at the moment when the Father had predetermined, in the sequence of cause and effect, that the wind should cease. I am not able, lightly, to put aside this supposition; but on the whole, it seems less likely than a supposition based upon the metaphorical theory. It is probable that shortly

[1] St. Mark viii. 17, 18.

after the death of Christ, the disciples returned to Galilee and remained there for some time. During their stay there, they would naturally resort to their old occupation of fishing, and it might easily happen that on one of their fishing expeditions they would be overtaken by a sudden storm. Now in the Fourth Gospel we find an account of an appearance of Jesus manifested to His disciples after His death, while they were pursuing their old occupation on or near the sea of Galilee. We may not be able to accept all the details of that account, but we may readily admit that it contains a basis of historical fact, viz. that Christ did on several occasions (as, for example, when He appeared walking on the waves) appear to His disciples while they were on or near that sea. Now we have only to suppose that on one of these occasions the disciples, while in a storm, besought the Lord to still the storm, and that it was stilled—and the source of the whole narrative seems clear. On reaching their homes in Capernaum after the storm, the first thing that the disciples would do, would naturally be, as they are said to have done in Jerusalem[1] after their first conflict with the authorities there, to meet together and praise God for their deliverance. Just as in Jerusalem they saw in their peril a peril similar to the peril that encompassed David, and their hearts naturally expressed their thanks in the words of the Psalmist, so would it be now. The words would naturally recur to them which describe how "they cry unto the Lord in their trouble, and he bringeth them out of their distress: He maketh the storm a calm, so that the waves thereof are still." Through many a home in Galilee the story would then be noised abroad how the Lord Jesus had been with His disciples on the sea in a storm, and had stilled it at their supplication. But when the question arose, "Why did the Lord allow the storm to rise and to imperil the lives of His disciples?" then, as the story passed from mouth to mouth, and as it came to attach itself to the earlier life of the Lord Jesus, and not to His appearances after death, the answer would naturally arise, first

[1] Acts iv. 25.

suggesting itself in the mind, and gradually becoming interwoven in the story, that "the Lord Jesus was sleeping when the storm arose, and was not roused by it till the disciples awoke Him." There is something so spiritually true in this last detail (exhibiting, as it does, the calm peace of Jesus and His perfect trustfulness in Nature) that it would naturally commend itself to all hearers; but clearly it would change the whole character of the narrative. Yet in all this process—supposing this to have been the actual process—it cannot be asserted with any probability that there was the slightest intention to deceive.

Improbable as the metaphorical explanation may seem to those who have not devoted years to the critical study of the subject, it will seem to many less improbable than the literal theory. It ought also to seem less improbable than the theory of falsification. The theory that the Gospel miracles are simply "lies" is, in my estimation, more incredible than the theory that they are literally true and supernatural. There is nothing whatever of the character of the "lie" about them. One can see at once the difference between them and the miracles of the Apocryphal Gospels. The Gospel miracles contain a spiritual truth, round which one can trace the growth of materialism and picturesque accretion. I know indeed that the metaphorical explanation of the miraculous element in the New Testament will seem unsatisfactory to those who desire to reject it altogether as entirely false. They may say, as indeed I have had said to me, "You speak of the spiritual truth contained in these miraculous narratives; the phrase offends us. If somebody told us he had seen you jump to the top of St. Paul's, the way to deal with that statement would be to say plainly, *It is a lie*, not to say, it contained the spiritual truth of your having an aspiring nature."

This objection is admirably adapted for my purpose, so well indeed that I should have suspected myself of partiality in accepting it as a specimen of sceptical opinion, but that it proceeds from a critic for whose keenness and love of truth—

manifested in the criticism of the pages while they were passing through the press—I have the sincerest respect. But I submit that it betokens an error, a very prevalent error, concerning the structure of the Gospels. We are dealing with sceptics. Now few sceptics that I know of, who have gone deeply into the question, suppose that the miraculous narratives, as we have them, were written by those who had "seen" the events recorded. If anyone had "seen" a natural event, and recorded it as a supernatural one, nothing could have excused us from dismissing the narrative as a "lie." But so far from this being the case, it would be generally admitted (and most readily by the most sceptical) that our written narratives were composed too long after the events recorded to have been composed (in the shape in which we have them) by eye-witnesses. This objection, therefore, so far, falls to the ground.

But it may be urged, that even admitting the supposed growth of the miraculous narratives from misunderstanding, from honest reverence, and from love of the detailed and the picturesque—we must still maintain that, though they may not have been lies to the narrator, they are lies for *us*. I reply that this may or may not be, according to your treatment of them. If, contrary to the testimony of his conscience and his understanding, a man persists in declaring that they are literally true, no doubt the miracles become lies to him. But if a man regards them as illusions, that is, as earthly integuments of spiritual truth, without which integuments it is probable that the spiritual truth would never have been preserved for us through the storms of the ages; if he in this spirit reads them as having originated from no mere lust for lying, but from the blended frailty and reverence of the human mind; if he looks on them not as proofs demonstrative that Jesus broke the laws of Nature, but as tokens of the deep impression of power left by Jesus upon the hearts of the generation following Him, then I submit that these narratives can still be read with reverence and edification, without doing violence either to the conscience or to the understanding.

It is therefore from no desire to erect a half-way house between believing everything and believing nothing, that I insist upon the truthfulness of the spirit, though not of the letter, of most of our miraculous narrative. I take my stand on Truth, and I say that to put aside the miracles of the Gospels as mere lies is nothing but a lazy perversion of truth, and a wilful determination to find a convenient short cut to certainty. If anyone wants to realize the spiritual truth of the miracles recorded in our Gospels, let him contrast them with the later miraculous narratives. In one example of these we find the infant Jesus "explaining hyperphysics and hypophysics" to a natural philosopher; making a living bird for a toy out of clay; paralysing the schoolmaster who attempts to flog him; striking dead a boy who runs up against him—with a hundred more miracles of the same sort. These, if we like, we may call lies; but to confuse these with the feeding of the five thousand is simply to ignore distinctions because distinctions are inconvenient. And the same distinction obviously applies to many other miracles, such as the destruction of the fig-tree, the type of Pharisaic barrenness; the walking upon the water by the Word of God whose "voice is upon the waters," and who "treadeth upon the waves of the sea;" the manifestation of Jesus to the Apostle St. Thomas vouchsafed at the moment when He was pressing with his hands the Body of the Lord in the Lord's Supper. Above all, this distinction applies to the details of the earliest chapters of St. Matthew and St. Luke, in which the First and Third Gospels enwrap the profound spiritual truth of the Incarnation expressed by the author of the Fourth Gospel in the saying that, "the Word was made flesh." Whatever view may be taken of the details of that narrative, one thing must be admitted by all students of history who have included human nature in their studies—that without the integument of the belief in the material Incarnation, the belief in the spiritual

Incarnation could not, humanly speaking, have been preserved through the dark ages of the Church so as to reach the apprehension of modern faith.

But to enter into any analysis of these or other miraculous narratives would lead us far beyond the limits of an Appendix. All that now remains is to point to the consequences of the adoption of the theory sketched in these pages. They are briefly these—first that in the Original Tradition (which is confessedly earlier than any of our four Gospels) there is a *total absence of the miraculous element*: and secondly, that the introduction of the miraculous element into the later written narrative of our Gospels is *compatible with the honesty of the narrators, and with the historical accuracy of the non-miraculous part of the narrative.*

THE END.

www.ingramcontent.com/pod-product-compliance
Lightning Source LLC
Chambersburg PA
CBHW022105300426
44117CB00007B/590